THE QUEST

Further Adventures in the Unconscious

Some Other Titles From New Falcon Publications

Aha! The Sevenfold Mystery of the Ineffable Love — Aleister Crowley
Bio-Etheric Healing — Trudy Lanitis
Undoing Yourself With Energized Meditation and Other Devices
Secrets of Western Tantra: The Sexuality of the Middle Path
Dogma Daze — Christopher S. Hyatt, Ph.D.
Rebels & Devils; The Psychology of Liberation **Edited by Christopher S. Hyatt, Ph.D.**
Aleister Crowley's Illustrated Goetia
Taboo: Sex, Religion & Magick
Sex Magic, Tantra & Tarot: The Way of the Secret Lover
— Christopher S. Hyatt, Ph.D., and Lon Milo DuQuette
Pacts With The Devil
Urban Voodoo: A Beginner's Guide to Afro-Caribbean Magic
— Jason Black and Christopher S. Hyatt, Ph.D.
The Psychopath's Bible — Christopher S. Hyatt, Ph.D., and Jack Willis
Ask Baba Lon — Lon Milo DuQuette
Aleister Crowley and the Treasure House of Images J.F.C. Fuller, Aleister Crowley, Lon Milo DuQuette and Nancy Wasserman
Enochian World of Aleister Crowley — Lon Milo DuQuette and Aleister Crowley

Info-Psychology   Neuropolitique   The Game of Life
What Does WoMan Want? — Timothy Leary, Ph.D.

Be Yourself - A Guide to Relaxation and Health
Dr. Israel Regardie's Definitive Work on Aleister Crowley, The Eye In The Triangle
Healing Energy, Prayer and Relaxation
My Rosicrucian Adventure
Teachers of Fulfillment
The Complete Golden Dawn System of Magic
The Eye in the Triangle: An Interpretation of Aleister Crowley
The Golden Dawn Audio CDs
The Legend of Aleister Crowley
The Portable Complete Golden Dawn System of Magic
The Tree of Life
What You Should Know About the Golden Dawn — Dr. Israel Regardie

Roll Away The Stone/The Herb Dangerous — Dr. Israel Regardie and Aleister Crowley

Rebellion, Revolution and Religiousness — Osho
Reichian Therapy: A Practical Guide for Home Use — Dr. Jack Willis
Woman's Orgasm: A Guide to Sexual Satisfaction — Benjamin Graber, M.D., and Georgia Kline-Graber, R.N.
Shaping Formless Fire   Seizing Power   Taking Power — Stephen Mace
The Illuminati Conspiracy: The Sapiens System — Donald Holmes, M.D.
The Secret Inner Order Rituals of the Golden Dawn — Pat Zalewski
Sufism, Islam and Jungian Psychology — J. Marvin Spiegelman, Ph.D.
Nonlocal Nature: The Eight Circuits of Consciousness — James A. Heffernan
on What is — Ja Wallin

MANY OF OUR TITLES AVAILABLE ON KINDLE!
Please visit our website at http://www.newfalcon.com

Other Titles by Dr. Israel Regardie

A Garden of Pomegranates
A Practical Guide to Geomantic Divination - A Small Gem
Attract and Use Healing Energy - A Small Gem
Be Yourself - A Guide to Relaxation and Health
Ceremonial Magic
Dr. Israel Regardie's Definitive Work on Aleister Crowley,
  The Eye In The Triangle
Healing Energy, Prayer and Relaxation
How To Make and Use Talismans - A Small Gem
My Rosicrucian Adventure
Teachers of Fulfillment
The Art and Meaning of Magic - A Small Gem
The Body-Mind Connection, A Path to Well-Being - A Small Gem
The Complete Golden Dawn System of Magic
The Complete Golden Dawn System of Magic Book 1 - Ltd. Edition
The Complete Golden Dawn System of Magic Book 2 - Ltd. Edition
The Complete Golden Dawn System of Magic - The Black Edition
The Eye in the Triangle: An Interpretation of Aleister Crowley
The Golden Dawn Audio CDs, Vol. 1, Vol. 2, and Vol. 3
The Legend of Aleister Crowley
The Magic of Israel Regardie
The Middle Pillar
The Philosopher's Stone
The Portable Complete Golden Dawn System of Magic
The Tree of Life
The Wisdom of Israel Regardie - Vol. I
  Selected Introductions, Prefaces and Forewords
The Wisdom of Israel Regardie - Vol. II
  Selected Essays and Commentaries
The Wisdom of Israel Regardie - Vol. III
  Selected Articles, Introductions, Prefaces and Forewords
What You Should Know About the Golden Dawn
Aha! (Dr. Israel Regardie and Aleister Crowley)
Roll Away The Stone/The Herb Dangerous
  (Dr. Israel Regardie and Aleister Crowley)

Copyright © 1984 by J. Marvin Spiegelman

All rights reserved. No part of this book,
in part or in whole, may be reproduced, transmitted,
or utilized, in any form or by any means, electronic or mechanical,
including photocopying, recording, or by any information storage
and retrieval system, without permission in writing
from the publisher, except for brief quotations
in critical articles, books and reviews.

ISBN 13: 978-1-56184-500-2
ISBN 10: 1-56184-5000

First Edition 1984
Second Revised Edition 2021

The paper used in this publication meets the minimum requirements
of the American National Standard for Permanence of
Paper for Printed Library Materials Z39.48-1984

Printed in USA

NEW FALCON PUBLICATIONS
2046 Hillhurst Avenue
Los Angeles, CA 90027
www.newfalcon.com
email: info@newfalcon.com

THE QUEST

Further Adventures in the Unconscious

A Psycho-Mythology Series

By J. Marvin Spiegelman, Ph.D

NEW FALCON PUBLICATIONS
LOS ANGELES, CALIFORNIA

"The Crowning with Thorns", Albrecht Durer (1471-1528)

*Dedicated,
with gratitude
to my
parents*

Table of Contents

Introduction to The Quest   xi

A Capsule of "The Tree"   xvii

PART 1   The Son of the Knight   1

PART 2   Mother and Daughter   69

PART 3   The Vessel   147

Introduction to The Quest

New Falcon Publications, booksellers and some others have told me that there is some question as to just what my books of fiction intend. My statement that they are just stories, and meant to be read that way does not suffice, since I am a psychologist and a Jungian Analyst and, indeed, my introduction to *The Tree* clearly affirmed that I thought of my work as "psycho-mythology," to blend a fiction and psychological fact, just as science-fiction or historical novels combine the knowledge of scholarly disciplines with story.

I stand guilty as charged, therefore, and feel obliged to give a fuller accounting of the trilogy of which *The Tree* was the first, I shall give some additional details in the matter. As some have intuited, there was, indeed, another structure and intention than is usually subsumed in a fictional work.

First of all, my "psycho-mythology" grew out of many years of use of Jung's method of "active imagination." This technique is described fully in the two essays which introduce my little book, *The Knight*, to which I respectfully direct those interested in origins. Here, let me suffice to say that the method is one of making conscious what people do all the time, namely talk to themselves. We are constantly engaged in a more-or-less conscious inner dialogue, talking or quarreling with ourselves, with friends and enemies, with loved ones and strangers. We also fantasize images and stories some of the time. It was Jung's genius to discover that one could consciously take up these barely aware quarrels and fantasies and pursue these "as-if" discussions with a measure of psychological reality. Such serious listening to our inner friend or antagonist, and sincerely continuing the relationship with a full measure of openness and commitment, ultimately leads to the discovery of all the archetypal figures of the psyche that Jung has written about–shadow, anima/animus, old wise man/

woman, Self, etc. This need not be just ego chatter, but can be a true encounter with the larger personality, of which the ego is merely a part. In the essays mentioned above, I noted that I had valuably used Jung's method of inner dialogue for some fourteen years when one day there was a quantum jump for me, in that the work was no longer merely for my own enlightenment and development, but suddenly took on the possibility of social usefulness. That, at least, was the opinion of an inner figure I was working with. Just after Christmas in 1966, a Knight–who had appeared in a dream many months before and had also made appearances in dreams and fantasies in early childhood and in my middle twenties–came forward and said that he had a story to tell, not just for my benefit but for others as well. There were additional people there in the background who also wanted to share their tales. The telling was to include me not just as amanuensis or transcriber, but as a participant in the work. I agreed to undertake this task, and spent the next four years, two days a week, engaged in the writing, thus producing three books. These were: *The Tree*, published in the first time in 1975 (eight years after its completion) and re-published in 1983; *The Quest*, published for the first time in 1984 (sixteen years after its completion); and *The Love* (scheduled for publication in 1985.

One might well ask why the publication of these books has taken such a long time, since these archetypal figures were of the impression that their stories would be of general interest and value. I certainly wondered about it at the outset. The answers that have come center around the idea that the time was not yet ripe or that the stories were not good enough from one point-of-view or another. I am unable to judge this. Some worthy people (e.g. Henry Miller) thought the stories were quite good indeed, others that they were too difficult. This puzzles me since the language used is generally accessible to persons with average education. It is true that some of the tales (e.g. that of Maya, the Yogini), contain technical terms from various spiritual disciplines. All of the latter are defined, however, so that most people seem to understand them. The history of the publication of the stories is fraught with frustration and rejection, much like that of mythological hero tales of which *The Tree* and *The Quest* are examples. I must leave it to the reader to arrive at his own judgement. For my part, I would like these tales to walk about on their own feet and endure their fate. I am pleased to know that they do reach out here and there and find their proper audience. I am grateful for the letters I have received from readers who have been touched by them.

Before I go on to tell more about the structure and content of the stories, here is a capsule version of *The Tree* for those who may not be acquainted with that book.

THE STRUCTURE OF *THE TREE*

The organization of The Tree is of ten tales, told by five men and five women. Each story is of a heroic nature, though the people are quite ordinary, of this world. They come from different times, spiritual origins, beliefs and religions, but each is a tale of individuation, of a pursuit of wholeness and meaning based on their own experience of the divine. The first three stories are by men with no name, but rather they have a quality or character to them. The Knight is timeless, but partakes of Jewish, Christian, and pagan qualities and mirrors best the theme of the Gnostic search for an answer to the question of evil. The Arab, who follows him, adds the Islamic skein to the picture, and pursues in the outer world what the Knight sought within. But the inner is not lacking in the Arab's moon-consciousness as he seeks and finds a transformation of his own passion and greed into love. The Ronin, the third male in this nameless triad, has the Buddhist slant on things. As a Japanese Samurai warrior without a lord, his quest follows the sequence of the ten Ox-Herding pictures, so well-known in Zen, and his psyche finds its wholeness in that process.

The three tales of women which follow are more personal in one sense–they all have names–but are also archetypal. They are meant to be quite characteristic of women, but also come from the stages of development of the *anima* (the image of the feminine in the male psyche), as described by Jung. Julia, the Atheist-Communist, is Mother and struggles with the issue of motherhood and creativity, although her spiritual battle is political. Sybilla, the Nymphomaniac, is Hetaira (prostitute into priestess and oracle), who reconciles the warring gods within herself. Maria, the Nun, is a spiritual priestess as Sybilla was an earth priestess. She overcomes taboo and the flesh and brings a renewal of the Christian story into the modern day.

This sequence of three males and three females is followed by four tales in which masculine and feminine are more blended. First comes The African, who is now a man with a name, searching for the spiritual origins of his existence and happens upon the alchemistic route of transformation. Next is Maya the Yogini, who takes up her traditional Hindu religion in the form of Kundalini Yoga, but does so alone and with a guru who comes to her from within her own soul. The Old Chinese Man is truly eastern and Chinese, Taoist, and sheds light upon himself and his name, as well as the nature of his faith by dialogue with a book, the *I Ching*. Finally, The Medium, Sophie-Sarah, goes into the depths of the Kabbalistic mystery and tries to answer the impossible question of the suffering of her people. She, carrying the image of Wisdom, completes the five stages of anima development described by Jung, following the *femme inspiratrice* stage of Maya, the Yogini.

These ten, meeting at The Tree of Life in paradise, all conclude that the task of humankind, at the present stage of evolution, is to realize the divine within themselves, and to become conscious of their own individuality and particularity. They all learn that the divine needs the human being for its fulfillment, just as the human needs the divine.

THE STRUCTURE OF *THE QUEST*

Just as *The Tree* represented the heroic mode and the seeking of salvation on an individual level, The Quest carries on this search, but now the stories are in pairs and multiples and the whole book has the quality of a single tale, the parts more dovetailed with each other. Rather than a totality of ten, there are three parts here. The first section takes up the story of *The Knight* but in a second generation. Here the Son of the Knight goes out to find his origins, but does so in the company of a dog, his friend and co-seeker. Thus, the section is called *Son of the Knight and Dog*. The parts of the tale have chapter headings, and the story is more like the early English and Spanish novel in style. The content, however, is also one of learning and healing, in which the *Son of the Knight and Dog* go through similar experiences–initiation by women, for example–but from different points-of-view. Through their experiences, both are redeemed and make the discovery of the divinization of man and the humanization of the divine.

The second part of *The Quest* is that of *Mother and Daughter*. Again a pair-story is involved, with mutual individuation and redemption the result. It may be noticed that the classical story of Demeter and Persephone is the background of this tale, just as the hero myth provided background to that of the *Son of the Knight*. This tale of the development of the feminine was also influenced by the story of Ben Hur, it may be noticed by some. Tarot card themes also play a role.

The third part of *The Quest* not only shows the union and surprising connection of the first two parts, but now takes up the problem of multiple integration and union, of all the figures of the tales. The story copes with the theme of "threeness", just as the previous tales resolved the issues of "oneness" and "twoness." Here, therefore, King Arthur, Sir Lancelot and Queen Guinevere serve as models for the search for that Grail of wholeness. The union achieved in the book stands by itself, just as that of *The Tree* did.

Suffice it to say that these books can be read separately but also entail a development in which the archetypes are fleshed out in story form and provide a panoply of a modern myth. I have said, perhaps, too little or too much, but hope that this short introduction will give some answers to the question of what an analyst who writes fiction is up to. Essentially, what I am describing, in story form, is an adventure into the unconscious, from which the themes of origin, good and evil, love and self-realization are revealed as both personal and transpersonal events. But now let the Son of the Knight and his friends speak for themselves.

A Capsule of "The Tree"

A Psychomythological Tale in Ten Parts, Plus Twenty-Odd Poems
By J. Marvin Spiegelman

I, J. Marvin Spiegelman, Ph.D., Clinical Psychologist, Jungian Analyst, have taken an archetypal journey, an inward exploration. In the course of this adventure, I have met ten different people, of other times and places, of other races and religions, each of whom has told me a tale of his own inner journey. I dutifully and devotedly recorded the accounts of their experiences in a six-hundred page manuscript which, in turn, proved to be the first of three volumes.

These ten people (and I) are eager to have their stories known, but, in the busy pace of the modern day, it seems difficult to attract attention to such timeless tales. A friend has suggested that a capsule version of the first volume, *The Tree*, might entice a person to look at the whole. Not knowing how to reduce their stories myself, I have asked these ten people to do so themselves, and the following is what each has had to say.

THE KNIGHT

It is true that I am a Knight, albeit a rather peculiar one, for I am of the ancient time and the modern age; I am both Jewish and Christian and acknowledge a pagan soul, as well. From a youthful life of joy and carefree play with companions, I was summoned by an Angel of God to go on a great journey to different places on earth and in the sea. The reason for this journey was because God was dead or abandoned, or split in pieces, and needed human help. In truth, God was a humpty-dumpty and the world was in sore pain because of it. I, therefore, under the guidance of my Angel, found what seemed to be God or Devil, under the sea. There, beneath the waves, he was a wise man who told a strange tale of self-sacrifice. He had helped men, lived with them as their king, wanted to be their brother, head even given his son as a sacrifice for them. But men still thought that he was the source of the evil in their lives, so he retired under the sea. Knights came to kill him, but upon hearing the story, they embraced him. They either kept silent or went mad with the thought that what men thought was God was Devil, and the reverse; for all were trained to believe that this King was the source of evil. My encounter with this King was even more shaking, since I learned from the Angel that God did not know of his own Power which dwelt in heaven–he was split off from this other half of Himself? Thus, I was faced with a paradox: God was unconscious and lived in two places, each not knowing where the other was. He needed man to help redeem Him, my Angel said

Next I found God under the earth. He had been a benevolent brother under the sea, but under the earth he was a suffering mother. Here she felt every pain, knew every fallen leaf. I sat and silently shared all these pains until I, too, knew in my own soul God the Mother, the suffering God.

And then I came to that same Power in Heaven, which was so fearsome and judging and awe-full, the very Eye of God. And Him I saw on a mountain triangle in the desert. He it was who shook me with his wrath and fierce judgment of men. But I stood and was not destroyed, though I felt the paradox of God's complexity and his separation into parts. I endured God's split and there ensued a softening and warming; the fearful father became benevolent. I then realized that it was the rejected first Son of God, called snake and Devil, who was at fault.

So, I went to the snake–or, rather, the snake came to me. This Devil-Son spoke of creation and destruction, of God's dark moods creating deserts, his tears forming lakes. He spoke, too, of God's need of a partner in order to gain self-knowledge, and of how this first son was the carrier of the same. The Devil-Son questioned and insinuated, probed and criticized. Therefore was he the despised and loved one, the needed and rejected of God. I learned once more that what was known as evil was not so. I grasped that what truly was evil was the separation of the parts of God from each other, and the separation of God and man. With this realization, there came a great vision of the union of God the

Father, God the Brother, and God the Son, in a great triangle, and I was relieved of my own division and gained some peace thereby.

But relief was brief. Once again I was summoned by the Angel. This time I faced, not God's maleness, but femaleness–beauty and poetry and love–in the form of God the Sister and God the Daughter. These I tasted and relished, but there then came God the Raging Mother, she who had been rejected, separated and far from God the wise. The female triangle returned with ferocity and rapine, as well as with love and beauty, and I knew what it meant to be raped by God.

At last the two triangles merged and made the Star of the People of David, and the Seal of the people of Solomon. I saw this sign upon a great Tree, whose roots went everywhere in the Earth and whose limbs reached all parts of the sky. And I saw that this tree contained all those symbols and signs of men's devotion and religion, of their belief and experience. It was the Angel who tole me that this was the Tree of Life, kept apart from men since the early days by the flaming sword, but now open to him who could understand, "Ye are Gods." And I knew, and told my tale: God needs man.

THE ARAB

My story is a tale of love and passion, of pain and grief, of union and reconciliation. A man meant to be a healer, I fell in love, but violated my beloved. A simple matter: there was more passion and greed in me than love. So I fled and wandered the earth. As a sailor, I sailed the seas and saw all manner of men and manners. I fed the raging hyena within me to satisfy all the lusts revolted and submitted. And I learned. At last, in a temple of the great goddess Kali in India, I came to understand the animal and its sacrifice. I learned of the taming of passion by its feeding and endurance, by its sacrifice. I learned of the taming of passion by its feeding and endurance, by its sacrifice and submission, by its transformation into the pearl of great price, into the jewel of a thousand lights, into the star-sapphire which fell from the moon. And I brought this jewel to my beloved who had loved me and knew of my love when I did not. But she, grieving in loss of me and waiting too long, had since married my friend. We loved in the moment and I was healed and redeemed. In later days, I married another love, and became a healer in truth. It was then that I saw my own star and crescent upon that self-same Tree which carried the star of the Knight. And I heard this tale. Hearing of his quest, I told some tales to edify him, and then told my own. But best of all, I spoke of God. In some poems I spoke, and in the colorful tale of where and what with whom I had my voyages, and what it was that I learned about my passion. For I learned to love.

THE RONIN

My story is brief, since I am a Ronin, a warrior and a monk of Japan, who fights and mediates and speaks little. My tale, beginning with the injustices done to me by my masters, is told in words to the famous Zen drawings, the Ox-Herding pictures.

I sought the bull of my nature. I found it, I wrestled with it, I tamed it, alone and apart. But then, I came to love the bull of my soul. I played the flute upon its back and came home with it. I found myself and my own nature, which just is. Then once again I went to the mountain and meditated. I gave myself up, for it was the "me" which was the source of pain and suffering. And I vanished, for I knew that nature, the Tree, was the Source.

At last, I came back to the market place and told my tale and lived my life and gave of my blessings to others. Then it was that I came to the garden where both Knight and Arab were telling their tales under that great Tree of trees. Hearing their stories, I told my own which, though brief, was most moving to them. They embraced me and I, though it was strange for me, embraced them in return. There it is for all to hear, but I cannot repeat it, since life moves on. The lion roars, the sword glints, and Buddha is.

JULIA, THE ATHEIST-COMMUNIST

My story is several-sided: it is a record of the life of a Jewish girl born in Poland, raised in America, who chooses Israel; it is a tale of barrenness and depression in a modern woman who is uncreative and must go deeply into a quest for self-knowledge; it is a tale of generations; it is a story of how one becomes a psychologist; it is a portrait of the atheistic and communist mine, the how and why of it. Finally, it is a tale of how the great diversity becomes a unity in the mind and in life; it is a story of how sickle becomes psi, how one could become an atheist for God, a communist for man. The story was told in the garden to all the others by that same Tree.

SYBILLA, THE NYMPHOMANIAC

Mine, too, is a tale of passion. A daughter of Greek and Egyptian, of Christian and Moslem, I was born out of wedlock, out of grace, and out of time. Gods took me. Gods of Greece and Egypt. They came and possessed me, and from an early age, I was nymphomaniac. I suffered and sought, was degraded and destroyed–almost. Near death from pain and horror, I wandered into the great desert until I came to a cave and met the rabbi who cured me. He, rejected by his people and himself, accompanied me upon the voyage of confrontation of those Gods and demons of Egypt who hounded me. Together, we saved ourselves. And a child was born.

Later, I went to Greece and met and loved a wild boy, who spoke not. I healed him of his pain and horror, and trained him and educated him and faced those Greek Gods. Those same Greek Gods did I face, those who lived at the Omphallos at Delphi where I was conceived one night in passion and love, and in violation of those same Gods. We faced those Gods. And a child was born. A child, and a healing, too.

So I, Sybilla, became a mouthpiece for God, a sybil indeed, and a true "nymphomaniac," a bride, handmaiden, and lover of the Gods. It was then that I came to Paradise where I saw the Tree, met and heard Knight and Arab, Ronin and Julia, and told my tale.

MARIA, THE NUN

Mine is a story of how a woman of the present day, religious and Catholic, comes to terms with her God, her faith, and her most sinful self. I hardly dare to summarize my story, for I must then merely list such things as incest (with father, with brothers), heresy (a coming to know God as Mother), deceit and disruption. But I beg you not to misjudge me. The facts are true, but all is redeemed in my tale, for I found the great Teeter-Totter of God, the cross upon which can live the light and dark of me, the maiden and whore, as well as my brother and spirits. Because, from the very Center of that Teeter-Totter there emerged She who could combine all of these, the great Rose beyond the most virginal, she who is the once and future feminine of God. And my tale was told to all under the great Tree, upon which many crosses grew, including my own.

THE AFRICAN

I chose the title, "African", and it is indeed true of me, by right of inheritance from my forebears, and from my lived experience, even though I was born and lived in Detroit, U.S.A. Mine is a story of how I came to acquire that title, and what the consequences were, but I shall only hint at it here. Enough for me to say that I was a black man full of rage. After much pain and effort, to find something–I was not sure what. I sought roots, identity, history, and other such cliches. In truth, I sought a cure of my anger which was like a Kansas wind, an African wild fire, or…but my words were not enough. A long voyage through the length and breadth of Africa was not enough. Nor was reflection. But then…but then…In Ethiopia, I met my woman; in Abyssinia, I met my queen. Sheba, she was, and Sheba she seemed. She and I became alchemists of the soul. She and I baked and worked and transformed ourselves in the ancient art which began upon our continent and is still pursued on our continent. We found animal, and vegetable, and mineral and transformed them. We found body and mind and heart and changed them. And we found ourselves. We found and made the precious Stone, and joined in love. Rage was cured. And, when sailing upon the ship to return to Detroit, U.S.A., we came at night to another Paradise, where all the others came to tell their tales. And I told my own.

MAYA, THE YOGINI

I am Hindu, though born of an English father. Raised in the India of modern day I lived a full and rich life, more varied. I would imagine, than any westerner would guess. In middle life, however, I felt the need for a retreat, for an experience of the spirit which is typically sought by the men in our country, but less so by the women. I longed for a guru and wisdom, but could find none that I valued sufficiently. From a dream, and from desire, I resolved to go into the seclusion of the mountains and meditate, relying upon the help of the great Lord

Shiva, Himself. So, I went, and I took with me mandalas and commentaries upon the great Kundalini Yoga. I took them and went off alone, leaving husband, children, lover–not irresponsibly, of course, since children were grown, husband had his own concerns, and lover was finding another.

I went and I practiced the Yoga of the Kundalini, all by myself, with only my supplications to the gods, with only my trust in Shiva and Shakti, with only my dreams and fantasies, and with only the pictures and commentary. Three years I remained. For three years, I meditated upon the centers, upon the Chakras, from Muladhara to Sahasrara, from anus to the top of the skull. I was alone and had many deep experiences, voyages in the soul and in space, in time and in dimensions one cannot speak about. Sexuality and hunger, passion and love, power and word, wisdom and vision: all these I faced. I confronted the transformations of God and Goddess, of Shiva and Shakti, as the Kundalini rose up my spine. And my story is a record of what I discovered. When I completed my work, I returned to Calcutta and my family, and was at peace. Suddenly, I was transported once again, but this time to the company of the seekers, the bank of Knight and Arab, Ronin and Julia, Sybilla and Maria, African and the rest. So, to them I told my tale, and there it is for those who wish to know of it.

THE OLD CHINESE MAN

Since each of my friends in this most esteemed company finds himself in a branch of religion or philosophy, albeit heretical, I suppose that I should also state my own. It is Taoistic, I might say, though I have a sone who is Christian, living far away, and my own education and experiences lead me to think of myself as a world-man. My tale, really, is a dialogue, between me and a book. Strange, you might think, for a man to speak with a book, but this is a very special one. It is called *I Ching*, our ancient and esteemed Book of Changes, which, indeed, is oracular and will respond to questions put to it. This text is no mere oracle, of course, but is a record of ancient wisdom and commentary from the Sages, including Confucius, himself. Now I, a man of the modern day, engaged this book, or the living "author" thereof, in conversation. I did not only put questions, but I spoke to the book directly, as if he were, indeed, an old man like myself. This extended conversation proved to be about myself and my arrogance, and about the book and its nature. And there were dreams and events, also. Much change took place, I think–in me, if not in the book. Yet, change took place in the cosmos, I think, in the family of the *I Ching*, in the family of my wife and children, and in the family of my soul. So, my tale is one of wisdom gained, by an Old Chinese Man.

THE MEDIUM

My name is Sophie-Sarah and my story is also with a book, though not entirely. Faced with the horror of the great Holocaust, and faced with my own mediumistic gifts, I resolved to take the dilemma of my people to the great text of Kabbala, itself, the Zohar, and to carry on a discussion with a Kabbalistic rabbi who came to me from Beyond. My tale is not a light one, and I do not believe that I can present a capsule of it which will either be clear enough to be valuable, or fair enough to the original. I can only hint that Hitler is to be found in the tale, and that the Names of God are there, and that mind and heart are challenged. The solution is my own, of course, and limited, but I am honored that the seekers have included me and that I found myself in their midst. I am awed to gaze upon the great Tree, which Kabbalists have always, always known. That tree grows with its roots in Heaven and reaches down into the world.

PSALMS

And, at last, there are poems, by each of the seekers. All try to express their experience, some in one poem, some in several. And these conclude *The Tree*, being the first volume, as it has been said, of a trilogy.

PART ONE

The Son of the Knight

INTRODUCTION

It is true that I am the Son of the Knight. But just because I am the Son of the Knight does not mean I am a chip off the old block. Far from it. I respect my father very much. I love him, though I have not seen him for the bulk of my life and he hardly played any outer role in it. I love him probably for the very things you might all love him for–integrity, devotion to his quest, his innocent valor and optimism. Yes, for all of that. I also think that his story is extraordinary; I am proud to have him as a father, I hope, even, that I have inherited some of his good qualities, if such traits of character can be inherited.

But, I must repeat that I have had no such high quests as the Knight. No Angel came to me in the middle of my wonderful and happy youth and dragged me off on a religious quest. No Eye of God looked down upon me and demanded obeisance. No Snake-Son wrapped himself and his deep darknesses around me and longed for my understanding. In short, I am no hero like my father. I know that he did not ask to be a hero or claim anything other than what he experienced. Still, and I think that you will all agree, he was a hero. Well–I am not. I am must an ordinary mortal and my quest, when you hear of it, is anything but heroic. I am just an ordinary mortal and my quest, when you hear of it, is anything but heroic. I am almost ashamed to tell you about it. When you hear of it, you might say: "Goodness, is that the Son of the Knight? Could he be related to the heroic figure who was able to confront God himself?"

I will answer, "Yes, that is me." "Why, then," you might ask, "do you bother to tell us your story at all?" Why indeed? I tell it because I have to. And because I am in accord with my father's suggestion that "Each tell where he is." He says this is important for us all, and I believe him. We don't all have to be "great" to have a story. There is a place for the little man in life. And even the Knight might have just a ordinary son, mightn't he? And he could love that son even though he was ordinary, could he not? "Yes, of course," you will answer.

So, then enough of my excuses and on to my story. My tale begins in a cave. In this cave there lived a very old man. How old? Sometimes I thought he was as old as God or Mankind. He sat in the cave and never even looked out. His eyes were fixed upon Eternity. It was as if he had seen and heard all the ideas of man for all time, and was contented to sit and gaze at an inner vision of eternity, never bothering to look up and out into the world to see what was going on. He seemed to know all about what was happening; everything was either illusion or would transform into something else; the highest values were Eternal, non-concrete and existed only in that far vision. For his deep blue eyes did see far indeed. At times, when I would talk to him I would look into those blue eyes and think that they were the same as the sky and that his eyes were really God's eyes. He would tell me wise things, in his cool and distant manner, and I was often struck by what he knew–of men and history and ideas. These were all vast and impersonal things. However, he seemed to know very little of personal things.

Like who my mother was! There! I have gotten it out! The main reason for my story is to tell you of the quest that I had to go on. Not heroic at all. I went looking for my mother! I found myself in this cave, was raised there as a little boy–though mostly I raised myself– and I did not know who my mother was! Well, I shall come back to my "quest" in a moment. I am glad I finally got it out, even if I had to blurt it out, rather than say it calmly and prepare you for it, as in a proper story.

As I say, this Wise Old Man lived there in the cave with me and educated me in "vastness", in "impersonalness", in the ideas of History and Eternity. He answered my questions. He was neither warm nor cold, neither close nor distant. He was like the natural laws of the universe and their wisdom: merely "there".

Also in that cave there lived a mother and her daughter. Believe it or not, both mother and daughter were nuns. They gave me to understand that they had been present at the Crucifixion of Christ and, as a result of that experience and that of Christ's Resurrection, they had become devoted Christians. Thenceforth they had been about the business of the Father and the Son. I did not know if this was true, or if they were using a figure of speech, or if they meant that they were there in a previous incarnation, or they were simply crazy. It doesn't matter really. I had a number of talks with the Mother, though they were brief. From these, I gained the impression that she was a great and devoted woman, constantly in the service of other people. She was always going out into the world and sacrificing herself for this or that person or cause. She was, indeed, utterly selfless, I am sure. She was radiant, deep and beautiful, but–and here was the tragedy–she was rather unavailable to either me or her daughter. The daughter was somewhat older than myself–in her teens when I was born–but she, like the Old Man, was always n a state of inner searching. She seemed to me harassed and sad and miserable, but very quiet, as well. She would wander around the cave, and away from it, in places I knew nothing about, so I saw her only occasionally and even then we did not speak to each other very much.

So there it is. As soon as I was old enough to reflect upon things–about the age of four–I became aware of my situation. I was living in a cave with an ancient man who could educate me in the eternal truths, but he was not my father, and was not involved with me personally. I was living, too, with an ancient woman who took care of people in the world, but not of me. And thirdly, there was a daughter, intense and deep, but a recluse.

So, who took care of me? But the time I could ask this question, I realized I had been taking care of myself! The old man of the cave, in response to my question, told me who my father was and why he was far from me, but that was all. In response to all other questions, who my mother was, why I was brought to this cave (or was I born here?), all those things pertaining to my personal life, brought only a shrug from him. I did not know if he did not know or did not want to tell me. My intuition was that these things hardly mattered to him and he may have felt that they should not matter to me either. He did take some interest in the adventures of my father, the Knight, and, apparently, my father met with his full approval, but he never enjoined me to be like him nor anything else. The older woman, the Mother and Nun, when I asked her questions, tearfully told me no, she was not my mother, and she could not tell me who my mother was. She was, she knew, a very good mother herself, but she could not take care of me. "Why?" I asked. "Just because," she answered, tearfully. It had been given to her in life to take care of others, and to do it fully and well. She could not take care of her own daughter, she regretted to say, the one who had been with her at the Crucifixion and the Resurrection, let alone me. She was deeply sorry but she could not. She did not say if it was Fate or God's will. But it was so.

And that is how things were. When I was little I used to dream and fantasy a lot, as you might imagine. The main vision I had, though, was not about having a mother. The vision I had one day, as I awakened from a reverie, was that I had a large Sun inside me like the Sun up in the sky. Afterwards, when I was told about my father the Knight, I knew my inside Sun was like the Sun-lion on his armor, and that I had inherited his sun-like nature. That gave me support.

All the same, I was not, as I have said, like my father, and I very much wanted a mother. So, when I was eight years old, I set out looking for my true mother. I was young but I knew how to pick fruit, how to tell which roots were edible and even how to catch small animals. Nobody taught me these things–I learned them by myself. Such is the power of nature and one's own instinct, I suppose. These things I learned from the age of three or four. How I existed before that, whether I was brought to the cave at that age, whether someone fed me or not–all that was a mystery to me. I was not given the answer to these questions.

I needed very much to know and experience a mother's love, however, and at an age when most boys are ready to turn away from the mother and join boys' groups, at that age I set out to find my mother.

So, you see the great difference between my father and myself. My father began in an ordinary castle, with family and friends, and was dragged out of that pleasant life by an angel, to follow an heroic quest. I, on the other hand, started out in rather unusual circumstances, with no mother nor father at my side, living in a cave with a man older than God and a woman who could mother everyone except her daughter and myself, and with a girl who was deeply within herself and cut off from me. Out of that cave, of course, I, who was really meant to be social and friendly and playful and ordinary, had to come. And the first thing I knew I had to do, was to find my mother. Thus began my very mundane quest.

DOG

I trust that this statement of how I came to begin my quest has affected you favorably. I left my cave with a little knapsack, made of an old bit of canvas I found. In it, I carried a knife, a few clothes and utensils, a cannister for water, and my collection of thirty favorite stones. These were little pebbles, really, but they represented all the colorful varieties of rock and gems in the neighborhood in which I had my childhood, and I took these along as my most (I almost said "only") valuable possession. I also picked some fruit from nearby trees and took a few edible plants. Not that I was worried about food. I knew that I would manage very well. It was just that I did not know what kinds of country I would come to, and it occurred to me that I might miss my native fruits and vegetables.

The first few days were uneventful. I had often wandered as far as two days walk from the cave, so I saw nothing that was in any way unusual or remarkable. There were water and fruit enough so that I could easily replenish my own supply. After the third day, however, the terrain began to change, and it grew more like a desert. I had never seen an arid and rocky landscape and I was rather amazed by it. As the days went on, it grew hotter and hotter, and I found it more and more difficult to find water. My supply of fruit and vegetables was beginning to run out, but I found the plants of the desert gave me sufficient nourishment and liquid to sustain me.

But I grew lonely and sad. This desert country was beautiful enough– nay, it was grand. And the nights, with their stars, were more glorious than anything that I had ever seen–but I was lonely. That may be difficult for you to believe, since I hardly had what one might call warm and cordial relations with anyone up until that time. But I was lonely anyway. Back in the cave, there ad at least been the warmth of another human being present, and of someone to talk to. Now, I was quite alone, indeed.

I am ashamed to say that I cried. I cried not just a little, but a lot. I felt chagrined that such a big boy, almost nine years old, should cry like a little baby, but that, in truth, is just what I did. I was lonely, and I wanted my mother–the mother I had never seem–more than anything. I longed to hear the voice of someone, like the Nun of the cave, but addressed to me, personally. I longed to have my forehead stroked, my tears wiped away, and to be hugged, but there wasn't anyone.

Each day I would walk farther and farther into the desert. Each day I would grow weary and more despairing. Each day I thought that I was foolish to go out looking for my mother. I had no idea where to find her, and I had given up the only real home I had known. Here I was, hot, tired, lonely, and cut off from every bit of human companionship. It had been very foolish of me.

I wandered a long time in the desert. I cannot say how long it was because I had no calendar, did not keep a notebook, and, after a time, one day was like another. But it seemed more like months than it was like days or weeks.

And, it seems to me that I cried very often. Not every night, of course, but often enough to make even me sick of it. Finally, there were no more tears. Or almost no more.

That is the strange part of it. The night when I thought I could cry no more, that finally the despair in my heart could no longer express itself in the form of tears, a strange thing happened. I woke up with a warm breath in my face. Someone was stroking my cheeks and forehead! I opened my eyes and was startled to see–not exactly "someone" but "something". It was a dog! The dog was shaggy and dirty, like myself, but he was obviously not just a wild animal, but one that had lived with someone, no doubt, and had gone astray or run away. The dog had deep brown eyes, very sad, but clearly glad to see me. Luckily, I knew what a dog was, since the Old Man had explained about such animals to me.

Well, I embraced this dog and enjoyed his warm and smell. He, in turn, liked me, and cuddled in closely. It was as if the world had provided not a mother, but another homeless creature, as much in need of mothering as myself!

Now, before you begin to think, "Oh, what a sentimental bit of garbage. What bathos!" Before, as I say, you begin to say that, let me hasten to tell you that this dog was no ordinary little mutt who came along to poor-orphan me and we got on jolly nice together, and all that.

This dog, as I say, was very special, indeed. As I looked into his eyes, I got the most uncanny feeling. I felt he was speaking to me, and that I could understand his language. He seemed to use a kind of non-verbal communication in which I understood perfectly what he was intending to say. I found that I could answer back in the same language, somehow, and get a response. Let you think, though, that I merely made the whole thing up or fantasied it, know that I tested this communication by asking the dog (without words) to do things, like pick up one of my pebbles and bring it to me, and he did it. Without one spoken word or gesture from me of any kind! We communicated in a language which preceded the separation of men and animals.

His story was rather phenomenal, and somewhat unbelievable, I think, but I believed it. And I think that you would, too, if you were to look into his deep dark eyes as he told it. In a way, his eyes, though dark and animal, had that same quality of eternity as those blue ones of the Old Man in the cave. If the blue eyes of the Old Man were the sky itself or God's eyes, then these dark ones of the dog were those of the deepest earth, and maybe of God's other half. But listen to what the dog told me.

This dog had been present, he said, at the Crowning of Thorns. He had been there when the Messiah had come, but was tortured and humiliated. The event was recorded in many ways, including that of an etching by the artist Durer. Did I know him? Well, not exactly, there had been no books nor pictures in my cave, but the Old Man had told me, of course, about the "Crowning with Thorns" and also about he artist Durer.

That a little dog had been present at that event, and at the Crucifixion also, had not occurred to me. Yet he had been there, he said, and he was so horrified, so chagrined, so pained, that he had chosen to wander through the world and not become a human being at all. He had been scheduled, he said, to become a human being in his next incarnation, but the vision of how human beings treat their Gods and how they are with each other was so terrible that he chose to remain an animal. Indeed, he allowed himself to be condemned to walk this earth in the same animal body until the horror of what he had seen could be expunged.

He had seen much in his wanderings, and there had been little to convince him that he had made a mistake. For the last few hundred years, he had been content to simply wander in the desert and forest and stay away from mankind altogether. Neither was he very fond of his own species, dogs. Dogs, he said, had been so trained and selected by man that they were hardly their own creatures any more, and had "sold out", for they had hardly any choice. They had been enslaved, really, because of their need to be close to man. He, however, had maintained his separateness, by choice. Why then, I asked, naturally, had he chosen to befriend me, to lick my tear-laden face and to confide in me like this? Well, he answered, with a sort of harumph, he had guessed that I was rather cut off from the run-of-the-mill human, and that as a lad wandering in the desert, I was as wounded and horror-struck as he.

I assured him I was indeed lonely, and looking for my mother, but I was not present at the Crowning of Thorns nor at the Crucifixion; but in the cave in which I lived, there had been two Ladies, a Mother-Nun and her Daughter, who had. I told the dog about the elder one, doing good in the world and all, and about how she sorrowfully could not be my mother, and he nodded.

When I told my new-found friend, the dog, about my quest for my mother, he grew soulful and sad, saying nothing. "You are behaving like the Mother-of-the-Cave," I said. "What is the matter? Do you know something that I do not, about finding her?" I said the foregoing, of course, in non-speak language.

The dog hastened to respond that, no, he did not have special information, he was just saddened at my plight. He had had a mother, he remembered, as had all animals, and it was hard for him to imagine how a being could survive without such tender and fierce mother-care. He surmised, however, that with People, this was possible, for they could even kill their own Gods, now couldn't they? It was easy for them, then, he supposed, to abandon children!

I hastened to correct him and point out that I was not abandoned. I had lived in a cave, was provided enough food and shelter, apparently, to sustain me until I was able to fend for myself, and had been taught almost everything by a very Wise Old Man. Besides, I was sure that my Mother had not meant to abandon me.

The dog was calmed, and agreed to accompany me on my quest for my mother. Indeed, he got it into his head if we were successful in this quest, he might be able, himself, to recover from the horror of What He Had Seen. Well, enough. This was what happened to me in the desert. I wandered looking for my mother, was on the brink of total despair, and I found, instead, a most remarkable companion, a dog who had seen the Crowning.

IN THE PALE CITY

My joy in my new-found friend lasted quite some time, as we wandered together in the desert wastes, in forests, and in the plain. Our instantaneous non-speak communication in no way interfered with our individual privacy. I was glad to find that out, because after the initial wonder at being able to communicate so readily with such a being, I began to have anxieties lest my private world be invaded when I wanted to be utterly alone. I had spent a great deal of time by myself, after all, and had known that I required this for my own well-being. So it was a pleasure to find out the dog also needed his aloneness and that each of us could fade off into his own inner world. In this way we could be both alone and together at the same time.

I found that Dog conveyed to me a kind of wordless wisdom which the Old Man of the Cave did not have. I cannot put into words what Dog taught me, for it is not that kind of knowledge. Nor is it of images. It has to do with bones and blood and smelling and such things. The language of sensations, yes, but not of eye and ear or taste. But I shall come back to that later on, when this language of bones and blood and smelling and such things. The language of sensations, yes, but not of eye and ear or taste. But I shall come back to that later on, when this language of bones and blood that I learned stood me in good stead. After we had wandered together for some time, when I was almost twelve years old, we came to a dark, pale city. In our silent, nature state, time had little meaning for us. Dog seemed to be "eternal" in his way, and I was just as "at home" with the nature-world as I had been in the cave.

The Quest

I had never seen a city before and Dog had misgivings about coming back into the habitat of Man, the God-Killer, as he called him. Still, I thought, how am I going to find mother if I stay out only in Nature? So, we came to the city. The Old Man had spoken of me, of course, about cities and how one lived in such places, and he was reasonably accurate about crowds and busyness and close contact. But there were lots of things in the city which the Old Man of the Cave did not tell me about: vehicles of strange design which ran without animal power, for example. Now I wondered: did the Old Man of the Cave simply not tell me about these things because they were not important, or was it that he was not really so all-seeing, and, were there new inventions which he did not know about? This introduced an astounding doubt into my mind: perhaps the Old Man of the Cave was not the total Authority I had believed him to be. It was true that Dog had taught me things I had never learned from the Old Man, but these seemed an extension, in other dimensions, of things that Old Man already knew. These were just Dog ways of expressing the same eternal truths. Now, I wondered if there might not be other truths than "eternal" ones, and if there were something like "progress", or if there was a wisdom of the "new" which Old Man, and even Dog, did not know about.

It seemed to be so, because Dog appeared to be rather frightened by the City, and now he huddled close to me at least as much as I to him. So, I thought to myself with quiet satisfaction, I must be growing up and becoming quite independent. I even had thoughts that, perhaps, I did not need to find my mother at all.

But this was illusion. I really did need to know.

What happened next is rather embarrassing to me and I hesitate to talk about it. But in light of the honesty my story requires I will relate it. This is it:

In that pale city, in that moon-covered, smoky city which seemed always to be in some sort of dark state, in that awful city, I went about from woman to woman, asking "Are you my mother?" That, I now realize, was a very foolish things to do. Dog knew that it was foolish, but he was so frightened and not at home there, among people, that he was unable to stop me from asking such a foolish question.

So, I went about asking all the ladies I would see. It must have seemed strange, this rather hulking youth of twelve asking women if they were his mother. Well, I got all sorts of answers. Some ladies smiled and laughingly said "no"; they were quite nice and human. Even Dog had to admit that and say that not all humans are potential God-killers. Others, though, were more like what Dog expected. These would look at me sourly, as if I were teasing them or trying to fool them, and walk off. Others would say, "Get away or I will call the policeman." I knew what a policeman was, Old Man of the Cave had told me, and I was not eager to have anything to do with them, if I could help it; they would put you in a cage. So I ran away from women who said that, and I agreed with Dog that such a person could be a God-killer.

One lady looked strangely at me, when I asked her my question and she said Yes, she was my mother. I was overjoyed. She took me home, but kicked Dog out and promptly began to use me as a sort of slave. She used me to do lots of work of all sorts, mostly menial, but gave nothing in return in the way of affection or even a kind word. I could not believe that this was my mother, and when I would sneak out to Dog to tell him of my suspicions, he agreed totally. I ran away.

I continued to ask for my mother, however. At last, I was taken away and brought to what I understood to be a madhouse. It seemed hard, but I understand it. A young fellow asking for his mother and disturbing all the ladies must be a nuisance. But why they just did not say, "Stop it, please, for you are nuisance!" I don't know. Perhaps it is easier to say "You are crazy" than to say the other. And both of these must be easier to say than face the fact there are such things as a husky twelve-year-old boy, and maybe even adult men and women, who have not had a mother.

THE LOONY-BIN: (1)

So I was brought to the Loony Bin. Now, this was not as bad as you might think. There were a lot of strange sorts there, people who didn't talk at all, others who giggled and talked to themselves, and still others who were very suspicious and wild some of the time, and quite clear at other times; as I say, all sorts. They were rather interesting, really. The orderlies, though, seemed rather rude and brutal and I wondered why they were there. Sometimes I could not tell who was who, for the orderlies at times seemed very much like some of the rough and frightening insane ones. But then, I thought, the insane ones have an excuse–they are mad.

And the doctors, the doctors. The less said about them, the better. All I can say in their defense is that they were only slightly less cold and inhuman than the nurses, and that they often seemed harassed. Besides that, they seemed mostly like machines. But they hardly mattered, since one saw them for only a few minutes a day. The rest of the time, when we were not herded about, we were left to ourselves.

Among the patients were a number of women, and I tried to get friendly with them. I did this mostly during periods of relaxation outside of the wards. At those times, the sexes and ages were mingled. At other times, I was kept with males. This was, apparently an enlightened mad-house, since I was kept with children the first few days, and then brought in with older youths and men, probably because I was so big for my age, almost six feet tall. You can see that it was getting increasingly difficult for me to be mothered, since I was becoming such a large fellow, with muscles and health from so much time in the open.

All the same, I continued my quest in the mental hospital. I tried to get friendly with some of the women patients. There were four sisters, in particular, with whom I became involved. They were not really sisters but I thought they were at first. This was only because that was their common diagnosis I took as the last name! Rather stupid of me I know, but what else was I to conclude when they would not tell me their names. When I went into their ward I saw a chart at the foot of their beds with the diagnosis on it. I, of course, assumed that they were sisters, all with the last name of "schizophrenia" and with different first names, such as "paranoid", "catatonic", "hebephrenic", and "simple". This last is what made me question if those were their real names, since nobody is called "simple" to his face, I supposed. Nonetheless, I thought this for more than a week.

But what I really want to relate is how they reacted to my asking them if they were my mother. I shall use their diagnoses, not their names, since telling their real names would be revealing a confidence and, perhaps get them in trouble. People who have mental diagnoses are rather suspect in this world I am told. Dog could not be with me during my stay in the hospital but when I discussed this with him later he felt human beings are terrible. They speak of mental illness as not shameful and as something to be helped, but then when people have such problems they are labeled, treated as objects, not as persons, and are then subjected to all sorts of insults and inequities. I have been in a hospital and I have seen that this is very often true. The doctors or nurses are not just cruel people, no more nor less cruel than patients nor anyone else. It is just that they are often harassed, indifferent, out for their own security, incompetent, unaware, or simply part of an institutional pattern into which people fall. Well, enough of my lecture.

On to what the ladies told me after some weeks. It is difficult to talk to people in a mental hospital, but the sister who was easiest to talk with was Paranoid. She was usually the most rational and intelligent of the lot, but she seemed inordinately sensitive and suspicious. When I asked her if she were my mother she first looked at me in apparent anger and turned away. When I repeated my question she looked at me quizzically and suspiciously. I pursued her and asked her again. Then she responded very angrily, asking me why was I doing this, was I sent by "them"? I did not now who "they" were, I assured her, but I was serious about my request.

I told her briefly about my adventures and my quest, while she looked at me with disbelief. After a time however, her eyes, which had been at once sad, fierce and angry, softened. She said, mostly to herself to think, but loud enough for me to hear it, "Well, you really seem sweet and open and honest to me, but you are such a big horse of a fellow, and healthy-looking. It is hard to believe you are really looking for your mother. I suspect most of the people in here need their mothers, or better ones than they had, as a matter of fact. But to be open about it seems so strange. I thought you might be one of "them' but I can trust that you are not. You are too straight and sincere-looking."

Then Paranoid said, No, she was not my mother, but she felt sorry for me, and perhaps she could do some mothering for me if that was what I needed.

Good! Here was someone who, although not my mother, was ready and willing to give me some mothering if I needed it. Perhaps I could be fulfilled by substitute mothers. Now there was a fine idea! I answered that her idea seemed splendid to me, at least until my real mother presented herself, but I was not clear about what kind of mothering she could provide for me. Paranoid said that she would think about this for some time and let me know. She suggested that I reflect about what I might want of her. Between us, we might come up with something valuable. I nodded happily.

After a day or two of serious pondering on both sides, Paranoid came to me. "You know, I have given the matter of my mothering you very serious thought," she said. "It is the first important matter which has aroused my interest for some time, aside from coping with the threat of 'them'. You are the first person in a long time I have been able to trust. Just being with you gives me a good feeling. I feel more open and loving and warm. Your clear, good face brings out feelings in me which I have not experienced for a very long time–since my son was killed by 'them' in war. For the first time, I feel warm and motherly again. You are really helping me, I think, by bringing out these feelings in me. I am grateful for that. But it is not enough that I feel motherly–it is important that what I give be received as well."

I was touched by what Paranoid had said. Here was a mother who had lost her son in a war–enough to drive anyone mad, I suppose. And now she was trusting me and being helped by my trust. That was odd. But what did I need of her, really? I could not tell. I told her this, that I was moved by her openness and honesty with me. I was glad, too, if I could be of help to her. And then I laughed, for I felt as if I were being a good mother to her! She laughed too, and then we were both overjoyed. We would often be together after that, and tell each other about ourselves. We had very good discussions together, and I learned much from this lady about wars, politics, economics, and how people are very bad with each other as a consequence of their social systems, their frustrations, and other things. She seemed to know things almost in the way that the Old Man of the Cave knew them, but she was more involved, emotional, an she also gave me much warmth and good feeling. It was a very educational experience.

With Hebephrenic, the second of the "sisters", I had more difficulty. Unlike Paranoid, she was neither suspicious of me nor did she take me seriously. She would talk on and on, in a most giggly and ridiculous fashion for long periods. When I would ask her if she were my mother she would look at me and laugh uproariously, as if that were the funniest thing she had ever heard. She would then talk in the strangest language about things which made no sense to me. I grew both hurt and annoyed, and told her so, but she paid no attention to me.

She was clearly not my mother, I thought, or she would listen to me, at least a little. Then I remembered my own mother obviously had not cared about me. This lady was also ignoring me and my interest, treating me with derision and lack of concern. Perhaps she was my mother after all. When I told Hebephrenic this, with some intensity and at some length, she paused in her giggling and rambling. She looked at me quizzically. She then said quite slowly, and with some effect, "You are the first person in a long time who has taken me seriously." After that she moved off a few paces and began to giggle, gesticulate and go on in a wild discourse in such a way as to make no sense to me.

I reflected upon this exchange and upon her behavior for some days. What did this mean? Why did she say that? Was she inviting me to be serious with her? Of course. I therefore began to follow her around every day, and listen, and seriously as I could, to all that she was saying. I listened both literally and symbolically. I tried to understand with all my might. Soon she ceased going away from me and laughing so much. Next she began to tell me about a whole other planet in which lived all sorts of strange and interesting people. It was quite another life which she lived. It was most complicated and fascinating. I got so involved in her story of this other planet, that I neglected to notice she was now also telling me about her former life on this planet. And by "former life", I do not mean a previous incarnation. When I neglected to notice this, she reverted to her giggly, inane talk. I soon saw my mistake, however, told her that I was interested in both lives, and we soon were having most interesting and deep conversations.

What emerged was that this lady was never taken seriously by the males in her life. Her father had been interested in her only as a kind of pleasant little doll at home and her husband treated her very similarly. She tolerated all this because she had a very rich imaginative life, and could discuss things with her female friends. However, when her son grew up and also did not take her seriously, she concluded–not consciously of course, this had merely "happened" to her–that she was not to be taken seriously. I was the first male to really take her seriously, to listen to her, not only about her imaginative life, but also her concrete life, and was overjoyed. She was very, very happy about that. I had provided what was lacking in her father, her husband, and her son, and she was deeply grateful.

Well, as you can imagine, I was quite moved by her story. I told her that I had found her and her story interesting and was glad I could help her. I discovered that my own imagination was greatly stimulated, to say nothing of the fact that I was required to use my mind to understand her. This was of considerable value to me. I had felt much repaid by the experience.

Now we laughed and giggled together, for we had a relation in which I was father and husband and son, to a woman whom I had asked, "Are you my mother?"

I concluded that she, like Paranoid, had indeed been a Mother-substitute, providing me with a challenge to use my mind and imagination. She had required me to be active in my thought, where Paranoid had been herself active in though with me!

How strange, I thought. I had been looking for my mother, and these two ladies had given me kinds of mothering that I needed but in most unexpected ways.

THE LOONY-BIN (2)

With the third schizophrenic sister, Catatonic, I had more difficulty than with either of the preceding two. Catatonic merely sat, sometimes in a foetal position, sometimes flat out, sometimes sitting up but staring straight ahead, but always with a blank stare and always in silence.

I suppose that I was beginning to get rather cocky by now, for I had "cured" both Paranoid and Hebephrenic and I thought that I would be able to do the same with Catatonic. What had happened with the other two sisters had not escaped the notice of the doctors. Without much talk about it, I was allowed to come and go through the wards as I pleased. One day I overheard a doctor say that it was an interesting procedure, that patients were curing each other. He was right, of course. But I rather thought I was "giving" more than I was getting in these encounters.

This one-sidedness was even clearer with Catatonic, who did not respond to any of my overtures. I was "giving", I thought, yet I was not only not receiving, but she too was not "receiving" what I was "giving". I asked both Paranoid and Hebephrenic what I could do about it, but they were of no help so I had to go it alone.

Some days I would sit alone with Catatonic in silence. Other days I would get annoyed with her and shout at her to talk to me. Still other days I would be in despair, and I would cry and call out to her to help me. None of these brought any response from her that I could perceive as different from her usual apathy.

As time went by, I felt and more removed from her and tended to drift off into my own imagination and fantasy. I missed Dog more than ever. He was out, God knows where, having his own adventures. More time elapsed, I do not know how long. I merely went to the same tree every day, the same one that Catatonic would sit by. I would also sit there and lose myself to the world.

One day, I felt two hands take my head by the chin and lift it up. I found myself looking deeply into the eyes of Catatonic. She no longer looked apathetic. No, far from that. She looked as if she were carrying within her soul all the suffering of all creatures everywhere. Her eyes had a lot of what Dog had in his own look–the silent suffering of creatureliness. I looked long and deep and began to feel in all my bones and sinews and muscles and skin and flesh all the suffering of loneliness, frustrated need, aching non-understanding of all of my young life. Nay, of more than that: not only of my own young life, but of what it means to be a creature. I remembered anew, as if I had forgotten it, that I had suffered the lack of mothering, and that my quest was to find my mother, not mother others or "cure" them. I looked long and deep and lost whatever cockiness that I had had.

I learned from that long look that even creatures with mothers, who have had the full natural loving and care of mothering–even they can have that look. "Gaze," the look said in a wordless way. "Gaze into the eyes of any creature, man or animal and you will see therein the silent suffering of being. No words to it." After this gaze of Catatonic filled my being, she began to stroke my face and arms and my back. She rubbed me gently and vigorously. I felt my bones and skin and muscles respond to her, as if they, were being reached in their cells and in their atoms. Her fingers had magic in them. They seemed to reach me in the non-verbal ways that Dog had reached me with his tongue and with his look.

Catatonic spoke to my pain with her fingers and her look. After a time I felt the magic of her look and her fingers crawl into me and I was moved to look at her as she looked at me. I too was moved to stroke her and reach her in all the areas of pain. My fingers went of their own accord. They seemed to know where the ache was, where the pain was, where the need was. I understood that the magic was in the letting go, letting the impulse and response be the guide. For her flesh and cells and skin responded to me as mine responded to her. And then I felt her rest, and I felt my own rest. The tension of the suffering of the cells was being reduced. And then there was sleep. Long quiet sleeps. Of the dead. Of rebirth.

One day Catatonic began to talk to me. She talked to me out of the blue, not out of a reasonable moment. Just as she had taken my head in her hands and looked into my eyes non-rationally, she began to talk at a non-rational moment. But her words were far from irrational. She spoke softly, slowly, but clearly and with feeling. What emerged was that she was not my mother, of course, but had indeed been a mother herself. She had loved a man deeply but was unable to go with her love since she was already married and had an infant son. She had not abandoned her son for her love, but she henceforth had not responded to her son's needs. She had cared for him routinely, without the sensitivity that would have been in her. At the same time she had only words of scorn and hate for her husband. In time the husband left her and the son died. And she was left with the sin of killing words and killing non-love. It was like a curse, but she did not realize it. She only knew that she must not speak, and must move as little as possible.

After a time, Catatonic continued, she became aware of me. She saw this strange hulk of a boy–who reminded her of her husband, her son, and the man she loved as well–she saw this strange boy doing all sorts of antics. She saw him talk and gesticulate and keep silent. She saw him make all these futile efforts to reach her. It was as if she were being permitted, at last, to look out of her dark, underground prison and see this foolish creature. Something in her made her look at the boy, hold him, fondle him. The rest I knew. It was a mystery. No words. But a healing.

Spontaneously, we both reached for a handful of moist earth and held it up. We looked into each other's eyes, and clasped each other's free hand, while holding the handful of earth with the other. We let the earth fall slowly until it left the hand empty. We then clasped both hands, looked into each other's eyes once more and embraced. It was a ritual. A union, and a healing. And it was over.

The experiences with Paranoid, Hebephrenic and Catatonic were overwhelming for me. I did not believed that I could accomplish much more in that mad-house. I had both given and received more than I had ever imagined. Indeed I was now losing the drive for the initial quest which had brought me out of the cave–the longing to find my mother. What more, I wondered, could an actual mother do than has been done by these three great women? They, together with Dog, and what the Old Man of the Cave had taught me, had prepared me very well for life. Yet, there was the fourth sister, Simple, and it looked as if the doctors of this hospital were not going to release me until something had happened between this last Schizophrenia sister and myself.

In some ways Simple was easier to connect with than any of the others. She was neither suspicious nor silly nor silent. She spoke to a person who addressed her but in a rather bland way. She was neither intelligent nor stupid. What was it, then, that repelled me? Was it her blandness? Yes, that accounted for a lot. But there was more. She had been a drug-addict and a prostitute. She had been a thief and a murderess. And she seemed to have no guilt nor remorse for any of her misuse of people or society. There was an odor about her which disgusted me. Literally! When near her I smelled the unwashedness, the stink of her amorality.

I was rather embarrassed by my attitude and by my repulsion, for I did not like to think of myself as a judgmental, holier-than-thou kind of person. Especially after my healing experiences with Paranoid, Hebephrenic, and Catatonic. I noticed, however, that the other three kept away from Simple as well. I did not know why, and none of them would tell me.

There was nothing for it, however, but to take the problem with Simple directly. So I summoned up my courage, tried to settle my aversion for her smell with the hope that I would soon adapt to it, and decided to involve myself with Simple until whatever it was that needed resolution would take place. I approached her with my usual "Are you my mother?" She laughed rather hollowly and said to me: "Why are you pulling that crap on me? You know I am not. And I doubt that you are still really interested in finding your mother. Unless it is 'mother-fucking' that you want."

Do not misunderstand. I was not so much disgusted with Simple as I was with myself. For the first time, I became aware of a feeling in myself which was one of self-loathing. I did not know why it was that I loathed myself, but there it was. And the disgust went deep, though I did not know the reason for it. What Simple said about "not really being interested in finding your mother" had truth in it, but "motherfucking?" I knew of course what was meant, but since I did not even know who my mother was, why should I be disgusted by "motherfucking?" Was there in me a natural revulsion against incest? And if so why did not Simple feel it?

When I told Simple these thoughts she simply laughed again. She had some interest in my self-loathing–when I told her that, she nodded, I thought even sympathetically–but the rest made her yawn. I retreated into myself. What bothered me about Simple? Her smell? Of course. Her coarseness? Yes. Her amorality? I did not know for sure. I was most interested in talking to her about her smell and her coarseness, but I was afraid that if I did she would talk to me again in that fashion which made me feel full of self-loathing. But if I asked her about the drugs and prostitution and thievery and murder, I would sound like a righteous moralist and I would be even more vulnerable to what I feared would be a very vicious tongue. What then?

I decided that all that I could do would be to tell her just what I had felt and thought. When I did this, when I told her just what my thoughts were she started to weep. I was dumbfounded by this, for it was the last think that I expected. Brutality, coarseness, hard truth, laughter–any of these, but quiet tears? From Simple? From Catatonic, perhaps, but from Simple? Quite unexpected. I was so startled, in fact, that I failed to comfort Simple at all. I apologized for my lack of consideration, and then listened to Simple's story. Did she smell? Well, it should not be surprising, for she had been dragged through all forms of human iniquity and degradation. Did I feel self-loathing in her presence? Good, then I might get a glimpse of how she had felt about herself for a very long time. She had pushed these feelings away long ago, the consequence being the blandness that everyone saw in her. She wept and wept. I remained by her in silence. It felt to me as if she would weep enough for a bath, or a lake, or even an ocean. But perhaps it was only enough for her to wash away the accumulated horror and disgust of a painful life.

She had been raised in an orphanage without any idea at all of who her mother or father might be. It was a loveless place, and she ran away from it when she had been about my present age, just before she was thirteen. The next twenty years found her in a life of being used by men and using them in return. She had become a thief soon after leaving the orphanage, learning how from other wanderers. Because she was inept as a thief, she was quickly caught and spent some time in jail, where she learned about drugs and prostitution. Later on she became a drug addict, longing for oblivion, and later yet, a prostitute, in order to pay for her drugs. What about her being a murderess? I asked. Yes, she said, several times. She had had several abortions, long after the foetus would have been a "person". She had also killed a pimp who had so misused her and deceived her that she could not tolerate it. It was then that she was sent to prison and from prison to the loony-bin. And here she had been for a year before I had arrived.

These were the "facts". Oh, she told them in more detail, but this was the outline of the story itself. Telling the tale seemed to change nothing. She had gotten relief, of course, from being able to weep and feel again, but the sordid fact of her life remained. She felt only self-loathing from it, horror at the men and events that helped her become this way; but still, what real morality was there? "Was life meant to be otherwise?" she asked.

Since I was not quite thirteen I did not know how life was supposed to be, and I had no answers for her questions. I did feel the need, however, of making her feel better. I told her of my life in the Cave, and of my search for my mother. I felt rather foolish in having such a quest, compared with the problems of her existence. It bothered me that I had no answers to her questions. Was man really like this? I had understood from Paranoid that men were very much distorted by their social systems, but then again, men had also created these systems had they not? Was man, by nature, bad or good? Or was this a silly question?

All that Simple was able to say to me was that she had been touched by me in two ways–the first was in my experience of self-loathing and the second was in my experience of being terribly vulnerable. These two experiences of mine somehow brought her back to herself; she could feel again. The rest, whether man was good or bad, whether social systems caused man's difficulty or vice-versa—about all that she did not care very much. She could feel again; she could, therefore, live again, and that was enough. She wondered, of course, if life was meant to be otherwise, but she was content to take it as it came. As long as she could feel. For her, life was simple: it was to feel and to experience.

I pondered a long time about what Simple had said. She taught me something: Life is Simple. The rules and regulations and the understanding are all part of it, of course, but the main thing is in the living. Well, I understood that. And then, something very deep hit me.

This quiet message from my experience with Simple suddenly and totally freed me from the authority of the Old Man of the Cave. He had been totally wise, knew all, and had retreated from life, was content with the eternal ideas. But now Simple had taught me that feeling was all, and life was in the living! Simple was as great an authority as the Old Man of the Cave. The Old Man now met his match (though, of course, he did not seek it) in this simple drug addict-prostitute-thief-murderess. Life was simple—in the living and the feeling of it! My old authority, already undermined in his monolithic unity by Dog, had now been overthrown by Simple.

And then I laughed. For I knew that in my quest for the Mother, I now had lost the authority, gained another, and in reality, had both two authorities and no authorities!

I was only one month away from my thirteenth birthday when I left the mad-house. I had been pronounced cured by the doctors. The Schizophrenia sisters had also been pronounced cured, and I had been acknowledged an important place in their treatment. We all left together, the "sisters" to take up the paths of their lives and I to continue my own.

DOG'S STORY

I emerged from the mad-house expecting to enjoy the light of day and my regained freedom. Indeed, it was almost a year to the day since I had been "imprisoned" in the loony-bin and underwent the experiences of healing with the mother-substitute, schizophrenia sisters. During all that time, I had not been with my good friend Dog. I am ashamed to say that after the first few weeks, I no longer missed Dog.

But perhaps there is a deeper meaning in all this, which eludes me. Could it be that I my deeper relationships with the "mothers"at this point that it was essential that I not, just not have the help of Dog? Was it a necessity that we both be separate at this time? I do not know, and I leave it to you for your opinion.

In any case when I did see Dog, as I emerged from the mad-house, I was very happy. Dog seemed older and even more haggard and unkempt than when I was with him in desert and city.

Dog was more glad to see me. He looked as if he had been through terrible suffering. In fact, he was so beaten up that I was afraid for his life. I nursed him back to health as best I could by providing warm blankets, good food, and peace. He was really unable to talk, even in non-speak, so I told him of my own adventures in the mad-house among the schizophrenia sisters. He looked at me with wide eyes and open mouth as I told him my story of the four sisters in the mad-house.

After some days he was finally able to speak, and then he told me the following tale, in no-word, telepathic, dog-speak, of course:

"You know, it is really rather fantastic. My own experiences during this past year have been quite parallel to your own. While you were coping with the four schizophrenia sisters, I, too, have had an experience of woman. I encountered someone similar to the ladies whom you describe. Indeed I could match in my experience, the labels of Paranoid, Hebephrenic, Catatonic, and Simple to an exact 'T', as they say. The difference is that I knew only one lady and she was not in a mad-house. In addition to that, my experiences did not turn out so well or favorably as yours. Indeed, I am lucky to be here with my life. What a paradox! You were in a mad-house, with people who were ill and emerged transformed. I, on the other, hand have spent my time in this pale city, with similar types, and have had nothing but pain, humiliation and agony–no transformation. Indeed, I am more convinced than ever that people are God-killers!

"After I was separated from you by the keepers of the mad-house, I wandered disconsolately around the city, trying to figure out a way to either free you or get to you myself. Within a short time I happened upon a strange lady who walked about with an umbrella all the time. She, too, it seems, was trying to get into the mad-house though her reasons were not clear to me. She was quite eccentric but the gate-keepers and hospital doctors either paid her no attention or joked with her. I could see she was eager to get in so I stayed with her for some time, following her about. She seemed more and more disturbed.

"At last I was able to ascertain that she had a son inside the loony-bin. Perhaps you were able to see him? No? Too bad. The poor woman was absolutely distraught with the fact that her son was inside and she was unable to visit him. I am not clear as to why this was. It seemed that her husband, who was a powerful man, had labeled her as mad and as a danger to her son, and therefore, she was enjoined from seeing the lad. She thereupon behaved as madly as possible, as if to prove that she was so and, therefore, entitled to be put into the mad-house along with her son!

"I had enormous compassion for this poor woman. Her goal was similar to my own–to free a loved one, or, at least join him if she could. But we were both doomed to defeat as a consequence of the powers of those who could decide these matters.

"This poor woman, unlike you, was unable to understand my language of dog-speak. I was therefore unable to comfort her, or help her in our common aim.

"Days and weeks went by, and she would neither eat nor take any solace at all. Even I, as I would follow her in agony, was seen as an enemy by her and she would shoo me away. I was forced to follow her at a distance. She became more certain that the 'powers', including her former husband, were working against her. She was absolutely correct, of course, and was called crazy. But she was also kept outside the mental hospital. She grew more and more despairing, as did I, who saw her suffering and could do nothing about it. At last one day she simply fainted from exhaustion and lack of food. She stayed in her little room and wasted away, as I went from person to person, trying to apprise them of the sad state of affairs. For my pains I got kickings and scoldings. Finally I gave up and simply remained near her. She died and was borne away, with no one knowing of the dark evil of her former husband or of the cruel society which treated her without an ounce of compassion.

"This terrible experience compounded the dim view I have had of people, the God-killers. I had, as you know, begun to change my view as a consequence of my relationship with you. Since you were not a vicious person, and certainly not a God-killer, I had to conclude that people, as such, were not necessarily God-killers. This experience with the poor umbrella lady, however, tended to fix me in my previous sour view of mankind. I was in very nearly total despair myself for many days after she died.

"I recovered, however, and gained the understanding that although life was hard, I had, somehow, to find a way to reach my only friend, hapless in the loony-bin. I realized that I had to get to the 'powers', those who really ran things. They were the people who would help me to get to you and would either free you or allow me to stay with you inside. But I did not know how to reach them.

"One day, I thought I was really going mad, for there, wandering about I saw the very same umbrella lady. Was I indeed mad? Good, I thought, then they will put me in the loony-bin too, where I can be with my friend, the Son of the Knight. But no, I thought, they probably are not so kind to dogs. They must surely simply kill mad dogs. Indeed, I had heard something about that in a song. Chastened by this bit of reality I advanced toward the woman with the umbrella. She seemed to recognize me. Even more, now she was able to speak to me–not as well as you do, but at least with the bare outlines of understanding. Perhaps her suffering itself enabled her to understand of dog-speak. But then, again, you have not suffered so much and you understand dog-speak, so it may be simply a mystery. Those who understand dog-speak are a rarity, are they not?

The woman with the umbrella had not, as I had thought, really died. She had been taken to a hospital, more dead than alive, but had recovered. They had nursed her back to health, but as soon as she was able to tell her story, she received the same treatment that she had suffered before. Only now it was even worse. She was befriended by one doctor who had managed an interview with her former husband. He, the brute, was able to convince the doctor that his wife was mad. And how was he able to do this? He arranged for the poor woman to see her son in the loony-bin for just a few minutes. The boy, apparently in a fit of pique, madness, or unreality, ran away from his mother and rejected her. This was sufficient proof for all concerned. So now our umbrella lady was wandering about, in a quite mad fashion. But now her madness was one of giggling, laughing, talking to herself, instead of suspicion. She believed that no one, husband, son, nor father would take her seriously. Well she was quite right. No one did.

"I sat and watched her giggling stupidly. I understood and tried to speak with her but she withdrew more and more. At last she was utterly silent and detached. She would neither laugh nor speak. She sat in total silence. At this point, I abandoned dog-speak and approached her as I did you–I licked her with my tongue and warmed her with my body. This seemed to bring her out of her total withdrawal, but when she emerged she was lifeless-looking. Her eyes were vacant and she was very bland in attitude. She apparently had decided to live, as a consequence of my animal warmth, but nothing more. I feel rather guilty even now as I tell this part of the story. Perhaps I should not have intervened at all. Perhaps I should have let her die in peace rather than try to help her as I did. If I had not meddled perhaps the subsequent tragedy would not have occurred. Well–no one can answer that question for me, I suppose. Except in Dog-Paradise where all questions are answered.

"But let me go on with my story and not try to soften it. She emerged from her withdrawal and then began to be concerned with her survival. In a mechanical way she would either steal money or food, or would offer herself as a prostitute in order to keep her unprecious life going. She was very decent to me, I must say, buying the kinds of food that I like and providing me with shelter. Other than that, her life seemed to be a progressively coarsening situation–thievery, immortality, exploitation of others and self. Through all this, there persisted her feeling of hurt and need for revenge. She seemed to grow madder and madder. One day she acted as if she saw her previous husband, the villain who had helped bring he to this miserable state. In reality, as I saw, there was simply a tramp of a man, who was reasonably well dressed at the moment, as a consequence of his own thievery. The umbrella woman, however, in her madness could not distinguish the man from her husband and when he approached her as one does prostitutes, she screamingly assaulted him with her umbrella and killed him. It may be hard to believe that an umbrella woman, with her own strength, can kill a man even if he is himself not too strong, but she did so. She did this in her accumulated fury, frustration, and agony. There was nothing that I could do to stop her.

"The umbrella woman was soon apprehended, brought to trial, and quickly convicted. She offered no defense. Indeed, she seemed strangely at peace. For she had, in her own mind, gotten her revenge against the devilish man who had ruined her life. I did not have been able to dissuade her from her illusion. So, she was condemned to be executed. Her madness now seemed to be of insufficient severity to free her from the guilt of murder. How strange are the customs of people! How cruel they are! How like God-killers they are indeed!

"I remained as near as I could be the umbrella lady. But there too I was frustrated. For she was kept in prison, every bit as inaccessible to me as your loony-bin was. At last, a week ago, she was executed. I did not see it, but I know of it.

"There was nothing I could do except to take up once more, my vigil outside your mad-house-prison. Here I have been for one week. I cannot say I have been despairing for you. No, I hardly had time to think about when or if you would emerge. I was so full of the experience of the umbrella lady. I am sure these past months have seen me go down-hill, so you see me ragged and unkempt.

"Well, dear Son of the Knight, this has been my story. One of sadness, frustration and despair. I am convinced more than ever that man is a God-killer, though I have now met two people, the Umbrella Lady is dead. Perhaps she too is a God whom the People have killed. I do not know. My experience, I must tell you, is similar to that I had at the Crowning. But you, dear friend, you are now free. Indeed you are not only free, you seem to have helped others as well. Perhaps it is fated that I should be with you. Perhaps you are the one to help me overcome this horror. When I am apart from you, it seems worse. I must confess, however, that we too have had our experiences of God-killers, even when we were together. Well, at least we are united once more. Only one year has gone by. And what is one year in the face of the eternity of God–and God-killers?

SON AND DOG COME TO COMMON GROUND

Dog's story horrified me. I was as deeply saddened by it as I was made happy by my positive experiences in the mental hospital. How paradoxical life is, I thought. But then that is what the Old Man of the Cave had taught me already. I realized again that even though the Old Man of the Cave was no longer the Authority for me he had, indeed, given me the benefit of great wisdom.

This, however, was no time for wisdom. What was needed now was to nurse my friend Dog back to health. He had undergone a terrible experience and his harsh views of Mankind had become even more ingrained. I, his only friend, had somehow to sustain him. He recovered physically in fairly short order, being basically a very healthy creature, but the sadness of his eyes increased. The first thing I had to do, I thought, was simply to show him creatures who were not God-killers. I proceeded, therefore, to search for the Schizophrenia sisters. I soon found them.

After Dog had spent some time with them, watching them, living with them, enjoying them, growing closer with them, he visibly softened. For these sisters, when I told them about Dog, were very eager to do everything they could for him. They washed and bathed and loved and stroked him and adored him and stood about waiting for his bidding. They mastered Dog-speak and attended to his every whim.

Dog was rather startled by all this and did not know what to make of it. He was suspicious at first but, at my insistence, he submitted himself to all this fussing and loving. We remained with each Schizophrenia sister for several months until it seemed clear that it was time to continue our quest. It was becoming "our" quest now.

While Dog was being fussed over by the sisters, I had time to reflect. I realized that I was still interested in finding my own real mother, but the goal was less intense than it had been. What had been taking place in my mind, rather, was the growth of a question: "Why are people the way that they are? Why did my mother have to abandon me, if indeed, that is what happened?" Now that my own needs for mothering had been fulfilled–at least to a great extent–I was now, I realized, concerned with larger questions.

When I told Dog of my thoughts, I was surprised to learn that he, too, had changed. His very favorable experience with the Sisters had made him aware that certainly not all people are God-killers; I was not, and the Sisters were not. But more than that, he was now feeling better, warmer, friendlier. This permitted him to ask himself the question: "Why are men God-killers at all? Clearly they did not have to be. What led them to do this in the first place?"

So, what had begun as a quest for my mother, now became an attempt to understand why men are so unloving. In short, we were both beginning to wonder why there was evil in the world. We now had a joint quest–a quest for understanding. We both needed to understand more deeply. We had been "cured" of our pain, but now we needed more for our understanding. The Schizophrenia sisters had given us much and had taught us much but they, as women frequently are, were contented with personal answers and did not need to pursue these questions further. Well, that may not be quite fair to them, when I say, "as women frequently are." Rather, let me say that they continued in a feminine way to understand and live their life, and at this point, both Dog and myself needed more in the way of a masculine understanding.

But where could we go? Who could teach us? Who, beyond the Old Man of the Cave, or the sisters, could give us the answers? Was I, at only thirteen, already finished with the world? No, I still needed to find my mother, but–then it struck me. I realized that in all my search for my mother I had forgotten that I was thirteen, and that I was not yet initiation ceremonies of tribes and societies. All of them had some way of making a boy into a man and usually at just about my age. But I was not initiated! Perhaps that was what I needed now, to undergo the initiation of a tribe in order to become a man, as part of their ritual. Perhaps I now was ready to undergo such ceremonies and receive such wisdom: perhaps this would enable me to understand why there was evil in the world.

Dog, on his part, was rather skeptical of any advantage that such an initiation would bring, but he acknowledged that that was the way of men and I should, indeed, seek a tribe and undergo such an experience. For his part he had already been initiated in the way of dogs very long ago. He was interest, however, in learning the answer to his question. We both therefore agreed to seek out a tribe where we could learn something about man and evil and where I, at least, could be initiated into manhood.

We agreed also that we should leave the City and go back into nature. As far as we could tell, all sense of tribe had already broken down in the City. It was clearly not very easy to get initiated there. Yes, we could get some form of it, as we could get some answers to the questions of evil, but I already knew what the City could offer along these lines. That sounds presumptuous, I know, coming from a thirteen-year-old, but it was, all the same, true. We were not so arrogant as to be unwilling to submit–indeed, we were seeking a tribe where we could–but not in the City.

So, we set off once again to our familiar native habitat of deserts, forests, and plains. But something had happened during our stay in the City. We were now finding it difficult to find true nature, untouched by Man. Everywhere we went we saw cities, towns, villages. It was as if the population of mankind had grown to enormous proportions during our comparatively brief absence from the country. Was this an illusion? Had aeons: he was not concerned about time as measured by a watch or sun-dial. For him, time was measured in terms of meaningful moments, or reincarnations, or aeons. I, on the other hand, being young and involved with such things, was very much aware of the passage of minutes, hours, days. At thirteen one is quite aware of the length of the day.

But more important even than this strange sense of time, induced by the apparent spread of population, was the fact that we had difficulty finding a real tribe. What had happened? Had all the tribes of the earth suddenly become "civilized" and embraced an urban life? Were there no more small groups of people living together in a cohesive whole, worshipping the same Gods and undergoing the same general experiences? Or was all fragmented, as we had seen in the City?

As we wandered we asked ourselves this question. And the answer always was Yes. There seemed to be only fragmentation, disbelief in Gods, or decadent beliefs and exploitation. Civilization there was aplenty, in terms of history, things and culture; but tribal unit, feeling, Gods? Not much. How then was I going to be initiated? And how were Dog and I going to get our answer to the problem of evil? We did not know. So we just wandered.

We wandered long after my thirteenth year was over. It seemed a great shame and a wrongness that I was not initiated during the proper year, but this too was a symptom of the wrongness of the times. My fourteenth year passed, and my fifteenth. Throughout our wanderings, we saw the same situation repeatedly, despite the difference in outer civilization. What we saw was the meaningless of the lives, the worshipping of Gods no longer truly believed in, or the disappearance of Gods, the accumulation of power and things, the absence of love. Now this was not true for everyone of course. We often saw people who were happy, loving, and content–well, not very often, but often enough to indicate that the blight was not total. The overall atmosphere, however, was very sad.

Still, I had to be initiated. What could we do? Find something less than perfect, was my thought. Dog looked at me in such a way to communicate what humans mean when they shrug their shoulders, "I don't know, what else?" So I decided to look for a tribe which would be as close as possible to my needs.

Now with that more modest attitude, we soon came upon a tribe living in a pleasant sort of place which seemed to meet our standards. There was nature enough all around, but there were buildings and comfort, and enough material and spiritual wealth to make people happy.

"Here," I said to Dog, "Here I will take my stand and be initiated." Dog seemed less sure, but shrugged his shoulders once again, and did not raise any protest.

THE SEARCH FOR INITIATION

In order to remain anonymous and cause no undue personal difficulty to anyone, as I was careful to do in speaking about the Schizophrenia sisters, I shall simply call the place that Dog and I finally chose for initiation, Town. For such it was, after all. It was situated in a larger region which one might call Rolificana, if one would like. And there was an even large region, immense actually, of which this too was only a small part. Let us call the larger region Cameria. As far as I was able to tell, one Town in Rolificana was much like another, and none of these differed very much from other sub-regions in Cameria. So, I will tell you of our experiences in Town.

Dog and I lived in Town for several years, from the time I was sixteen years old. I want to tell you about Town, its inhabitants, and how it governed and took care of itself. This, after all, is the arena in which my initiation finally began.

First I need to describe what the population of Town was like. I came to these observations only after a period of time–it was all too confusing at first. I very much needed. Dog in all of this, since the inhabitants of Town tended to misuse language; they would speak, say, of Peace and mean War, or of Freedom and mean Restriction.

Were it not for Dog and what he taught me, I would have fallen victim to the meanings of these words, as many of the deluded populace had, and would have lived in illusion. This would have been no worse than not living in illusion–no, far from it! I did not see that the enlightened ones were any happier than the deluded ones. In short, Town was far from an ideal place to live. Not because of the place but because of the people. No, not because of the people, really; they were basically like you and me with all their faults and strengths and capacity for good and evil. It was not because of their social system either, though that had a lot to do with it. The reason that they were in such bad shape will emerge later on.

It strikes me that I am having difficulty staying with my story. I think I am rather ashamed for having to describe the people and the system of Town in the way that I have chosen. It seems a rather unfeeling and barbaric way. For you see, the way that I am going to describe the people is one that I learned from a book of one of the doctors when I was in the loony-bin. They are the names of various kinds of mental disorders, such as the various psychoneuroses. These labels are not kind, I know, but, I am afraid, that is how things really were in Town. I do not mean to denigrate these people; they were no more to blame for their condition than the people in the loony-bin. However, they were allowed to walk around and even put others in the loony-bin!

Enough of my apologies; on with my story. I am now going to describe the people of Town. I hasten to add that those of whom I speak by no means constituted all the types and classes of the People of Town. Many did not fit into my categories. But enough of them did to make things look that way.

I will start with the Older People. These, I thought, should have been the ones who could enlighten me with wisdom, teach me of the sayings of the past and tell me the truths of their Gods, as the Old Man of the Cave had. But could they? No. They were, according to the book, Depressives or Psychosomatics. Many would look glum and sit alone, or complain bitterly about life, or how the young were no longer respectful, or about the lack of law and order. Others would speak mostly about their aches and pains and the various kinds of doctoring they had had. They all seemed narrow and pasty in complexion, and man and tight-lipped. Not all though; some were Pollyanna Hysterics, saying that everything was all right, and going to be fine, that there was no reason for the bad things going on in the world except that some people were bad, or that the government was not like it used to be. Need I go on? Probably not, for you can readily see that the Old People could really tell me nothing about the problem of evil. All that I could learn really, is that here is another example of tragedy–people grow old and have learned nothing, can enjoy nothing, and simply wait to die. Dog and I both "shrugged our shoulders."

Now, the Adult class, both Young and Older, constituted the bulk of the society. The former were primarily characterized as Anxiety States, and the latter as Manic-Depressives. Both were pre-occupied with their status in society, the achievement of things and power. The Young Adults were anxious lest they not get things or not enough of them, and the Older Adults were, by turns, manic in their pursuit of enjoyment and pleasure once they had things and money, or depressed that they had not achieved what they wished. Both Young and Older Adults drank a lot. Whereas the Older People mostly took pills for their pains, the Adult group took pills of various kinds and a great deal of alcohol, as well. Dog and I were not very happy with the Adults, Young or Older; I knew that there was little chance to be initiated meaningful there.

It was not so much different when one looked at the Youth. These one might characterize as Passive or Aggressive, or at best Passive-Aggressive. Those that did not totally swallow the meaningless values of their parents, went to another extreme and sat all day and took other kinds of drugs, not alcohol. They begged for their livelihood, not out of conviction, but out of lack of desire to achieve anything. Their visions also seemed meaningless. There were still others who simply tore down everything, attacked the system without much sense. They too were not impressive; but I had a certain sympathy for the Youth. They, at least, were quite clear that the Gods were dead, and that the lives of their elders was meaningless. Indeed, Dog and I both saw that the death of their Gods was the cause of the suffering and senselessness.

Dog became sympathetic. He saw the God-killers suffering from their crimes. They had killed their God and now they were feeling the emptiness of it.

But let me go on. I have described the People, but not described their leaders and wise men. The leaders are easily described as Psychopaths. They were interested mostly in power and its achievement, techniques of getting what they wanted. They would use all sorts of phrases with high-sounding messages but did not mean them. These were the people who meant War when they spoke of Peace, or confinement when they spoke of freedom. They who seemed to have no moral sense spoke most often about morality or law. They were the frightening ones, for they had the power. The Wise Men very often had contempt for the Leaders, but they too, were not so endearing. They were largely Obsessive, continually concerning themselves with meaningless Research or Scholarship when they were not using their skills in the service of the war-machines of the Leaders. Or there were the Compulsives who interpreted the law, commented for the People, carried on dried up rituals of the already dead or gradually dying religions. Clearly these Wise Men were no longer wise at all.

Where, then, were the initiators? Well, there were the Teachers, who were very often, Oligophrenics. They were, characteristically, not intelligent enough to get the jobs or professions which would bring in more of the "things." Or, they were teaching the values and the facts of the centuries long past, in ways that would kill the desire of Youth to learn. So they clearly performed no meaningful initiation.

What about the religious? The Shamans, or the teachers of the soul? Well, those who were not Compulsive were either priests of the churches and Hysterical, or they were analysts of the mind and were Schizoid. They sat in their chairs and dredged up more and more dried-up, meaningless data about the causes of pain of the soul. These clearly could not initiate anyone, except into the meaningless aspects and the pain of self-reflection.

Who, then? I not only was not going to find my mother, I was apparently not going to be initiated either. There were, as I have said, many who did not fall into the above classes. These were the artists of various kinds, of course, who tried to express the general horror, out of their own agony, and apprise the people of their condition. There were, too, the Athletes who at least kept their bodies in good shape and did not look pasty and half-dead. But they could not initiate any more than the Artists could, since they had to serve the going concern. Besides I was neither Artist could, since they had to serve the going concern. Besides I was neither Artist nor Athlete. How did I know that? Well, I didn't, really. Perhaps I had something of both in me, but I felt in my bones that I needed initiation. How to get it, and where to go?

THE SEARCH CONTINUES

The more Dog and I searched among the People and Institutions of Town, of Rolificana, and of Cameria, the more despairing we became.

We did what we could to accept their achievements and values, but we were not successful. No, that is not true. We were quite successful, indeed, but our successful. No, that is not true. We were quite successful, indeed, but our success left us ever more miserable. Our search went on.

At last, we met a man from Pueroa. He seemed to understand the malaise of the Camerians and he was a Healer. He had become a Healer in Pueroa, the origin of most of the ancestors of the Camerians, and had come to Town to do his work. His manner of healing was to help a person look into his own soul, his dreams, his fantasies. Well, Dog and I both needed healing, that was clear. And the teacher of this Healer, in Pueroa, seemed very much like the Old Man of the Cave to me. So, I placed myself under the Healer's care.

In the course of time I discovered that I too should become a healer, for that is what my soul seemed to say. Dog and I went to Pueroa, therefore, so that I too could become a Healer–Healer of the Soul.

Dog and I remained in Pueroa until I was twenty-one. That, of course, is when a boy becomes a man and so, I suppose, did I. For I learned much in Pueroa, and so did Dog. There we learned the source of the pain and suffering of the People–their Gods had died. Not only, as Dog had supposed, because they had killed their God. The Gods had died a natural death. Gods are creations of the soul too, are they not? And, when people grew up, and outlived the images of their Gods, then the images died, and new ones were needed. Clear enough, is it not?

And Evil; why was there evil? Evil was a man cut off from God, and God cut off from man. For the image of God was within man, even his evil side. But the worst evil was the separation, the division. Man had to find his Gods within, reunite with them, and engage in the common struggle of humanizing them.

All of this made sense to Dog and to me. We spent a very deep and depressing full life by going daily into the depths of our souls, to find the Gods and deal with them. Since there were many others in Pueroa pursuing a similar task, we were not lonely. Indeed, we thought we lived in the center of the world. And perhaps we did. For I became initiated, which was what I was after. I became initiated as a shaman, as a healer, in short as an Initiator. I who had need of being Initiated, would Initiate, and that in truth would be my continuing Initiation. I would do this by helping others to find the God in themselves. What could be better? For this, moreover, I had the help of Dog, for he too was a God was he not?

So it was. At twenty-one, I came back to Cameria as a Healer and I became famous in Town. For I was helping people, was not? Yes. And no. It was strangely disquieting. Healer I was, yes. Helping people, yes. Initiator I was, yes. And there were many like me. But something was missing, I could not say what. Dog and I were satisfied with our understanding of evil, of dark and light, of the condition of the world, of the soul of men. But this dark and light, it was pale, wasn't it? And the other Healers, they were pale too, weren't they? Or dark. By now I was in my mid-twenties; I knew that I would continue to be initiated during my life. But something was missing. What? Did I still long for my Mother? Yes, but I was not moved to find her anymore. What was it then?

Then, of course, I knew. It was Love. You would all know that, of course. A young man in his mid-twenties without love–that is death, isn't it? Indeed, it may be death for a man to be without love in his mid-thirties, or mid-forties, or fifties, sixties, or seventies.

But I am jumping ahead of my story. This is what I later discovered. At this point, I realized I knew nothing about Love. Of course, I had had many sexual and love experiences before. Sometimes I had the one, sometimes the other, and sometimes–the best, of course–together. But now I knew that in becoming a Healer I was initiated only partly. There was something else I needed to learn, and it had to do with Love.

I sought among my colleagues, and discovered that few of them knew much about love, even though they talked a great deal about aspects of it. But they talked about "stages" and "patterns" and "disorders". When I inquired of them I discovered that most of them had had even fewer love experiences than I, and that, in truth, they did not know very much. They only had ideas concerning it. What to do? I was disconsolate until one older colleague who had been observing me for some time finally asked me what the trouble was. When I told him he nodded sagely, and agreed with my observations not only of my colleagues but of the people of Town. He felt that Love was indeed lacking, but that I might go to the people of the Blues in order to find out about it.

The Blues were among the most rejected members of the society of Camerians, for reasons that were not clear. The Blues held menial jobs, were oppressed, or else were so much like the other Camerians as to lose their particularity. Others were highly rebellious. I did not know why my colleague thought the Blues might help me, but I agreed to try it. It was hard to find Blues who would be interested in initiating me in Love. When I spoke about it, they thought I was crazy, or looking for a prostitute–things which they well understood from most of the Camerians–or that I was out to continue the routine exploitation of them in a new way. I could hardly blame them. At last, however, I met a Blue who had been in Pueroa, had freed herself of the oppression of the Camerians, but had not lost the value of herself as a Blue. Indeed, she had so much admixture of the other races and groups, that one could call her an "International Blue."

THE LADY OF THE BLUES,
AND THE SEQUEL: INITIATION BEGUN

I did not need to travel far to find this Lady of the Blues. She lived right in Town, in a region where many other blues also lived. As a matter of fact, it was not I who found her at all. She found me. One night, as I was sitting at a party, this Blue lady came up to me and said she saw something in my eyes that interested her. Was I a Rolificanan or Camerian? I did not look like it. Had I been in Pueroa? I looked at her carefully and saw that her deep, dark eyes had an extraordinary glint in them. Fascinated by those eyes, I saw them change from a deep black color to a dark blue. They warmed me and frightened me all at once and I could not say why.

I spoke very little that evening. Indeed, during the period of my relationship with the Lady of the Blues I hardly spoke at all. Nor did she. Once our understanding of my need to be initiated in the ways of Love was understood, words seemed both unnecessary and a barrier. That first night I knew that she would be initiator and she understood this as well.

That first night there was the look of her–dark and rounded and curved and supple. I did not have long to look, for she was upon me like a cat and I was enfolded in arms and hands and lips. I did not know whether to fight or embrace, to lash out or possess. In answer, I did not know whether to fight or embrace, to lash out or possess. In answer, I did both. I felt pulled upon and drawn out, scratched and sucked and stroked from every place of sensitivity, from every opening. I did not know if my soul were being drained out, or if I were being filled up with the liquid energy of the moon. In the end it was all the same. I fell exhausted–as if I had been in the midst of a thunderstorm and had been fully spent in both fighting and being this electric storm. So it was that first night–a look and a storm.

The second night there was the smell of her–earthy and musty and damp like hay after a rain. If the storm was her force of thunderous nature, then the dampness of her smell was the rich wetness of her fecund black earth. But this too was hardly less gentle than the first night–for the smells were of her and of me, in every place where we could sniff, like cats, or dogs in heat. She was upon me and around me and, again, I lay back exhausted, as if my nostrils could take in no more.

The third night there was the taste of her–briny and tart, salty and sweet. Now this and now that, depending upon where one tasted and when one tasted. I was not only tasted by her, I was devoured. I was as a delicious bit of fish for a hungry cat, a sweet for a child, breast for an infant, meat for a raging lion, and manna for the starving pious. And I lay back devoured, and exhausted.

The fourth night there was the touch of her–her touch upon me, my touch upon her. Crevices and openings, hills and valleys, hard little protuberances and softnesses beyond all belief. Each touch was as finger meeting finger, no matter where it went. Each cell had pseudopodia, reaching out to embrace me at every turn. Her fingers made me cringe and leap forward, every pore of me saying "come closer", "more" and "stop it, but don't stop it." The touch was of madness and delight. To say ecstasy would be to deny the ecstasies of the first three nights, and this was not how it was. Is infinity plus one greater than infinity?

The fifth night there was the sound of her. Not only the purring, not only little whelps of delight, not only the shrieking and screaming and barking. All of these; but now, too, there came whispering and a humming. And now the sounds of music from her throat–the Blue Songs of the Blue Lady. Sounds of sadness and despair. Songs of sultry passion. Songs of anger and revolt. Songs of God. She sang and sang until my ears were full with her sounds.

The sixth night there was the totality of her. The passionate sounds of soul, and touch of trembling, the taste of tartness, the smell of smouldering smegma, and the look, at last, the look of love. For not only did I see her beautifully rounded forms, I looked deeply into her dark and miraculously changing blue to black eyes–and I saw therein the soul of the World. I saw the deep blue of dark heaven and deep sea. I saw the blackness of moonless night and rich black earth. I saw the soul of Nature. She said nothing, but I knew. I knew. Never before had I had an experience like that. Never before. My soul had been awakened, my body had been awakened. I had been awakened and drained and renewed. I had been plumbed and driven to both ecstasy and exhaustion. And I knew; I had been initiate by the Goddess of Love.

The seventh night we rested. We lay in an interlocking embrace, of warmth and closeness and tenderness but no passion. It was good to feel this gentleness and tenderness, for mostly I had felt as if swept up in a great violent storm of nature and had had every millimeter of skin and flesh touched and transformed by fire. We rested and slept. For the seventh night was the end of the beginning.

For on the seventh night, the Blue-Black Goddess told me that my initiation had only begun. I had been spent and coaxed and drawn upon and exhausted. I had been embraced and drained and awakened and kneaded. I had known the totality of fulfillment. I had known the plenitude and intensity of nature and of the Goddess but I had to learn more. I had to go on to Another. But I hardly knew her, I protested. Once tasted, this joy of her would not let me keep my peace, I would awaken of a night, I told her, and long for her. She must not send me away. She nodded gently and said that when the Initiation was completed, I would know what I do, where to go, how I would feel. But now, the Seven Days of Creation were completed. She had done her part for the Goddess, had incarnated Her, now I must go on.

And to where? I wondered. What more can one want than this? To the Red-Brown Lady, she responded. I had only to wait, and she would present herself. I had only to listen and obey. What else could I do? So next morning I awakened to find the Blue-Black Lady gone.

I returned to my daily round of life and reflected much upon the experience. The Old Man of the Cave had told me nothing of this! And even the experience with the Schizophrenia sisters paled by comparison! But then, I became chagrined. If one likes Durer and Goya, does one compare them? No, they are only different!

As I thought of Durer I realized that Dog was no longer with me. Indeed, I had lost track of him the night I met the Lady of the Blues. I trusted, however, that he could take care of himself and return when he felt ready. And why should I blame myself if I had lost myself totally? Those seven nights were out of space and time, out of the round of being, into the Creation of the World.

But the Creation, as the Blue-Black Lady told me, was only beginning. As she had promised, four weeks later there was introduced to me, by a most unsuspecting friend, a Red-Brown Lady whose body was as rounded as Blue-Black, if this could be believed: but she was smaller and more delicate, soft but wiry. A chill of wonder and anticipation overcame me as I met her, because I knew that it was She. Nor could I imagine what delights, what experiences would be mine with her, this Red-Brown Lady. She was at once, a Yogini of the Orient and an Indian of the New World. Yet she was placeless and timeless, and her small voice said little. But she knew who I was, as I knew who she was. She summoned me to her place and I went as full of anticipation as would a lad of thirteen. And then I laughed. For here I was, well past the time of initiation of any known tribe, feeling the hungers and wonders of a lad of thirteen! But what lad of thirteen is lucky enough to be initiated as I was being? Blessed be the Goddess for sending me these gifts! Blessed be She: though She deprived me of a Mother, She had sent me that which no mother can provide.

Red-Brown was as different from Blue-Black as the colors are from each other. With Blue-Black I had known wildness, and intensity, and the spending of myself until I was exhausted. I had known no limits until the end. I was awakened and devoured. The nights were our clime and profuse spending our aim. But with Red-Brown, it was different. No opposite, but different.

For the mornings were our time. Great long hours from dawn until noon after which we slept the hot afternoon away. We awakened of an evening to the delights of–but let me tell you how it was. For it was not "on the first day" or the "second day." Nay, it was days and days. I felt myself losing track of time again but not always in joy. For Red-Brown taught me control. With Blue-Black I battled another and had only to fight to possess another; with Red-Brown, I had to learn to master only myself and keep still. In short we did a Yoga of Love. She taught me, Red-Brown did, of the rising of the passion of the Kundalini, from anus to genitals to belly to heart, to throat to head and beyond, and back again in a whirling circle. She taught me to contain my semen, to contain my soul, to master every movement, every breath, every whim. She taught me to restrain my passion and go with a delicacy and touch and slight murmur. And she raised it to a height which would be unbearable, only to let me sink again to a quietness. For to this Goddess, to be wild, to ejaculate, to go free, was as great a sin and a devastation as restraint had been with Blue-Black. And we sat, Red-Brown and I, in Lotus position, day after day, in intensity, waiting for the right moment. Control did not mean lack of desire. Oh no! The opposite; for it meant the raising of desire to the highest pitch, of its elevation from center to center, and containing it, thus living in continuous, unendurable ecstasy. And this for hours, from dawn to noon; this with the speaking of fantasy, of the telling of desires, and wild thoughts, and all that went through the mind. And all for the sake of the elevation of the Kundalini. Yet she was the same Goddess, I knew, this Red-Brown incarnation, as her sister Blue-Black. When I could not contain, when the semen rushed, when I was devastated, it was forgiven. To start afresh, a new. For her, creation was of the spirit, and of the elevation of the energy.

At noon, as I have said, we slept. We slept until evening, when there was dancing. We watched her friends dance, in a soft, sultry way, building up so slowly that one did not know that the pace was increasing. For the dance too was an elevation of Kundalini. We watched her friends dance, in a soft, sultry way, building up so slowly that one did not know that the pace was increasing. For the dance too was an elevation of Kundalini. We watched, and ate of sweetmeats and rice and those liquids which would clear the head, not drown it. We ate and drank lightly to sustain us and pleasure us, not surfeit us, for ours was an initiation of the senses and the body to greater heights of voluptuousness. And after I learned control then Red-brown would dance, and I would drink in the wonder of her movements, of her fineness, of her language of love to the Gods, to people, to animals, and to me.

When I was stirred to such heights that I thought I could no longer bear it, when a look or the slightest gesture of Red-Brown would thrill me, when I thought I could contain no more, she taught me to dance. She taught me to move, to express, to flow and to allow that passion to seek its way, not only up and into the higher centers, but throughout the body. To let each pore and muscle and bone have its say, and to be its willing victim. So I danced, not with the subtlety of Red-Brown, but with a movement of my own that spoke languages. First I danced alone, to express; then I danced together with her, achieving a union of movement. And then we slept. I felt the juices grow alive in me, warming me, and I felt frustration less and less.

There emerged in me, above all, a desire for union, a desire for totality with myself and totality with another, greater, even, than the freeing of oneself, the exhaustion and fulfillment. And this was a mystery of Love that I had not known. I had learned battle and surrender. Now I learned mastery and submission anew, but of myself not another.

The days wore on, until Red-Brown and I were living in ever more complete levels of union. At last we could flow freely, sometimes sitting together in a lotus position, sometimes dancing, sometimes only looking, sometimes only sharing our fantasies. And at our last union of body and spirit was such that we could look into each other's souls and feel the union therein. The God was with the Goddess, the Goddess was united within herself, soul and spirit and body were one, and the flow came together, naturally, quietly. I was spent but not exhausted, for the union went on.

And then the Initiation by Red-Brown as at an end. Was it better than with Blue-Black? No. Only different, a second language of love. I bowed to my Goddess, joined my palms before my face and knelt to her. What more, O God, what more could one want?

But my Initiation was not finished, said Red-Brown. No, I could expect another soon.

THE INITIATION CONTINUES:
GOLDEN YELLOW AND GREEN-WHITE

Several months passed after my leave-taking from Red-Brown. I often thought of that rich brown body, that intense red dot on her forehead, those doe-brown eyes, so shy and sensitive, yet speaking of a powerful soul. I thought too of Blue-Black, of the intensity of the passion, of the depths of those black-blue miraculous eyes. I thought, "What more can one know, what more is there to the mystery of Love than been taught to be by those two?" I trusted that another would come as promised, but I was so contented that I would not have complained had nothing more transpired. I could spend the rest of my life, I knew, merely reliving the experiences with those two.

And then one day a commanding knock boomed out upon my door and I opened it to Golden Yellow. There before me, slight and slender, imperious with a hard and cold yet beautiful look, stood a Lady of golden yellow skin and black hair. She nodded to me and beckoned me to follow her. I knew who she was and did not even reflect upon how she knew who I was and where to come and find me. I merely followed her as any willing dog would accompany his mistress. I walked behind her some paces as if without being fully aware of it, I was making up for past affronts. I said nothing and did nothing, but wondered what labor of love, what initiation awaited me now. Golden Yellow was beautiful, but cold, and I could not fathom what I was to do or to experience.

We walked until I was exhausted. At last we came to a house which had no particular merit. Even inside it had an austerity which was the opposite of what I had experienced with Red-Brown. She motioned me to sit in a chair. She seemed far less tired than I but waited some minutes until I was resting easy. Then she began to talk, in rather harsh tones, and with an unexpected air of cynicism that I was startled to hear. "You have been taught, I am told, about Love," she began. She smiled, wryly or bitterly or contemptuously, I could not tell, but continued: "You have been wooed and taught and loved. You have been given much. Now you must prove what you have learned. Now you must woo. But I warn you, I am not an easy mark. I am bitter and angry with men; your task will not be easy." She stopped as if waiting for some reply. I did not know exactly what to answer, but I though that this unexpected task in the Initiation into Love made very good sense. I told her so, and told her that I would do my best.

I looked Golden Yellow over carefully and decided my task would be pleasant. She was a very attractive Lady and if that icicle about her heart could be melted, the rewards would be great. I therefore began.

I began by telling her now she looked at me–her beauty, her strength, my wonder at her coldness. I told her, in short, what I had learned from my lessons in freedom and restraint. That is, that in the flow of Love one should trust what happens from moment to moment, believing that true Love is a union of these. When the flow begins, love itself seeks and finds its right place. So I talked. As I spoke I seemed to heat up my own desire, and I moved to embrace her. She rejected me coldly. Chagrined, I started again, still telling her of my feelings, of being chagrined and hurt. Perhaps I was too forward, perhaps too conceited? Such laughed in my face. I grew more hurt and angry. I told her of my anger and how I would like to just take her. She laughed again and I wilted. But she did not leave and I persisted.

I went out and brought back flowers and fruit and sweets. She took them and put them aside without a word of thanks. I told her of my hurt and feeling foolish. No answer. She looked at me as if in desire and I burned for her. Again I moved toward her but gently. She sneered at me for not being man enough to simply take her. So I grabbed her and threw her down. She bit and clawed but I felt the moistness of her, and I thought, "Aha, now I have found the way to her." I took her quickly, with quick passion. After the climax, she sneered at me, calling me a brute who had profited not at all from the loving instruction that I had received from great Ladies. I acknowledged that the Ladies had been great, that I was inept, foolish, and had apparently learned nothing from these great Ladies. I bowed in humiliation. What did the great Golden Yellow Lady want of me? I had tried to woo her and had failed. I had told her of my feelings and had reached her not at all. What were her feelings? How could I reach her?

"At last, fool," she generously said to me, "At last you ask a question, rather than act and woo and tell your own feelings! At last you give some glimmer that you have learned something from Blue-Black and Red-Brown. Did they no search out your feelings, your needs, your desires?" "Yes," I responded, "But Blue-Black pretty well took me and asked questions only later!"

"Nonsense, Golden Yellow continued. "You are just like all men, wrapped up inside yourself, conceited, expecting to be served, and coaxed and loved and petted, but of Love, you give nothing!" I thought that was unfair and told her so, but she ignored me. Instead she took me out of the house.

She led me by the hand to a nearby house which was sumptuous by comparison. Inside were great numbers of books lining most of the walls, with swords covering the wall unlined by books. Seated near a window, busily poring over thick tomes, was a handsome man, obviously a man of both strength and scholarship.

"Here," said Golden Yellow, "Here is the awful man who was my loved one and lover. But what is he? A warrior and a scholar. There is no love in him." She turned to him in contempt. He glared back at her in counter-contempt.

A war of words and hatred then began which I was powerless to stop. Or was I? The gist of the conversation was the contempt of the one for the other, that the one was not a man, and the other not a woman. Finally, I intervened, and said, "This battle must stop. It is of no avail. What, Madame, do you want? Please, Sir, let me mediate this senseless strife."

Golden Yellow pointed to the bookcases and said, "I want to wear the pants!" I held back the scholar, and I said, "Then take them!"

Golden Yellow, without another word, reached behind the bookcases and found a pair of trousers. She put them on and grandly walked to the wall with the swords and shields. She selected one especially beautiful shield, clasped it to her breast, and sank to her knees, saying, "Thus do I claim the rights of the Goddess."

At that moment it was as if a miracle happened. The cold, bitter, Golden Yellow Lady was transformed into a soft, warm creature, like the geishas of long ago. She wore pants, it is true, but these were the silken ones of a woman, not a man, and the shield was transformed in her hands to a great round tray filled with delights.

I was so stunned at the transformation of the Golden Lady that it was some moments before I saw that she was now serving with love and adoration the Scholar-Warrior who had himself been transformed. He no longer wore pants, it is true. Nor was he at all involved with books or battle. Instead he was dressed in the feminine robes of a monk, and he sat in deep inner contemplation. I saw that he was transfigured into a Buddha, actively searching within himself, having abandoned both battle and books. And Golden Yellow was serving him with adoration.

I stood in wonder. Was this the next lesson of Love? Yes, I saw it in both of them: Love in the service of God; Love in the Service and Adoration; Love in the spirit. So did my third lesson in the Initiation of Love come to an end. I bowed and silently withdrew after gazing upon this wondrous scene.

But hardly had I walked the miles back to my own place, hardly had I recovered from this strange experience of Love, when I was accosted by a Lady who said that she was Green-White. I was now accustomed to strange names, and when I saw this lady was fair and green of eye I thought, "Well, there is some sense of these names."

I did not know what to expect from Green-White. She was a winsome lass and smiled gaily. "Do not be frightened, O Solemn Son of the Knight, for I am not so fearsome or fierce." She laughed gaily, and took me by the hand out of Town, out into the country. She took me up into the forests, where the trees were green, the grass was green, and even the lakes were green from the reflection of the leaves. She ran and she made me run, and she laughed.

What did I need to learn from Green-White? She laughed, "To play, silly." Play was the work of the Gods, and of men, when they love. It is good to be solemn, it is good to be wild and restrained, adoring and controlling, serious and in service, it is good to be wild and restrained, adoring and controlled, serious and in service. But to Love is to Play.

And play we did–in the mountains, on the beaches, even in town and Pueroa. She taught me to play although I was a difficult pupil, always wondering about the meaning of things. Searching after the meaning of things, it seems, is to kill play. One plays for the fun of it. And we did. We made love for the fun of it. We danced for the fun of it. We talked for the fun of it. And we loved each other for the fun of it.

When at last I learned this, Green-White brought me back to my place in town, and there in my rooms were Blue-Black, Red-Brown, and Golden Yellow waiting for us. Four Goddesses. And I knew as I looked at them adoringly that they were all aspects of the One Goddess, and that She had taught me to Love.

As I understood that, the Goddesses vanished. But they did not really vanish, for they found a place in my soul, and if you look you can find them there yet.

A FURTHER INITIATION

For a long time I was happy in my place. I had a secret–not a secret which one is enjoined not to speak about–but a secret which could not be told even if one wished. For I had experienced a Mystery and that is a secret that one can only allude to, suggest, circumambulate but not divulge. It made me happy.

Dog had not yet returned, and I was beginning to grow worried about him. But, strangely, my loneliness was not acute and I trusted that he would come back when he saw fit. He who had witnessed the Crowning of Thorns would surely be able to survive many other trials–and who, really, would want to harm Dog, who had hurt no one? Thus I rationalized my lack of care, and I proceeded about my work as a Healer. My work improved greatly now that I was able to understand Love more deeply. I could enter into the agonies and problems of those struggling with their love, and I could do with more compassion. At the same time, strangely, I felt less certainty, offered less advice than I had therefore. For in Love who knows of certainty? Who can say how Love must go? Who can say how it must be expressed and to whom? This view seemed to be helpful for I could, at times, arouse the capacity to love. I was a Healer and a Lover and I sometimes did not know which was the more important.

I was lonely as a man and had little male company apart from those I entrusted to heal. But the healing relationship was not the same as friendship, and though there were several women with whom I was on a basis of equality, there were no men with whom I enjoyed an association. Dog was no longer there to be my friend, confidante, and sometimes guide; I was lonely.

I sought out my older colleague. I had earlier informed him of my experiences with the Goddesses and he had been dumbfounded. He had heard of such things, but had been disinclined to believe them, had thought of them only as a "myth" or a "story." He believed me; but after that he seemed to keep his distance as if I were, somehow, unreliable. When I approached him with this observation he simply pooh-poohed it, but my sense of his withdrawal remained.

Perhaps he was right. The withdrawal may well have been my own, for these experiences with the Goddess somehow set me apart. All the same I was lonely. I remembered fondly the Old Man of the

Cave and once more sought out my older colleague. I told him I still felt the need of initiation; there was something in the man's world which I did not grasp, did not feel part of.

My colleague shook his head. What more could one wish in the way of initiation than to be a Healer, and a Lover? He said that since I had enjoyed good luck when he had recommended to me the Blue people, perhaps I could also have good luck if I went to the Golden People. They also lived in Cameria but apart from all the others. I would have to travel to those places of desert and forest and prairie where the Golden ones lived. No one had much respect for those people who had anciently occupied the Camerian land, but they were said to have mysteries.

I snatched at this bit of information and resolved to set out for the country of the Golden ones. It did not take me long to reach their lands, part of the last places in Cameria which had not been gouged by the unloving hands of the men of Commerce. The land of the Golden ones was beautiful. It was desert–a golden desert of yellows and reds and browns. It was prairie–a golden prairie of undulating crop land, irregularly cultivated with love and respect. It was forest–a sunlit golden forest of mountains and trees maintaining their majestic primacy over Man.

But the Golden people were suspicious. Whereever I went in the land of the Golden ones they were suspicious, and like the Blues, expected only exploitation, lack of understanding, and no good from me. It helped when I told that I was not originally a Camerian, but they also said that I looked like one. I could not even claim to be a Pueroan, although surely my father, the Knight, was either a Pueroan or descended from one. And why couldn't I? Because I did not know who my mother was! It was this fact, that finally softened the hearts of some of the Golden people toward me. This seemed to them a great tragedy and I was indeed to be pitied. So at last in the red, golden desert where some of the Golden people lived, I found a small group which would accept me.

I told the Chief and the Shaman of his small group about my entire history–about the Cave, the Old Man, the Mother and Daughter, my quest for my Mother, the meeting with Dog, and our adventures in City, in the loony-bin, in Town, in Pueroa, in becoming a healer, and at last, with the Goddesses. They were very interested in all of this, particularly in Dog and the Goddesses. They exchanged knowing looks when I spoke of Dog, but they did not tell me what they had in mind. The Shaman was most interested in my training to become a Healer, but he seemed a sniff a little when I told him that the healing was done mostly through words.

It was at this point that both Chief and Shaman nodded and agreed that I needed further initiation. They informed me that they were of the opinion that the Camerians were indeed–as I felt when I was looking for my mother and confined in the loony-bin–quite mad. And why were they mad? Because they tended to think only with their heads. Everything was of the head and cold, without nature and without love. One knew of course that a true man had to think too with the heart. Indeed the center of thought was all over the body, was it not, said the Shaman. He nodded approvingly to what I had learned from the Red-Brown Lady, about all the centers of consciousness and experience. He said that she was indeed of a common heritage with him and that he too knew that unless all the centers of the body, including, of course, the head, are connected that a man is just a wisp, an airy fragment, no more alive than a rock. It was sad, but in spite of all my experience I was indeed less initiated than some of their boys!

I shook my head ruefully at what they had to put myself at their disposal. How could I be initiated by them? How could I become a true man, in their lights?

The Chief and the Shaman nodded their willingness to undertake this task. There were two stages of becoming a man in their tribe, which were undertaken by all the youth–Physical Man and Spiritual Man. These initiations began when the boys were six or seven. Both the physical and spiritual initiations took place simultaneously, with the physical emphasized earlier in development, the spiritual taking on more importance later.

What were these initiations? For the Physical Man, this meant becoming totally at home in one's body, as the place where the Gods would come to dwell. It meant first and foremost, physical health, and knowledge of herbs and other remedies for ordinary care. It also meant stamina, endurance, and strength. Those were achieved in games when one was a boy, in contests of various kinds in adolescence, and in the skills of hunting, fishing, woodsmanship. All of these were accompanied on the spiritual side by teachings of the meaning of these activities, their place in community life, and what aspect of the Gods was being served.

The spiritual side was taken up in discussion with the Wise Men and with the older ones of each generation. Finally, there was the initiation of Aloneness, where the man would come to his own spirit. This took place at about age eighteen. These achievements were expected of all males in their tribe. There was a third stage of initiation, but for only one or two in each generation–those meant to become Shaman or Chief. These initiations were very secret and limited to the ones whose identity was revealed in dream or vision either by the Shaman, the prospective Shaman or the Chief himself.

Where would I fit into these procedures and rites? Well, they answered, mine was a special case. Not only was I older and already a man, but I had already been initiated into mysteries of the Goddess which had been heard of in tribe, but had not taken place for a very long time. I was already a Shaman in my own right for another Tribe even though it was for the Camerians. Still, from what I had told them, they felt I had been well-trained, had had the "calling" from dreams and was indeed a collegial Shaman.

I was advance spiritually even though there was still room for growth. I also had learned a great deal physically and spiritually from the Goddesses, but my hosts would have to do much to bring me up to their level of Physical Man. It was foolish for me to learn the methods of their tribe, related to hunting and fishing and woodsmanship; for these were merely methods of surviving in the world. I already knew a good deal of it, and this knowledge did not constitute the reality of where I would live in Cameria or anywhere else outside of the land of the Golden Ones.

What I did need to learn–or re-learn–was stamina, endurance, and to be at one with my body. As a boy and a youth I had fended for myself in the natural would and was in good condition. In later years I had become soft and sedentary like most of my fellow Healers, which was a great shock to the Shaman. How could anyone heal anything if he was not at one with his own body? He shook his head.

The remedy in my case was easy. I had merely only to take the necessary steps to become fit and to have stamina. I thereupon began a daily course of swimming, increasing the distance each week until I covered at least a mile every day, without fatigue. I was also enjoined to run. I would run and walk in spurts and in turn until I could go many miles without becoming tired. It was with great pleasure that I did this. The swimming and the running had not only a quickening effect upon my health and upon my body, I approached it also from a spiritual standpoint; it had much symbolic meaning for me: to carry great wind in the chest, in the region of the heart, to be big spirited, and to endure. I could also meditate while running or swimming and I saw the great goodness of all this. I felt the energies run up and down the center but in a way different from that taught me by the Red-Brown Lady. I felt it as a deep and pure Physical Man, my cells breathing and feeling in a non-sexual, non-passionate way. It was an inner strength. When I said this, the Shaman nodded. It was a mystery, not to be understood, except as one experienced it from within. I had no need for the competitions, the games, the other ways of men battling each other–both Shaman and Chief acknowledged this. In a ceremony in which I ran many miles, hiked many miles, and swam many miles, I was initiated as Physical Man.

INITIATION CONTINUES

The completion of my labors to become a Physical Man left me in very good spirits, but I was well aware that I had not yet passed the initiation in its totality: there remained the work connected with becoming a Spiritual Man, as well. My guides, Chief and Shaman, were hard-pressed to find the right tasks for me to accomplish as I was not going to remain with their people; therefore I did not need to know all the correct rituals and beliefs attendant upon them. In any case, they averred that I was far more developed spiritually than any of their tribesmen and belonged, by right, in the company of Shamans and Chiefs. They therefore decided to initiate me into their own secrets, but as to which of these to reveal they were uncertain.

Should Chief teach me the ways of being a Chief with his tribe? When I was surely not going to remain with the tribe and be a Chief? Should Shaman teach me the ways and rites of his contacting the Gods? When I was already a Shaman in my own right, did not approve–for myself–of the use of the sacramental drugs as he used them, was not going to be Shaman to his people?

They decided to leave these matters in the hands of the God, who decided all such important things anyway. They agreed to take me to the secret sanctuary deep in the desert, reserved for prospective Shamans and Chiefs. The customary rite was for the initiate to remain at the sanctuary for 30 days and nights, all alone. He was to fast for ten days, eat lightly for ten more, fast again for the remaining ten. On the thirty-first day, it was expected that the God would appear and tell the initiate both his state and his task: it would be the God himself who would initiate the Spiritual Man into Shaman or Chief. This was the last of the usual rites, but they agreed that such a one would be appropriate for me.

And so I was led deep into the desert. After some days, I was brought to a large cave at the base of the mountains which ringed the desert. I smiled at this, for had I not begun my life in such a cave? Had I not spent much of my boyhood in such a place, alone and fending for myself? Of course I had. But the God of this place was not the same, I supposed. The Shaman and Chief said nothing of such matters, but I knew that my experience with my own Cave and with the Old Man of the Cave would be different than here in the land of the Golden People. Furthermore, I had often been alone for long periods, and had even fasted on occasion. But this rite, of the ten days of fasting, this I had never done before, Armed only with my knife and with provisions sufficient for the ten days of light eating, I waved goodbye to my friends Shaman and Chief and prepared myself for my vigil.

The first few nights I slept fitfully, though the days were peaceful. There was indeed something strange and numinous about the cave and surroundings but I could not tell just what it was. During the day I wandered about the area and drank in its atmosphere. The place was beautiful in an austere way, with its golden brown sands, stark cliffs, and suddenly rising, steep mountains. There was a great cleft in the mountain behind the cave which looked ominous to me. I did not try to climb it; something in me said I should not.

The first ten days passed uneventfully, and I felt an increasing stillness in my being. I was glad to have this time of full aloneness–it seemed a very long time since I had experienced it. I missed only Dog, my old companion in my wanderings, and said a silent prayer for his well-being. After the first tens days, I enjoyed eating once again, and I relished the simple food which I was given. Once again I was able to eat slowly, to savor each mouthful and, as the Red-Brown lady had taught me, to nourish myself of the prana, the spiritual goodness of each bite of food. I felt easily well-fed and even had some provisions to spare at the end of the second ten days.

The third ten days passed much like the first, in walking, meditating, and sitting silently before the Cave. My dreams began to return as I slept less fitfully. These were of varying character, some pointing to previous periods of my life, some pointing portentously to something in the future, unknown. None of them was a "big" dream such as I had experienced at various times in my life nor, as I was led to expect, I might have now.

So, all led slowly and quietly to the thirty-first day.

On the night preceding the thirty-first day, I slept fitfully once again. There was a charge in the air, and I was filled with anticipation. Would there be a dream? A vision? A concrete appearance of the God? And what God was it who occupied these precincts and would tell me of that which would initiate me as a Spiritual Man? These questions, which had been with me for all the thirty days, now seemed to insist themselves upon me and I could hardly contain myself with the trembling and anxiety that they engendered. Only one thought came in, which made me feel even worse: perhaps nothing at all would happen; perhaps the God would not manifest at all. Perhaps I would not be initiated, as I wished, and I was doomed to be one of those who would live his life as only half a Spiritual Man. With that thought, as it entered into my being, as it went down from my head through my throat, to chest and belly and genitals and anus, as it settled itself into me, I grew strangely calm. I realized that I was ready to accept that, too. Then I laughed to myself: my acceptance of being not-visited-by-the-God, of being "half a Spiritual Man", of being just the ordinary mortal that I really was–simply realizing that I am not a Hero like my father but an ordinary fellow who did not even know who his mother was–the acceptance of all of this in itself made me a Spiritual Man!

Can one understand that? Can I convey this mysterious secret? At that moment of the experience of the non-God I felt that I became a Spiritual Man. I knew that I could leave this cave and this mountain, could leave the Chief and Shaman, could leave the land of the Golden People, could return to the workaday world of Cameria, of

Rolificana, of Town, and live my life in my own way. In short, I was already initiated into Spiritual Manhood. With that, I fell peacefully asleep and rested deeply from all desires, anticipations, and fears. I was at one with myself.

    I slept peacefully that night–that is, the first part of the night. Toward dawn, I had a dream in which a whirlwind came and swept me deep into an abyss and then high up on a mountain. During the first part of the dream I was with a guide and then a Voice spoke out, firmly and with authority. The Voice came out of a thunderstorm but it was not the storm itself. The Voice bade me climb the mountain and "Embrace the Fire." At that moment, I had a vision of a large monster-like being which was itself made of blue and red fire, but was spitting a fiery stream of green and yellow fire.

    The Being changed shape and flowed like an amoeba, around itself. It had myriad eyes, like the tail of a peacock, and then on great Eye. Its fire lashed out at me and I fought it. I struggled with it and struggled too to contain myself and be the Spiritual Man that I had come to be the previous evening. As I struggled, I awakened to thunder claps and the beating of rain upon the ground outside the cave. A great storm had come up in the dawn which was unusual for the region, and it seemed to give with my dream. Half-awake, the dream went on, and I heard the Voice command me to climb the mountain. I could not do otherwise than obey so I immediately began to climb.

    All morning I climbed and as I climbed I felt myself struggling in a very concrete way with the Fire-Being who was enveloping me, burning me, paining me, crushing me. But climb I must. I arrived at mid-morning at the great cleft in the triangular mountain. And it was here that I thought I saw a great Eye which looked at me as if it would penetrate every part of me. I felt over-powered and even more enveloped, if that were possible, than I did by the flame.

    As I clambered to the cleft I suddenly understood that I was at a place where my father, the Knight, had been. I suddenly understood that I was facing the God of my father, and his fathers before him. I understood that and I wept. I wept with knowledge that I was in the same place and meeting the same God. The weeping racked me, but reduced the pain of the fire. I felt my bones ache, my heart break with the wonder and greatness of it, and the salt-water of my tears made bearable the fire-heat of the Being.

On I climbed to the very top of the mountain as the storm continued and the rain washed away both my tears and the feeling of battle with the Fire-Being. At last I arrived at the top of the mountain and collapsed. Then there seemed to be one last gasp of battle between me and the Fire-Being, and I thought I had killed it. But with a last thrust of one tentacle-arm of fire, the Being reached out behind me and struck me in the small of the back. I bent over in pain, losing consciousness.

In my unconsciousness, I seemed to dream once again. In the dream I was walking peacefully down an ordinary street when two men dragged me through a door. The men were dressed in the green-mesh clothing of Knights, and bore yellow lions on their breastplates. They grabbed me and brought me into a large amphitheater, circular in shape, in which many people were gathered. Among the people, I caught a glimpse of my father the Knight, there with his black suit of armor, also with a great yellow lion on his chest. He waved to me warmly and happily and once again I wept, for I knew that I was one with my father. There are no words nor explanation that I can give for this experience. Then at the next moment the two green Knights were beating me with the branches of a tree. The beating was rough but not painful, as if the beating contained the symbol of my being initiated by a tree.

The beating ended and I was confronted with an absolutely tremendous crown bejewelled on every side, and heavy with gems and colorful stones. I was about to be crowned and all the people there seemed very happy at this prospect. The crown, however, seemed far too large for me and I shrunk back from it. I tried to speak, to say something about what I was feeling but the words would not come out of my mouth. The people changed their mood from joy to disappointment or sadness and it was as if the world or time had come to a standstill. Among all the people only my father continued to look at me with warmth and compassion. He waved at me as if both bidding me goodbye and God's speed, as if he knew, better than I, what all this was about.

I awakened in tears and in loneliness with the words of the people echoing in my ears, "He is too young" and "He is not worthy." I could not speak, and my lips trembled. As I awakened, I felt the electrifying thrill of being touched on the finger by the God. I trembled with it and, at the same moment, saw a lone tree on top of the mountain, burning. It seemed as if lightning had struck the tree and it was burning but the fire did not seem to destroy it. Was this still my dream, or did it exist in itself out there?

INITIATION CONCLUDED

All the rest of that thirty-first day I rested upon the mountain. The storm had subsided and the sun reappeared, hot. I was exhausted and could hardly move myself to find out if I was all in one piece. I slept now and again. Toward evening I was sufficiently rested to climb back down the mountain, past the cleft, and down to the precincts of the cave. There I rested once again and ate what remained after my second ten days. I stayed that night, the next day, and the night after that, trying to recover my strength and my mental balance. Although a Shaman myself, I could not bring myself to interpret my own experience. I knew only exhaustion, pain, stiffness in the small of the back, and wonder.

At last, after several days of recuperation and when my supplies were exhausted, I returned to the place of the Golden People.

Chief and Shaman were there to greet me and they did so warmly. The looked at me searchingly and with compassion. They later told me that my face had changed markedly and that, indeed, whatever I had experienced in the cave and on the mountain had affected me deeply. The sign of the Spiritual Man was no longer just within but showed as an intense dark look of the eye, as a jutting of the jaw and as a lining of the face.

They were as eager to hear of what I had experienced as I was to tell them and avail myself of their understanding. But I was too weak–whether from the fasting or the experience, it was hard to say– and I was allowed to rest.

Some days later I had recovered, except for the fact that the small of my back was weak, sometimes stiff, and would occasionally require me to bend over double. Shaman showed me how I must perform certain kinds of exercises which would take the pressure off this spot. I needed to strengthen my upper legs and upper back, which could carry the weight and pressure, thus relieving me. In short, I had to improve my "posture" from one of being "beaten down" and "bent" to one who could "stand erect" and carry his total weight well.

I was eager to tell Chief and Shaman of my experiences. I told them of what happened in the cave on the thirtieth night, when I accepted that the God might not appear at all, that I was an ordinary man, yet my own Spiritual Man, whether He came or no. Chief and Shaman nodded in deep understanding and appreciation of this.

I told them then of my peaceful sleep and of the Voice awakening me, of the dream of the battle with the Fire-Being, and of being summoned to go up the mountain alone. I told of my painful climb and battle, of approaching the cleft, and knowing that I was experiencing the God of my father and his fathers. I told of my fears and of coming to the top of the mountain. I told of the storm, of the continuing dream, of the green Knights, and of seeing my father in the Amphitheater. I told of the beating with the branches of the tree, and of the Crown. I told of my withdrawal, and of the statements of the people, "He is too young" and "He is not worthy." I told of my father waving to me with compassion. I told of being alone and lonely and being unable to speak. I told of being touched on the finger by God, and of the vision of the tree burning without being destroyed. All this I told, and of the end, and coming back.

Chief and Shaman listened carefully to my story and they wept. Weeping is unusual among the Golden People, particularly the men, so that I knew that their weeping was a mark of especial brotherly love and compassion. They waited long, however, to comment upon what I had told. I think that this was out of respect and regard for me and for the numinousness of the experience itself.

Then Chief spoke to me first. "Your dream tells me that you could have been a Chief and a much greater chief than myself. That you withdrew, I understand, for to be such a chief, to be a great King even, is a most heavy task which very few do well. That you are 'too young', as they said, may be true. That you are 'unworthy' is, I think, a presumption and not true. But perhaps you were found 'unworthy' because you 'killed the God' and that is your sin. Yes, I think that is true. No one, of course, can really 'kill the God' forever, but you have gone against the God of your forefathers and that is a sin. You have battled and wrestled with the God and now you bear the mark of having been humbled. Perhaps you will never be a King or a Chief, but I do not believe it. I think rather that you will be, like your father, a

'King without a Crown', I acknowledge your Chiefdom, for you have fought the God, killed the God, and been touched by the God. You, my fellow chief, I embrace you and I bow to you."

With those moving words, the Chief embraced me and we both wept unashamedly.

Having concluded his deep and moving words to me in which I felt the God speaking through him, the great Chief moved back and then the Shaman began to speak:

"I knew that you were a Shaman like myself, before. But now I know that you are a greater Shaman than myself, and touched by the God to a degree that has not been vouchsafed me. You are indeed a 'King without a Crown' for that, in truth, is what we Shamans are. We represent, on earth, the God of the most high, but our authority is in our mediation, in our healing, in our prophecy, and in our leading, like a Chief. And you, sir Knight, you are a Shaman of the great God, of the Voice, and of the Fire. And you will heal, and 'touch', and speak with fire even though you need to be healed, and touched, and cannot speak. For you are a Healer in need of healing, a Lover in need of loving, a Physical Man in need of physical help and strength, a Spiritual Man in need of spirit, and you are a Speaker in need of healing words and fiery voice. All of these you have, and need, and give. Oh, fellow Shaman, greater than myself, I bow to you, my brother, and I embrace you."

With those moving words the Shaman embraced me and we wept, unashamedly.

Thus was my initiation completed. I was now a man, a man touched by God. I was a Healer, Lover, Physical Man, Spiritual Man and Speaker, in need of healing and being healed, of loving and being loved, of physical and spiritual strength–giving and receiving, and of speaking and being spoken to. And I saw and fought and killed and was touched by the God of my father. I was both the Son of the Knight on my own. My quest was not my father's quest; I was my own Man.

IN WHICH DOG REAPPEARS

Following the completion of my initiation a great feast was to be held to celebrate the event. Preparations would take several weeks, since Chief wanted to have special foods from other tribes of the

Golden People who lived elsewhere, in forest and prairie; also he wanted to have other Chiefs and Shamans present for this event. I protested; I wanted to have our celebration small and intimate. And I felt that these other Chiefs and Shamans, although I would be honored to have them present, would really have no role nor interest in he particularities of my initiation. Chief reluctantly agreed and, instead of the great feast, we had a small intimate one made up only of Chief, Shaman, and myself. Well, that was not quite all, since Chief and Shaman promised me one surprise guest who would make up the fourth of our masculine feasting.

So several days later we three sat down to our feast which, while not made up of all the great dishes of all the Golden People, was elaborate and delicious anyway. Before we could even toast each other with the special drink of the region, the door opened and there appeared a quite swarthy man. His skin was either a very dark brown or a light black. His features were rather like those of the Golden People, strong and severe, though sensitive. He reminded me of someone I once knew, but I could not remember who it was. He was muscular and well-proportioned, though perhaps a head shorter than myself.

I turned to my hosts, Chief and Shaman, to introduce me to this impressive man. They merely smiled and asked if I did not recognize him. I replied that he looked familiar to me, but no, I did not know who he was. The stranger than came forward and shook my hand and looked deeply into my eyes. He then startled me by licking my forehead! The look–and the lick–told me at once that this was–but no, how could that be? It surely was the look of Dog, and the lick of Dog, but here was a man. Even if his skin coloring was exactly that of Dog, it surely was not possible that Dog could have become a man!

The stranger laughed at my discomfiture. He seemed to read my mind as did Dog of old. And then he said, "If God could become a man, why is it so unbelievable that Dog might become a man, too? And look, my friend, at the name of Dog itself? Is not God contained therein?" I was startled by the comparison and the statement but had to admit that all things were possible. Had not this same Dog been present at the Crowning of Thorns? Why could he not become Man as well? So I nodded. But I looked questioningly, I suppose, for Dog then continued:

"You will want to know what has happened to me, how it is that I have changed my form since I last saw you. It is many, many months since I have seen you, but Chief and Shaman have been good enough to bring me up to date on all your experiences. You too, my good friend Knight and Son of the Knight, have changed drastically, but the outer sings of it, though present, are less pronounced than those you see in me deserve to be compared with what you have experienced, I leave to you. I will simply tell you my story, as I did of old, and let the facts be the measure.

"You will recall that I vanished from your side some weeks before you, yourself, came into the hands of the Lady of the Blues. Shortly after you consulted your older colleague, unknown assailants captured me and dragged me off to a brothel in a part of Town which is rarely visited by its respectable inhabitants. In this brothel, I became part of a show for the entertainment of its visitors. I performed sexual acts with the Blue-Black Lady under their eyes. To me these acts were quite ordinary and pleasant, and well within the purview of what we dogs were used to experiencing, but now I saw that these same acts could be used as a form of humiliation and degradation and could be viewed as being wicked and taboo. The suffering of Blue-Black was very great indeed. I felt what it was to be a human being, to be degraded and humiliated and to have one's ordinary sexual desires perverted by vicious attitudes. I also understood what it meant to be enslaved. For just as Blue-Black was enslaved by being required to perform and exhibit herself in humiliation, those who so enslaved her were themselves enslaved by the use of power without compassion. Those who paid to watch her were, in turn, enslaved by sexuality without feeling. And they were all enslaved by the absence of love. Then I knew what it was to be human and what it was that the humans did who killed their God, as I watched. And I had compassion both for them and for myself. I knew what it was to be human and to be enslaved by sexuality without love.

"After some weeks, I was taken from this brothel, and bought to the precincts of the Red-Brown Lady. There I was part of an ordeal by priests and priestesses who kept restraining my desires, after arousing me. I felt all the tortures of my pure animal soul put to wicked experimental measures of men who cared only for transformation, for the use of the power of nature to increase their own sense of power.

I knew, in short, the horror of being a man enslaved by the lust for power, at the expense of his own animal nature. And I felt compassion for the Red-Brown Lady, who was misused, just as I. I knew what it was to be human and enslaved by power without compassion.

After several more weeks, I was taken from this temple to the home of the Golden-Yellow Lady. There I was trained to merely fetch and carry and do all the tasks of the Scholar and his Lady. They were cruel. And they used me so because they, too, were merely being used by the God. And I knew what it was to be human and enslaved by the Spirit, by the God, without adoration and love.

"After some more weeks, I was taken to the Green-White Lady of the Forest. There I simply played, as was my nature as a Dog. We played and played and played, and then I saw the uselessness of the Green-White Lady, and of myself, to merely play and have no more meaning in life than that. And I knew what it was to be human, to only play, and thus have a meaningless life. I knew what it was to be human and enslaved by meaninglessness.

"As if all these experiences were not enough, I was brought to this region, by one of the Golden People. Here, at last, I was told that my experience with the Ladies was an experience of the Goddess, and of this, men suffer and die. This, I was told, is what happens among the People, even among the Golden People. This is what it was to be a man. I, who was so horrified by the experience of the evil of Men, the God-Killers, now I saw what it was by the experience of evil of Men, the God-Killers, now I saw what it was that men experienced of the God, and the Goddess. Was this not what the God experienced of Himself? Was not the Goddess part of the God? And did not the God-Man suffer the fate of being human?

"Given this realization I repented my anger at men, and I grew in compassion and fellow-suffering. We animals, it is true, suffer greatly at the hands of People, but People suffer more deeply and totally than we animals. No wonder it was that God chose to become Man, and not Dog. For Man suffered God's nature more than any other creature. I did not give up my animal nature nor abhor it nor think it any the less divine, for I shall always be Dog, but I did, in truth, understand what it was to be Man.

"Chief and Shaman brought me out to the Cave and to the Mountain where you, good Knight and Son of the Knight, had your experience of the God. And there too did I dream. For Dogs dream just as humans dream, did you not know that? And there too did the Voice come to me and command me, and there too did the Voice come to me and command me, and there too did the Fire-Being come upon me.

"But I, good Knight and Son of the Knight, I did not do battle. I did not fight nor did I wrestle. Why I do not know. Perhaps it was because I had felt so deeply what it was to be a suffering human. Perhaps because the nature of the Fire-Being was so close to my own animal nature. In any case, for whatever reason, I did not do battle. I was simply embraced by the Fire-Being and enveloped in it. I was warmed and heated, until I felt every pore of my body being transformed by this fiery heat. But the heat was of an electric goodness and healing. It was a cleansing from suffering, rather than a further suffering. And in the course of being embraced by the fire, I felt myself transformed.

"I saw myself brought into an amphitheater, where there were many men and animals. It was something like Noah's Ark, where two of each kind of creature were present. And there, on one side of me, was a dog, much like myself, who held a branch of a tree in his mouth and beat me with it. On the other side of me was a man, one looking very much like you, my good friend and companion, Son of the Knight; indeed, I thought it was you and I was overjoyed to see you again. But no, there you were among the spectators, and you waved at me warmly. Were there two of you, one beating me as part of my initiation, another there to observe, with compassion? I did not know. I knew only that I was being beaten and undergoing further transformation.

"And then I saw a tree, itself burning. It was burning strangely, not being destroyed by the fire. And, to the sound of trumpets and the great good shouts of the assembled people, I was put into the flame, and I lost consciousness.

"When I awoke the dream was over, and I found myself in the cave. Had I only dreamed? Was all the same? No. I looked down at myself, and I saw the creature you now see before you–a man. I understood what it was to be human, and by a divine mystery which I do not understand, I became human. I, the Dog, who had seen the horror of God becoming man and being crucified by man; I, the Dog, who had known what it was to be human and to suffer and cause suffering; I, the Dog, had become a Man.

"So that, dear Knight and Son of the Knight, is my story. I am still Dog and will always be Dog, and I am still your brother and will always be your brother, but now I am also Man and will be by your side.

LYSIS

You can imagine how overjoyed and moved I was at hearing the whole story of my friend Dog. The intertwining of our fates, the commonality of the experience of the same God. Dog's remarkable transformation–all of those combined to give me a sense of completion. Indeed, all my experiences–of the Schizophrenia ladies, of the four Goddesses, of my initiation among the Golden People, of Dog himself–seemed to be unexpected and marvellous rewards en route to finding my mother. So valuable were these that I was ready to say that I no longer needed to find my mother, as nice as it would be to know who she was.

I communicated these thoughts to my friends Chief and Shaman and they nodded sagely. But they advised me not to abandon my quest. They pointed out that these great things which happened to me occurred only during the course of my quest, and if I were to abandon my search, who knows what would happen? The god has His own strange ways, after all, and we have to be true to what he brings to us. I responded that no doubt they were right, but perhaps the God now wished me to simply abandon my search and be satisfied with what had already been achieved. But as soon as I said this I felt a pain. I knew that I was still in need of healing though a healer, still in need of finding–what? Mother? Healing? Wholeness? Yes, in search of Wholeness, and perhaps, that Self I was meant to be. Now, united with my friend and brother Dog, I was open to the future.

Chief and Shaman said nothing. Instead of words they crossed their hands, each in turn, and embraced my crossed hands. Chief, Shaman, Dog, and I, did this each with the other; four crossed pairs. We then put hands, one on top of the other, alternating, creating a mountain of eight hands in one. We then laughed and separated. The ritual was completed. We were all one and separate, in pairs and united, fulfilled in ourselves and open to the continuous quest.

The next day Shaman came forth saying that he had a dream. The dream was simple; it said that he, Shaman, along with Chief, should bring Dog and me back to the Cave. We should enter the Cave and go through the remotest darkness of it–which no one had done before. There Chief and Shaman were to bid Dog and me goodbye and allow us to go deeper and deeper into the darkness. It was so bidden. That was the Voice.

Despite the frightening character of the dream, none of us had any difficulty in accepting the reality of the demand of the Voice and its fundamental rightness. I trusted Shaman totally and was prepared to follow this Voice and its fundamental rightness. I trusted Shaman totally and was prepared to follow this Voice, even if it turned out badly. For we were brothers in the Spirit and either would gladly give his life for the other. Yet the task seemed strange to us all. No one of the tribe had ever been deeper into the cave than one could see by sunlight. This because the Cave's special numinousness. It belonged to the God. The tradition of the Golden People said that the Cave led ultimately into the depths of the earth, perhaps to the Underworld itself, but no one knew for certain because none had gone that route. We were to be the first.

So it was that some days later Dog and I, rested and well fed, equipped with food, candles, and our meager belongings, went to the Cave along with Chief and Shaman. There was nothing in the dream which said that we could not have candles, so we took them. We went in a remarkably festive mood, laughing and joking. Even inside the Cave we did not feel the awfulness. Only sa we penetrated into its depths, farther than had ever been penetrated before, only then did we sese the eeriness, the anxiety, the unknowingness of what lay in store for us.

At last Shaman said that something told him this was as far as he and Chief could go. His dream had been fulfilled; now we must be on our way.

Our parting was brisk and to the point. A touch of the hand, a smile and nod in the candlelight, and we were off.

Dog and I walked on into the darkness of the cave for a long time without any words passing between us. Now that Dog was human, we still had good non-verbal communication, but we did need to speak together and our understanding was not the same as it once had been. This, we both felt, was all to the good for we were, in truth, different selves.

Hours and hours passed while we walked on. The Cave itself seemed not so remarkable any more; an ample passageway with plenty of room all around, some source of air which made us breathe freely and only occasional crossings with other passageways which caused us doubt. These other passageways, however, were invariably filled with streams, or were much smaller, or were of the dead-end sort, so we had no trouble keeping on our way. We ate of our provisions and continued on.

We only began to grow worried when our candles began to run out some days later. But we had to continue on our way. At last we ran out of light altogether and had to proceed in the dark. Even this was not so bad when we got used to it for the floor of the cave was reasonably smooth. So we walked for an unknown period.

And then we came to a crossing, far larger than anything we had yet encountered. Here was a body of water, not rushing, but clearly larger and wider than anything theretofore. We could not see, we could not guess which direction to take, or how far the body of water extended. For a moment both Dog and I wished the Dog were truly an animal once again, for perhaps we would guess the answers to these questions, as animals sometimes can. But he assured me that if he once could, he could not now. What to do?

I remembered my collection of thirty stones which I had carried with me ever since I set out on the quest for my mother. I did not know why, except that those stones–only a few of which had been gems–were my chief treasure at that time. Now they were to come in handy. I could throw rather well, and with them we could at least tell how far ahead water still lay, and if there were walls about.

So we abandoned what remained of our provisions, leaped into the water and started swimming. Dog was a natural swimmer, and I was now glad that I had become, indeed, a Physical Man partly through swimming every day. We swam as straight as we could for a time; then, with Dog's help I rose up and threw a stone in each of the four directions. To the rear we heard the sound of a stone in water. The same ahead of us. On both sides we heard the clang of stone upon stone wall. That was reassuring; at least we were swimming straight ahead and still on our path.

We swam on for a period which seemed, perhaps, a mile; once again I threw a stone in each of four directions. The results were the same. We repeated the pattern a third time, a fourth time and a fifth time, and began to grow fatigued. I guessed we had swum some six miles and wondered if stones or energy would be depleted first. But we repeated our pattern a sixth, and seventh time. Same results.

Now we had only two stones left. I decided we could safely continue our pattern of swimming, staying reasonably straight, and throw the stones only ahead of us. So I threw the twenty-ninth stone, and the thirtieth. Still water, and no relief. We were growing up tired. We floated more than we swam, it seemed. We now were concerned about falling asleep from exhaustion and simply sinking like two water-logged vessels.

I remembered wondering if I were a fish or a vessel when I heard Dog exclaim, "Land!" I awakened from my hypnogogia and dove ahead to feel once again the hard stone of the cave floor. Its hardness was as pleasant as cotton to me and I clambered into it with great joy.

Dog and I rested there a little, then we began walking once more. Very soon we saw a glimmering of light way off in the distance. We hastened our steps and saw the light grow larger and more vivid. At last we came upon a large room which let in the light of the outer world.

An uncanny feeling came over me. Had I been here before? Was it deja vu? No, this seemed like the Cave of my childhood!

As we came closer to the opening, I glimpsed two forms which shifted and changed and then I saw it was the Mother and Daughter from my childhood. Somehow we had come from the Cave of the Golden People, under the strange mountain, and arrived at the Cave of my childhood!

I exclaimed this to Dog and was going to collapse with both shock and exhaustion when the Mother rushed up to me and embraced me.

"You have come home, at last," she said, "and on your thirteenth birthday as was predicted."

I looked at her in astonishment. I realized that I must indeed be about thirty at this time. I wondered vaguely if there were any connection with my thirty stones. I also wondered why it was that the Mother of the cave, who had never shown me any affection was now embracing me.

I looked at her in astonishment. I realized that I must indeed be about thirty at this time. I wondered vaguely if there were any connection with my thirty stones. I also wondered why it was that the Mother of the cave, who had never shown me any affection was now embracing me.

I looked at her questioningly and asked, "Are you my mother? And where is the Old Man of the Cave?" The woman smiled and said, "That is a long story. I will tell it all to you, but you and your friend must rest. Rest and be fed and then we will tell stories!"

With that I laughed, for she sounded indeed like a mother. Then Dog and I rested. We slept and ate while we were waited upon in every warm and cozy way, by both Mother and Daughter. When we were finished resting and being cared for, we told our own stories to the clucking sympathy of the Mother and the serious and rapt attention of the Daughter. Both women had changed since my childhood; not so much as I, perhaps–though they both recognized me at once– but a good deal all the same. The Daughter was a woman, perhaps in her middle forties. She was stately and tall and full, and queenly. The Mother was warm and loving and now, best of all, much of her warmth was directed at me.

So we told our stories to both of them and received their rapt interest and appreciation. When we finished I said, "Now it is our turn to hear, to be both informed and entertained. I have waited long enough!"

"Indeed you have, Knight and Son of the Knight," said the Mother. 'We shall now tell our tales.' Now, may I present Mother and Daughter, to tell their own stories.

PART TWO

The Mother and Daughter

A BEGINNING IN DESTRUCTION

We, too, O Son of the Knight, have stories to relate, my Daughter and I. I have been very glad to hear your tale and I hope that our stories will be of interest to you. You will, I think, find some answers to your questions. And even you, Sir Dog, may find a link between your life and ours.

It is true that the fate of Daughter and myself has been intertwined, and we have had, at times, a deep connection which some might term symbiotic, others would call mystical. All the same, we are different. We have achieved a separation into two distinct people. We are individuals. I can only speak for myself, what I have experienced–Daughter will have to tell her own story.

The early part of my life need not be dwelt upon. Suffice it to say that I was born of a noble family in Israel about the same time Our Lord Jesus Christ was born. My husband was also of noble birth. We married young. We soon had a son and a daughter and lived our lives as did people of the time who were privileged and well-to-do–that is with a certain grace and charm. But I suppose all people of leisure and education and nobility have lived thusly, even the dastardly Romans. There is a charm and benevolence, yea even a goodness among the enlightened aristocracy everywhere. They are rarely cruel. Their excesses come from loss of purpose in life. I have found, in contrast to the power-hungry, cruel sort who come out from classes seeking status.

Our lives were pleasant and interesting, though we were concerned about the fate of our fellow Jews under the Romans. The times as you know were not easy for the masses. My own temperament was that of a helper and a server so I was involved with the poor, with the downtrodden.

It was in the performance of such tasks that I became acquainted with the sect of Christians and their message. It seemed a good message to me and embraced their view of life. I need not go into my conversion at this point, what dreams and experiences led me to it–that I might do at some other time if you like–but I do wish you to know that this is what occurred. I was also instrumental in the conversion of my husband, my son, and my daughter.

But the time I was thirty-three years old my son was seventeen and my daughter twelve; my husband was several years older than myself and we were all devout Christians. We lived our lives in a spirit of goodness and peace, wishing only to carry the message of love and of the incarnation of the Messiah as best we could.

But there was persecution, and we lost many dear friends to slavery, to the cruel games of the Romans, and some vanished, we knew not where. When our collaboration with the Christians was found out we lost our house and lands; the suffering became our own rather than merely observed. My husband and my son were taken off to Rome, to a fate of which I knew not, but I presumed it to be death.

Our personal loss, that of my daughter and myself, was almost insupportable, but we took solace in our Faith. When our Lord was crucified–and we witnessed this–it was as if the end of the world had come. We wandered, my daughter and I, as if already dead, or more accurately, in the daze of those who have had good fortune and cannot believe it when all is lost.

During the three days after He died and was placed in the tomb, we spent our time among the lepers, waiting, hoping, and knowing that our Lord would be resurrected, for He had told us so. On the third day, He rose. We did not see this, but we were told and believed, and we were overjoyed. When we went to the tomb, to the cave where He was buried, we saw the rock was removed and the body was gone, which we already knew. I know not indeed why we even sent to that place. What strange impulse of God or man was it which led us to that cave?

Was it merely the wicked curiosity of woman which led us there? Or the deep interest in our Lord's actions? Or was it something deeper over which none of us can have any final control and is part of the divine will–not known, sometimes, even by the Will itself? I chose not to speculate further just now. I only want you to know that I have given the matter thought, and have no answer. In any event, the whole course of our lives was deeply changed thereby.

You will say, "Going to the tomb changed their lives? When the presumed death of husband and son did not? When observing the Crucifixion did not?" My answer is, "Yes." All of those things changed us, but our lives, somehow, continued. The events at the Tomb and the Cave, however, brought about a total transformation, a complete change.

"And what did happen there?" you will say, wondering what this was. I will tell you in a moment. It is shocking, even now, and hard to speak about but I will.

First, however, I must say that when we arrived at the Tomb-Cave, we saw nothing. The rock was removed, no one was about, and there was only a peace and tranquility about the place which calmed us. We felt that the Lord was no longer here, would be about His business with His apostles, and we decided to simply enjoy the peace which pervaded the area.

My daughter picked wild flowers of various sorts which abounded there and I sat quietly with my sewing. I idly watched her as she gathered the flowers and, just as she was about to pick a particularly beautiful narcissus, we heard a rumbling as if there were thunder.

But there was no thunder. We looked up and saw the sky was clear, and the noises we heard were coming from men. I pause as I say "men" for these noised were hardly those of men, at least as I had known men. They seemed unearthly and wild and demonic. There were shouts and cries and then they were upon us, on top of us, and all over us before we could even make out who or what they were.

And they took us. In every way. There were, perhaps, twenty or thirty of them pouring out of the Tomb-Cave like vermin. They dragged us back into their place in the Tomb-Cave, deeply into it. It was dark and frightening; what horrified me most of all was the very brief glimpse that I had of my daughter. She looked at me with utter helplessness and terror. There she was, not yet thirteen years old, about to be–what? Raped? Of course that. Killed? Very likely. Tortured? God help us, I thought, spare her that! I spoke out a prayer, asking that my Daughter be spared this horror and that it all be heaped upon me. I felt, in that moment, what our Lord suffered, taking the sins of others upon Himself, offering Himself up as a sacrifice. It is not because one is so good and self-sacrificing and a martyr, but because the pain of one's loved one's suffering is so much greater than to suffer the same event oneself. How much greater then must God's suffering be, because He loves so much more! Strangely, these rational and understanding thoughts went through my mind in the midst of the terrible manhandling by these ruffians. I prayed that the agony of my Daughter be upon me, and I prayed with all my might and all my heart and all my soul.

But there was no answer. Or the answer was 'no." I cannot tell. For my daughter and myself were both raped by all the men and tied to stakes, there to be handled and raped again. The torment was great. There was physical pain at the roughness of the men. There was emotional pain at the degradation and humiliation. And worse of all for me was the anguish of watching my daughter undergo all these agonies and being unable to do anything about it. I wept and I screamed until I could not. I called out and shouted until I could not. I fainted. I returned to consciousness and fainted again.

At last I was aware that we were being kept in this Tomb-Cave by these wild men to be used for their pleasures, not just once but many times, and for as many days and nights as they wished, until we either died or they tired of us. There was no talking, no compassion or feeling of any kind. They looked like men, but they treated us–not like animals, for one would be more kindly towards an animal–but like objects. I could not look at my daughter. I now prayed for death but that too did not come. I knew only pain and further pain. Then after the waves of pain had ended, I knew only nausea, hatred, and callousness. I was becoming a "creature"–neither human nor animal, but something else–like these men. I was turning into some kind of devil or demon. Then in the fullness of my despair and hatred and non-humanness, I cursed God.

I did not curse God in the ordinary, human way which we all do when annoyed, angry, frustrated. I cursed God from the depths of my being with full consciousness. I cursed the Father, I cursed the Son.

I cursed the Holy Spirit which ran through both. I cursed men and I cursed male Gods. I cried out as if in a last piercing scream against the God of my Fathers, against the God of my choice, against, indeed, all Gods. I longed for a Goddess. I called out to Mary, the Mother of God, I called out to her, as a woman and human and vulnerable, like myself. I called out to her, as one who had lost a son, as one who had been forced to watch the suffering of her child, I called out to her, not as one who could help me, but as one who suffered like myself–not more than myself, but like myself. And I called out, like some pagan, to a Goddess if she existed, to intervene, to at least stop the pain. And then I fainted again, but this time it was a total darkness and there was no more pain.

A VISION

When I regained consciousness, I found myself outside the Cave-Tomb alone, lying in the same field where I had been sewing some hours before and my daughter had been peacefully gathering wild-flowers. But was it some hours? It had seemed like an eternity of violence, yet it was outside of space and time. I could not tell how long it had been.

The field was different. When we had come to witness the scene of the Resurrection there had been green and flowers and all manner of beauty, but now the field seemed desolate. No flowers grew, the plants were dried and brown. The air was cold, frighteningly so for the region I was familiar with. Indeed, I had an uncanny feeling of being in a place which was familiar and also utterly strange. I was afraid to move, to think, to do any single thing. I had enough life to be fearful of further damage. It is amazing how life seems to persist and protect itself, even after near-total destruction, apparently, and even when on wishes to die.

I did not want to reflect upon anything, so I closed my eyes to the barrenness, cuddled myself in my shredded clothes against the cold and tried to blot out all that had happened. I wanted only darkness, surcease from pain and consciousness. So I fell asleep once again.

But now I dreamed. I dreamed that I saw Mary, the sorrowing Madonna of Our Lord. I saw her in her agony, and I saw her come to me and embrace me like a sister, or like a mother herself. She wept with me and comforted me with her own weeping. But was it Mary? Or was it a Goddess? It did not matter. In my dream I wept and wept and was comforted. And I felt the pain in my bones begin to diminish. As it diminished the figure of the Lady grew larger. I shall call her Lady since I do not know if it was Mary, or Demeter, or Goddess, Pagan Ancestor or what. The Lady began to take on dimensions of grandeur and glory such as I had never seen before. Around Her was an aura of glittering and dazzling light. She was indeed a Goddess. But She looked at me now, not with compassion, but in a matter-of-fact fellow-feeling, almost masculinely detached sort of way. She spoke:

"You are a Mother, like myself. And you have suffered, like myself. You will understand." With those simple words, explaining nothing, not even showing compassion, She vanished.

When I awakened I thought long about the dream. My understanding was that the Lady, whatever she was, was no longer comforting me, she was declaring my equality with her. She was implying that I had a task even like her own. I was fully awake when I realized this. And now I imagined that I saw the Lady and that She was nodding in agreement with my conclusion. In a wordless way I understood that I was now going to live both inside and outside time, like a Goddess. I understood that for a period of nine-something–nine hours, days, weeks, months, years, I did not know–I would wander and try to do good. I would wander and try to find my daughter. And in my wandering I would have the Lady by my side.

This vision and this understanding gave me peace. I had no answers; I still had the same anguish for my daughter and felt the pain of her absence; my memory still shook with the horror of all that I had experienced in loss of husband, son, home, and now, daughter. But now I could bear it all with a certain calm. The Lady Blessed be She, was with me.

It was almost with a foreknowledge that I would find nothing there that I walked back to the Tomb-Cave. And it was so. No rock before it, no one inside. I walked inside as far as I could see, as far as light could penetrate, but there was no sign of anyone having been there in a very long time. Indeed, this confirmed the reality of what I had experienced in dream and vision, I , therefore, went back outside the Tomb-Cave, ready to undertake the nine-fold wandering, promised by the Lady.

OF TREES AND HUNGER

It was strange as I wandered about from place to place. The world had changed. I was, indeed, both inside and outside time. I found myself among the old places, but nothing was the same. None of the people weer there, and few of the buildings. All was desolate, as if I were living in a perpetual winter.

I longed for green and trees but could find few. When I came to a forest all the trees had been cut down. Only stumps remained. It was a terrible, terrible sight. I had seen how beautiful these old trees had been, how refreshing for the soul it was to wander through them, to smell of their scent and to feel the leaves underfoot and to gaze into their tall beauty. I had seen forests cut down wantonly by the hand of a greedy man; but I had never seen such a wanton rape of a forest in this way. Here, in this destroyed forest, I saw the symbol of the cold and devastation which had surrounded me since I emerged from the Tomb-Cave.

As I wandered through the stumps of the forest in disbelief, I thought I heard the screams of agony of–what? Man or beast? I was frightened. Then I saw a man going zigzag through the trees, darting here and there in sharp gnawing terror. When he approached me I was suddenly dumbfounded; he looked very much like the leader of the gang which had raped Daughter and me. It could not be he, yet it looked much like him. Horror and hatred came over me and I wanted him to be torn apart, to be shredded and to suffer every bit of pain possible. My feelings shocked me for I had always been a very gentle person and had never experienced such fury before.

Then I looked at him again, and I was touched by his misery and grief. It was probably was not the same leader of the gang, I thought; here was a suffering creature, afflicted perhaps even more than myself. I looked at him with compassion.

The man appeared afraid of me at first, but when he saw that I meant no harm his features changed and he looked at me imploringly. "Have you any food?" he asked.

I gave him what food I had with me which he devoured quickly. He continued to look imploringly at me, as if to ask if there was any more. I shook my head, sorrowfully. He began to weep. I took his head in my hands and tried to comfort him, my own tears falling as well, without knowing why it was that he was so wracked with pain. Then he began to tell his story.

"It is terrible, terrible," he began. "No matter how much I eat, no matter how much I devour and stuff myself, I am continually left in a state of hunger which overwhelms me. It is a gnawing, aching, ravenous clawing from deep in my belly which is never sated. I wish I could die but I cannot do even that."

I looked at him quizzically, wondering how this terrible condition came about. He continued as if in answer to my question:

"My work has always been in forests. I have prided myself on being a man who could fell trees as good as anyone. And I felt even more pride since my father has owned forests and grown rich in the sale of the lumber. I was both the son of the great owner and strong enough and skilled enough to be the workers as well. I had great pride. Life was good.

"I was working with twenty or thirty of my men in this forest one day, cutting away at the trees, when a woman looking remarkably like yourself came up to me along with a daughter of perhaps twelve or thirteen. She said that she had very much enjoyed the forest and had hoped that I and my men would not cut it all down.

"In my arrogance I laughed at her, saying that forests were meant to be cut down. Furthermore, all my men had been apart from women for some time, cutting in the forest, and they looked greedily upon the woman and her daughter, I too was hungry and found her attractive, but I was not prepared for what happened next.

"Before I had even decided it, before I could even weigh the desire which was upon me, there was a great sound from the men as if a wolf had possessed them all, and they came at once, all of them, to possess the woman and her daughter. And I, and I–I weep now with the shame and humiliation of it–and I, too, joined in the violence. We raped the women and her daughter, right here in the forest. We took them and possessed them and used them, and not just once, but many times. Nor was it only a passion of the moment for my men and me. We took them again and again. And we enjoyed it.

"I fell into a deep sleep and dreamed that a great Goddess came to me in rage and fury. She frightened me so in my dream that I thought that I would go mad. I feared she would tear me apart. But no, She simply looked at me and froze my blood. Then she spoke,

She told me that I and my men had committed a horrible crime. I was a raper of trees and women. I was a raper of the soul. My punishment was to be, that for my excessive greed, I was to suffer greed. I was to ache in hunger unfulfilled. My greed was not to be for power or wealth or sexual pleasure, it was to be only for food. I would hunger and starve and be ravenous but I would never be appeased nor satisfied. With that threat the Goddess vanished and I awakened in terror.

"I looked about and saw that mother and daughter were gone, and that my men were all asleep. Somehow, the two women had freed themselves from the post to which we had tied them, and had fled. I was rather relieved after such a dream to find them gone. But I began to feel gnawing of hunger in my belly. These hunger pains increased and I ate at once. I ate all that I could find but was not satisfied. I took horse and left the forest for the home of my parents who were wealthy from the sale of trees. I ate all that there was in the house. My hunger was such that they had to sell everything they owned in order to feed me. And none of it was enough. I ate and ate. When all was finished, when my parents were ruined, I was still hungry. I went through the streets of the town eating all that I could find, even the offal in the streets.

"At last I was driven from the town and I tried to kill myself, but I could not. I came back to the forest, here, hoping to free myself from the curse of the Goddess; and here I have been wandering in pain and hunger and agony without surcease. I can neither die nor get relief and now you see me, driven in the deepest humiliation and deepest despair that one can imagine!"

Having finished his story, the man wept uncontrollably; his sobs seemed to come from the same place of emptiness in his stomach–a place of horror and death and gnawing ravenousness. At last he cried himself to sleep. Sleep apparently was the only thing that gave him relief from pain for his face relaxed a little in his sleep.

I sat there watching him and was overcome with compassion. I wondered at the parallel of the experiences and even at the similarity of our appearance. I knew full well, of course, that this man was not the same as the leader of those who had raped us in the cave. But even so, I thought, the punishment had been enough.

I believed that I knew the Goddess that had come to him in his dream. It was the Lady, Herself. So, I prayed to my Lady;

I begged her to forgive this raping creature. I begged her to have compassion and to come again to the gentleness and loving kindness which was She.

In the midst of my prayer the Lady appeared to me. She looked at me with calm and asked, "Do you forgive your rapist?" I responded, "I do." "It is done," said the Lady, and She vanished once again.

At that moment, a peace seemed to come over this forest. Where cold and clouds and darkness and barrenness had been, I now felt a late afternoon sun just as it was going down. I saw that there, around the stumps of the trees, were new growths, new little trees were appearing. Indeed, there, not far away, it looked as if some trees had already grown up in a miraculous way.

I looked, too, at the man, the one who had been a leader. His sleep was peaceful and his features had changed. No longer fierce, no longer agonized, no longer ravenous, he now looked strong and peaceful and handsome. The marks of the suffering were there, but now he even looked beautiful.

He awakened. He looked at me wonderingly. "I have just had a dream," he said, "in which the Goddess appeared and forgave me. She also said that a woman close to me though not my victim, had been a 'victim' and that she had implored forgiveness for me. And this was granted. You must be that 'woman close to me' for no one has been close to me since my affliction. You I thank, and the Goddess." Once more he wept, but with relief and pleasure this time.

Again I held him close, this former tormenter of trees and women, this former werewolf of hunger, and I felt my love for him and his for me. And there we made love, in the middle of the newly growing forest. Where rape had been, love emerged. There we made love. We made love and both were healed of pain.

OF SUN AND DARKNESS

My sojourn with this man was brief; too brief in fact. Within a very few days I felt compelled to leave this idyllic place. I missed Daughter terribly and no amount of tenderness and adoration from the Leader of Tree-Fellers could heal that wound. For this was a wound of separation, a grief and pain at loss, not a wound of penetration and humiliation.

I had no choice but to leave my lover and proceed to look for Daughter. I soon felt the weight of my separation and loss even more than before. Neither Love nor Daughter had I. I resolved to fast until I found some way or word which would direct me to my beloved Daughter.

Days and nights went by and I wandered without a sign. I could no longer find the place of the Tomb-Cave. All sign of Daughter had vanished from the earth. Even the Cave itself had vanished and I could not show anyone where we had been raped and abducted. It was as if the Earth herself had swallowed up Daughter and I was in fear of never seeing her again. I wandered in the days and nights, sleeping hardly at all, neither eating nor drinking. By night I would carry two torches to light my way, and I held them until my hands hurt. By day I would use the light of the sun, the one hot eye of heaven who looked mercilessly down upon me.

The lack of food and water, the mere shreds of sleep in the fabric of the days, the dryness of the sun–all of these tended to make me delirious. But it was not in delirium that I prayed to the Lady to assist me once again. I devoutly asked her to give me a sign that Daughter was still alive, to tell me where she was, who had her, and how I might reach her.

My prayer to the Lady was once again answered by a dream. But my dream told me that the Lady, even if she were a Goddess, was not all-knowing and certainly not all-powerful. For the Lady appeared in her tragic form and said that She knew not where Daughter was. Then She looked meaningfully toward the sun itself, as if that orb which observes all might know the answer.

I awakened from my dream and looked toward the hot sun. Now in my delirium I saw it as a great and powerful Eye which looked down upon me with a withering stare.

The Eye formed itself into two lips and then spoke in a powerful and authoritative manner:

"You are honored, O Mother, for your daughter has been placed above other women. Your prayer has been heard and your daughter has been freed of her entrapment by demonic men and joined in marriage to the Son of God! Fear not, for she of the lovely ankles, she of the dark and passionate mien, she of the goodness of heart, she, your daughter is honored above all the women of Jerusalem!"

I trembled before these words from what was an Angel of heaven, or even perhaps God the Father Himself! I must indeed have been mad, I thought, for can it be that my Daughter has become a Bride of Christ? Has she indeed been wed to the Son of God? Or was this Eye of Heaven a demon, or the Devil Himself, deluding me and creeping into my weakness of hunger, thirst, and lack of sleep? I called out to the Lady, She whom I trusted, to tell me whether my Daughter had been so honored or whether I was merely mad with grief.

Then I saw the Lady, but in alternating shapes. First she appeared in her sweet, compassionate, but sorrowing Madonna form, looking at me with great love and kindness. The She looked like a kind of Hecate, or even a wild Medusa, with hair as snakes and with wild demonic eyes. The eyes flashed and her lips opened with cackle. The two visions repeated back and forth as if one were looking at the at the profile of a vase from an "outside" and an "inside"; both were true, it depended which side one focused upon. The two faces merged after a time into one great and powerful Face of the Lady. But faces merged after a time into one great and powerful Face of the Lady. But this was the Lady of Sorrows and the Lady of Compassion, at the same time this was the Lady of Joyous Frenzy and Passion. She spoke:

"It is true that your Daughter has been wed to the Son of God. It is true that the Father has given His Son. But it is not the Lord whom you knew no. Neither is it the Lord, Sun of this world, no. It is His brother, the Lord of the Underworld. It is His brother, the Sun of the Night!"

With these words ringing as if struck upon a great gong, I fainted once more.

When I awakened I could hardly manage to keep myself in one conscious whole. I had either to faint once again and flee from what I knew and understood, or else be wracked by a greater pain than even before. For my daughter, my lovely Daughter of the passionate mien and beautiful ankles, was the Bride of Satan! What help was this in answer to my prayers! What had the Lady done if She had not opposed this? Was this not worse even than our being raped and beaten by twenty or thirty men? They were after all only men, and not the Prince of Darkness Himself! I tore my clothes and clawed at my hair and face. I wanted to tear myself to bits, but then a cool and crisp voice from the Lady Herself came into my soul to calm me, and stopped me right in my self-destructive tracks. She spoke:

"What do you do, O Mother of the honored Daughter? Have you not seen my two faces? Have you not seen men as tender and compassionate? Have you not seen me as wild and cruel? And do you not know me as you know yourself? And are not the two of me as One? Are not, then, the Mother of two Sons the same? And can not the Mother, and that same Father beget two Sons who are as One? Can you not guess at the mystery?"

The Lady then looked right through me and I was silenced. I was not spared my grief nor spared my anguish that my Daughter was wed in the Underworld. But I was strong. I was aware that the Son of the Night was also a Sun in the Night. I spoke no more.

The Lady fixed me in her gaze for a long time and then said, "But you will know in the spirit what your Daughter will know in the flesh." This was both a promise and a threat. It chilled me a bit but I smiled, for it seemed ironic: The Eye of Heaven had stated that what was an "honor" for my daughter was going to be repeated for me. "Thank you very much, but no thank you," was my immediate thought and this too made me laugh.

But my laughter died upon my lips; I felt an earthquake, a real one, and saw the ground crack open near me. I started to run. I saw boulders falling from above, which could kill me, and splits in the earth into which I could fall and be smothered. Something hit me–a rock? All was darkness.

My darkness was a strange one. I was in a dream or in a borderline state which was neither sleep nor wakefulness. All was dark, yet there was a dim and suffused light all around, which allowed me to make out shapes and outlines, but not details. It was as one might imagine the experience of a person who is going blind, or what one sees immediately after coming into a darkened room from full sunlight. And, as happens when one comes into the darkened room, in time I could make out more detail in the shapes and forms, but never was there clear light.

I thought I saw what one might think of as a moonscape: rock and sand and mountains and caves and pocked surfaces. And silent, very, very silent. As if the earthquake which I had seen had shaken the entire earth and changed its structure and appearance. No life. Not even the remotest bit of green. And quiet. But suddenly! Harshly! The sun itself, as a Great Eye, as a Monster of shapes and changing fire forms, comes leaping out of no known place. It comes to me and burns me, scalds me, embraces me in a kind of rape of every pore, and I struggle and struggle, until I am broken in every part of my body. It leaves. I lie pained and aching in every small part of skin and flesh. I pant like a sensitive animal whose skin is so tender that it can not stand the barest breath of wind. I pant quietly. Then thundering out of the barren earth appears a huge horse-like creature. He is a gorgeous, Pegasus-like horse with wings and is frightening with his great hoofs and enormous organs. He falls upon me as if to take me. I cry out, for I am only a woman, and cannot. I am only a woman and human. I seem in my madness to change into a mare, and am taken by this Dark Stallion. I am taken and am overwhelmed by unspeakable–dare I admit it? Yes, I am overwhelmed by unspeakable ecstasy.

Days, weeks, months later–I awaken fully. The world is as it was before, quiet, somewhat barren, but I have had an experience of which I cannot speak. It was as the Lady had said. I look about, dazed. It is winter, deep in winter. All is bare, but there, over there, do I not a see a single ear of corn growing? Yes. I smell it, and taste it. And I eat it. I am quiet, and healed. I am chilled, and warmed–and–silent.

SHE COMES TO THE CASTLE

In the days and weeks immediately following this numinous even, I wandered in a strange kind of ecstasy. I felt as if I continually thirsty, yet fully sated by having drunk the most refreshing water of the clearest stream. I felt as if I had tasted the greatest sensual delight which it is possible for a woman to experience, yet I felt virginal. I felt a freshness of breath, of spirit and of being, in relation to the night especially and to the stars over all, yet I felt old and beaten and tired. All these I felt. All these opposite kinds of feeling had I. All were true, simultaneously. Was this, I wondered, the experience of the God, the Son of the Night? Was this anything like that which the Madonna Herself had felt when touched by God? I dared not make these comparisons yet I felt both honored and humbled. A final pair of opposites which I did not try to unravel.

But the original longing for my daughter returned, unassuaged by the good things that had happened to me. It was as if the grief of loss, of separation, of feeling my own pain and that which I imagined she was undergoing–all of these took away the goodness and left only the harder, more aching feelings. I felt guilty for having had pleasure at all. I was plunged into more dreadful and gnawing grief.

Thus I wandered, neglecting my appearance, until I looked old and haggard. I wandered far afield, far from my original place–though in fact I could not tell if it were different or the same, for the world was changed. I wandered among cities and the places where men lived and worked. The Lady was still with me, in spirit, though vague, and seemed to guide my footsteps here and there and everywhere.

At last She guided me to a town where I sat down in fatigue and grief beside a well. There the people of the village drew water, and there I sat in the shade drawing what cool pleasure I could under a lovely olive tree. I was told that this place was named Well of the Virgin, and I was satisfied. For such is Your name, O Lady, who is both divine and human. Such is Your name, whether called Virgin, Goddess, Madonna or–as I do–Lady.

As I sat in stillness four lovely maidens approached me. They spoke to me:

Where are you coming from, old woman, and where are you going? Why have you left your home? And why do you not come into our palace, the palace of our father, the King? There, within its happy walls, you would find more shad than here, and there you would be at home in your old age, just as the young women there are happy. We would be good to you."

This speech of welcome touched me, but I wondered why these four lovely young maidens were so good to me. Was this the typical hearty welcome of the people of this place, or did they see the hand of the Lady about me? I did not know. Nor did I wish to tell them the truth of my story, for either I would not be believed, or they would treat me with an honor that I was not prepared to accept. I therefore spoke to them in half-truths.

I told them that I had been abducted by pirates and brought thence from my native home. When the pirates landed near this place, and while they were preparing to carouse with other women, I escaped. I concluded my story by saying that I was indeed looking for help and hospitality such as the four maidens offered. I was also eager to be of help, if I could Perhaps there was a child in the palace who needed a nurse, and perhaps I could teach handiwork, too.

The four maidens responded beautifully. The said that the King and Queen would be happy to have me, and that any of the lords of the land would be glad of the chance to have me in their household. But I should come straightaway to their own palace. Their mother would be delighted for she had recently given birth to a sweet son. Anyone would be glad to nurse this son; there would be great rewards for this new and only-begotten Prince.

I gladly accompanied the four maidens, each of whom was prettier than the other. They all had names which I had difficulty in pronouncing, but three of these names began with K. So I called them K-1, K-2, K-3, and D. The sisters were so lovely as they walked that I thought they were dancing. They carried their brazen pitchers on their heads in such a way that the vessels seemed as valuable s gold and delicate as porcelain. They walked like Goddesses and I wondered if the Lady, Herself, had taken their forms to guide me. As I watched them walk I was amaze at the differences among them. One was dark, another light, the third brownish, the fourth golden, yet all these differences were very slight and one knew that they were sisters. I was sure that they were Goddesses. I lifted my veil to observe them better to adore their dance-like steps. I could adore them, these wonderful maidens, but then I was reminded anew of my daughter, who was indeed a match for them all. For sure was dark and light, brown and golden, and he was more a goddess than any human creature I had ever seen. And with that thought, that memory of my lost daughter, I was plunged back into the gloom which had been lifted by the kindness of the maidens and the prospect of being of some use as a nurse in the castle.

With this attitude, I crossed over the threshold of the palace into the room of the Queen. As I did so a startling thing happened. I saw the Queen sitting before me with the child, her new son. But between us in transparent glory, was shiny and glimmering Lady Herself. She filled the room with divine light and spread her glow around us. I felt warmed with the rapture of Her appearance, but the Queen was stricken with awe and was terrified. She rose up and, to my astonishment, she bowed to me as if I were the Lady! She treated me as a

Goddess and insisted that I sit in her Queenly chair. I refused knowing full well that I was no Goddess and that the poor Queen had become confused by seeing the glow of goddess upon me, when She was merely between the Queen and myself. I did not know what to do so I stood in silence with my eyes cast down, until a handmaiden set a stool before me and put a sheepskin upon it.

I sat upon the stool for a long time in deep grief. It seemed that nothing could console me. My despair affected the Queen and even her daughters, the four maidens, until there was only gloom in the room.

All was still in the room and dark, until the handmaiden, whose name was Iambe, suddenly danced into the middle. It looked to me as if she grasped a last trail of the glory of the Lady as She passed from sight. Iambe took it to her lips, put it behind her head, and did a provocative little step which was both audacious and modestly girlish.

And she began to recite:

"I would begin my ditty here
And so the Mother please;
Her grief is great, my friends, I fear,
It puts us on our knees."

With the introduction of Iambe I looked up, and was surprised to see that she was solicitous of me, but also mocking. I became aware of the self-enhancement of my depressed state and ruefully gave her a half-smile. She continued:

"The Mother smiles as she despairs.
A martyr's face shows she;
The goddess wreath she will not wear
From fear or modestly."

Now I began to feel hurt and angry at Iambe. Was that reference to "martyr" an unpleasant one? False modesty? Was I just enjoying my depression? Certainly not! Iambe giggled and went on:

"Depressed. Confessed. Despairs. Repairs.
Our Mother has come home.
No wrath, I pray it's glee, we see,
When martyr's hood is foam."

When martyr's hood is foam"–What did she mean by that? My sadness is a cloak to be lifted and no more substantial than foam? Yes, that must be it. But that is not true! I miss Daughter very much!

> "Alone. It's hard. But has rewards.
> Two sides, the martyr's cloak.
> But let our warmth replace the swords
> And love, the hood to soak."

Yes, Iambe, I see your point, and I see your love and humor, too. But can I just drop my sadness and mourning for Daughter and accept your love? Besides, how is it that you know that? The Lady must have told you! Did She?

Iambe continued:

> "The Lady speaks through all of us
> In each a special way
> The Goddess lives, why make a fuss?
> To her we all do pray
>
> In love, and grief, we joy and mourn
> And both are there at once.
> The Goddess knows, as we sojourn,
> For She's like us, no dunce.
>
> So come and dance in quiet mood
> And share our Woman's fate.
> The Maidens Four are 'Daughters–food'
> They need you 'til they mate.
>
> So can you come, O Mother, dear?
> And join us in our play?
> We'll dance and sing and shed a tear
> In union spend our day."

After Iambe had said these gracious lines, what could I say? I made myself more comfortable in appreciation of my hosts and what they had to offer me.

No sooner, however, had I relaxed upon my bench softened with sheep wool, when a lady called "Belly" came forward. She stood before me, fat. She was very full-hipped and busted. Unlike Iambe, who had looked at me warmly and lovingly, if a little mockingly, "Belly" looked straight at me in a most vulgar and earthy manner, which made me feel that I was a "virgin" indeed and very prudish as well. Belly began a lascivious dance, shaking her ample hips and rolling her huge breasts, while walking about as if she were strutting before a number of hungry and panting men.

She started to sing a song whose words I could not grasp entirely, for they included slang usages of pornographic sort and I did not understand all the references. The song seemed to be about a man who had lusted after her, had longed to couple with her. Belly egged him on, since he had no money to pay for her loving attentions, and had gotten him close to his desire when she turned her back upon him and broke wind in his face.

This stanza was greeted with uproarious laughter by all the women present, including the Queen. I was shocked and surprised and grew even more uncomfortable. I was feeling silly because of my prudishness.

After Belly finished her song about the poor man, she did a dance with an imitation phallus as a partner. She looked longingly at it, caressed it, put it to her cheek, pretended to have intercourse with it under her arm. She winced as if this were to painful, and then tried to put it in her ear, her nose, and then in her mouth, as if she did not know into which orifice to insert it. This uncertainty also brought loud guffaws from the ladies. Belly then licked the phallus with great gusto and pleasure to the equal pleasure of the assembled ladies. Finally, with a pseudo-ecstatic look, she placed the phallus between her legs and pretended to have intercourse. She let out a very loud sign and was greeted by the audience with a similarly full and ecstatic sign as they identified with her.

I still did not laugh the way the other ladies did, though I must confess I smiled often at her terrific earthiness and fine disregard for the male as nothing other than an "object". For me, the whole show was "enlightening" about my experiences with males. It was a story of What Women Go Through, rather than being hilarious. I saw the performance as an assertion of our power as women rather than anything else. So you see how priggish and prudish I was.

Despite my lack of responsiveness Belly went on with the entertainment. She danced and she swayed. She shook her hips, she shook her breasts. She placed the phallus between her breasts and rubbed them against it. She went through an ecstasy of relationship with this phallus-partner to the great delight of all the women present.

To the delight of all, that is, except me. I grew more and more morose and prudish and felt ridiculous in my moroseness and prudishness. I closed my eyes and pleaded with the Lady to come to me. I prayed that She relieve me of this painful split in my feeling which was making me humorless.

With my eyes tightly closed, I saw the Lady, and I saw her sorrowing. She spoke:

You are like me, O little Mother. You sorrow, you pray, you are passionate, you are compassionate, but little Mother, so am I. You are rueful too, and so am I. There, you see Belly, a great and good sister, and she is marvelous indeed. I envy her. For I cannot be that way. Do you know why? I will tell you. It is because my own Mother was just like her–great and earthy Belly, a great and vulgar one. And I, "special' I, was chosen to rise 'above' that and reach the spirit. And so I have and so I have. For I have given birth to God and a Goddess. But lo, little Mother, now you see me, limited, and not so great as my own Mother, who was wild and vulgar and earthy and not afraid. Most of all, She could laugh. So little Mother, Daughter of mine, you, like me, can laugh only a little. Submit, if you can, to Belly and laugh."

With these words the Lady vanished. I looked up to see Belly still in her dance of gyrations, with the rhythmic clapping of hands of all present. Then they all looked at me as if encouraging me to join in the dance with Belly. Belly too, the Great Fat Vulgar One, summoned me with a flutter of her fingers, saying "Come hither." And then I rose from my stool. I rose as if moved by a power greater than myself and I came forward. Forward I came and I embraced and was embraced by Belly. She handed me the phallus, and I smiled.

I smiled and kissed the phallus-partner, for I was beginning to feel something move inside me. I felt a movement of lovely vulgarity. What else can I call it? I started to dance and let this vulgar thing take over. But was it vulgar? Was it not my own mother who was dancing inside me? And was it not perhaps the equivalent of the Lady's

Mother, too? So I think. And so it went. I danced. And I swayed. And I gradually removed my clothes in the most seductive way possible. I bumped my organs forward and back. I ground them around as if they were chewing up and digesting a most marvelously huge penis. I thrust my breasts and circled them. I did this and that. I grew more and more confident. Then to my great surprise I broke wind. It was not just a mild and feminine little squeak which might be thought cute. No, it was a loud and raucous wind-breaker which would be a credit to a donkey!

Then I began to laugh. I laughed and laughed, along with all the women present. I laughed with them as we began to dance together. We bumped and turned our organs. We shared the great phallus, and we made wind-breaking noises with our mouths and, whenever we could, with our behinds. And we danced a great dance with dark and hairy Belly. Belly was our guide and we followed her. Belly was our laughing and joyous guide–the earthy mother of us all. And then, I imagined–or was it so?–that Lady joined us. And I thought that her Mother, too, the Great Earth Goddess joined us. Indeed, I could not tell the difference between Belly and the Earth Goddess. And we all danced, the mighty Dance of Women, the mighty and uproarious dance of Wind-Breaker, of the Phallus-Holder.

We danced until we were exhausted. We danced until we all fell on top of each other in laughing and exhausted merriment. And we fell asleep in an intimacy and warmth of arms, legs, buttocks, breasts. We slept the sleep of the warmth of the earth, and of the body. It was a great, good, smelly sleep.

When I awakened I saw Belly again. Now she was warm and gentle in her dark and bosomy hairiness. She looked at me with tenderness and love; I saw a deep sensitivity in those black eyes and a deep joy. But I knew too that there had been profound suffering there. I knew that Lady and Belly were One. That Mother and Daughter were One. And then Belly gave me a drink. It was a drink of deeply refreshing and fulfilling barley-water. And I knew without words that the barley-water was our drink. It was the drink of the women who knew of the underworld, the women who had known the Underworld God, but had experienced the Mothering goddess of the Earth Herself. And we, we women, we did not need the Vine. We did not need the grape, we did not need the wine. No, we had that already in our flesh, in our breasts and thighs and bellies. We had that wine-spirit built into us–at least when we had Belly! And for us, the drink of refreshment was an after-drink and a before-drink, of barley-water, mixed with delicate mint. So I drank and my thirst was quenched. I looked deeply into the eyes of Belly, and our souls were One.

THE PRINCE: APPEARANCE AND DEPARTURE

The peace which Iambe, Belly, the Queen and her four daughters gave me filled me with gratitude. There was still a secret mourning in me for my daughter but I was brought to an acceptance of life, of death, of loneliness, and of my own limitation by these lovely women. I felt a woman among women and loved, and I longed to do something for them in return.

The Queen, when I asked her what I could do for her and her entourage, answered that I would do her a great and wonderful service by being nurse to her son. This son, coming as he did out of her later years, long after the birth of both her three older sons and four daughters, this son was very special. She did not tell me in what way she thought that this son and four daughters, this son was very special, but she made it very clear that he was in some way extraordinary, and that she wanted me, especially, to look after him. When I asked her why she thought that I in particular would be worthy of this honor, she merely looked at me with a smile, a little archly. It was a secret between us, she seemed to be saying. I wondered if she meant my connection with the Lady was the special reason, but I knew that I could not mention this. For this was a secret I could not divulge; it was either seen and known, or it was not. I had to trust that this was what the Queen meant with her smile. I agreed to nurse this young Prince as best I could.

And so I did. I took this sweet, dark-haired young Prince, and held him to my breast which became fragrant as soon as it was near him. I held him on my lap which became soft and warm and containing as soon as he was in it. Indeed, everything that I did for him seemed to suit him perfectly as if he were made for it, or produced it by his presence. I marvelled at this. Was the Lady responsible for this, or was I in the presence of a young God? But I did not question my great good fortune of being able to give a wonderful Prince all that his infant heart seemed to require.

He waxed strong and handsome. He was bright-eyed and courageous, of a loving and open temperament which was at once deeply human and sweet and also god-like. I was happy. One night, however, I had a dream which shocked me.

In my dream the Lady came to me. She told me that with Her help I was doing very well by the young Prince, but henceforth I was to supplement my care of him in a special way. Each night I was to expose the fine young Prince to the full strength of the fire, like a billet of wood that is being made into a torch, or like a lamb which is being gently and slowly browned over a warm blaze. I was shocked by this instruction from the Lady, and shook my head strenuously, saying no to this. "Oh, Lady," I said, "This young Prince is like my own lost son. He thrives under my care, grows like a young god. But he is mortal, I think, and would become mere roast lamb under such treatment!"

The Lady responded: "Little Mother, you forget who it is that speaks to you. Why do you suppose that the young Prince thrives under your care? Why do you suppose that he grows like a young God? Why do you think that the Queen was so eager that you, the sorrowing little Mother, should care for this Prince, the apple of her eye? Do you think it is because of your virtues? Do you think that you, indeed, are a Goddess?"

I hung my head in shame and could not answer. Indeed, I knew that all this that was good through my hands was because I had the Lady about me. I knew that what love and sweet care and nourishing growth came through me was a direct consequence of my link with the Lady. Should I not trust this same source of goodness? Was what seemed dangerous and awful to me only so because of my limited understanding? Would the Lady mean evil as well as good? My answer, strangely, was that I did not know. I knew the two faces of Lady; she could be a Hecate as well as a Demeter. I, as a woman, knew that no female, even if she is touched by a God or Goddess, is devoid of the capacity for evil. But all the same I had to trust Lady.

That night, therefore, when everyone was asleep, I took the young Prince and warmed him upon the fire as if he were a billet of wood for a torch, or a lamb to be roasted. Strangely, miraculously, the Prince slept on peacefully and made no outcry. Indeed, he seemed to be warmed and even cleansed by the fire. I was amazed and deeply relieved by this miracle and thanked the Lady for it. Secretly, I was prepared to snatch him away from the fire at the first sign of whimper from him or the appearance of a reddish glow upon his skin. Thus I both trusted and did not trust the Lady; I would have fought her like a like a tigress should harm begin to come to my young Prince.

Then I saw Lady in a vision, smiling. "You have done as you should, little Mother, even to not trust me, while trusting me. For that is as it should be. Thee I love." With that I saw her gently touch the body of the Prince, and come to me and kiss my head.

Every night after that I would repeat the strange ritual of the toasting of the Prince. And he continued to wax strong and loving and handsome. For all practical purposes I became his true mother, and the bond between us seemed great.

Then one night just before his third birthday, the Queen came into the great hall with the fireplace and saw our fiery ritual. Why did she do so? Cat-like curiosity, unspoken jealousy, or merely chance occurrence? What made her do this thing, I do not know. Perhaps it was "meant" as are all great events, meant by the gods in their scheme of things. In any event, our peaceful, happy household, our recovering bond of family and female closeness was shattered by this perception of the Queen. For now she saw. And she screamed. Naturally she screamed. Would not any mother scream were she to see her son being roasted upon a spit? Did not even our Lady Mary scream, when she saw her Son crossed-up upon His nails? Is any explanation adequate to deal with one's fear and horror at this event?

So the Queen screamed, and in terror beat both hands upon her thighs. She called out, "Oh, my son, my prince, this stranger plunges thee into the fire and me she lets waste away into a living death!" Thus lamented the Queen.

I was startled and stood dumbfounded. I was sympathetic with the Queen and felt her bereavement, knowing that what she saw and what seemed to her as a hell was, in fact, the opposite of what she feared. But I could not speak. I stood with my mouth open.

Then, I thought I saw the Lady once again. She came out of the fire, it seemed to me, and walked toward me. Then, to my amazement, She, this great Lady, Mother of God, Mother of a Goddess, came into me. She literally entered my being, crawled into my skin and into my small body and used me as her vessel to speak. She spoke to the Queen through me, thusly;

"Ignorant are human beings and thoughtless, for they can neither understand nor foresee good and evil. Thoughtless are you, Oh Queen, for you have not trusted. I would have made of your son a true immortal, who would have remained eternally young, and I would have won for him imperishable fame. Thus was the fire that he suffered–a burning, painless fire of eternal life. And it was no fire in the ordinary sense, and he did not suffer it. Now, thanks to you and your fears, he shall be mortal like any other, and know the pain of the fire of passion and suffering and error, and go through the burning of learning of good and evil. Nor can he avoid death, both the many deaths in life, and the rebirths–in life and in the end. But he shall receive reknown, because he was warmed in my arms and slept in my lap. For the little Mother, whom I have used, did him warm and contain, through me. Thus will this little Prince receive fame and be great. But he will be an ordinary mortal as well. And you, Oh Queen, you and your whole people must erect a great temple, and an altar to me, to the Lady, to the Goddess. And it shall be above the Well of the Virgin–my well–and near the dancing place. And, because you did not trust the Goddess, you shall offer worship until you learn to trust, even as the little Mother, did trust."

Thus spoke the Lady, through me. And as she did so, I felt myself as no longer an oldish woman, but as young and bathed in beauty. I was aware of a desire-awakening fragrance upon my body, and my hair was as golden as the sun. I knew that when the Goddess entered into one, one was truly eternally young and immortal. At that moment I was aware that the Goddess and I were both separate and united, dual and unitary. And now you will readily see without any further words from me how it was so.

The Queen, poor creature, fell down in a faint. She lay there at my feet, making no sound, for a very long time. Gradually the aura and grandeur of the Lady departed from me and I saw that the four daughters, having heard the weeping of the little Prince, now away from the fire, and having heard the speech of the Goddess coming through my lips, went on caring for the little boy. One daughter put him on her lap. Another lit a fire. A third ran to the mother, helped her to her feet. All of them–and, I, too, when I came back to my ordinariness–looked to the Prince. We busied ourselves with washing him and comforting him and surrounding him with love.

But the Prince would not be comforted, for now he had worse nurses. I, even I, who had been the carrier of the good things which nourishing him, could not comfort him. So, we all, Daughters, Queen, and myself, spent the whole night praying to the Goddess, and trembling with fear.

As we prayed the Queen wept quietly, often looking at me with great sadness. At last she spoke to me:

"Oh, little Mother, I must speak to you and confess. The words of the Goddess, the great lady, as they came through you sounded harsh and unloving. Perhaps, as their vehicle, you do not feel guiltless. But I must tell you that Her words were true. It was, I, even I, who was as She said, ignorant and untrusting. So hear my tale. Now I feel that I must tell you; you, little Mother, are a vessel for the Lady; you, perhaps, will intercede for me. Pray, listen a little and be gentle in your judgment.

"I must first confess that the Prince is not my physical son, though I love him greater than my own. Long did I pray for a son in my older age, for I had been an inadequate mother, I thought, much involved with my own pleasures and adornments. My sons, born first, did suffer thereby, though my daughters did not. I prayed for a new son and heir who would be a tribute to the Kingdom and one upon whom I could lavish the care that I had not expended before.

"One night, in a dream, a great Goddess, but appearing much as yourself, little Mother, though more grand and gorgeous, approached me and said that my wish would come true. She said, however, that I was to be mother to a child born of God and Woman; I was to care for this child, even though it was not my own. My true test was to care for him as unselfishly as I had been selfish. I was to love him even though not of my flesh, as much or greater than I would love my own. The Lady told me further that in time She would appear to me in human form and that I was to let Her take care of the little Prince and to trust Her.

"I awakened from this dream in a very gripped state. I felt that I had been touched by the most profound experience of my life; I had to believe that the dream contained a truth. I was to be allowed to redeem my motherhood, and in the most selfless and spiritual of ways.

"I said nothing to anyone about this, not even my husband; I did not know how this grand little Prince was going to be made manifest.

I did not have long to wait, however. Three days later, my maids reported that a sweet little infant boy had been fished out of the well, the Well of the Virgin. No one seemed to know his parentage, but he had the mark of royalty. At once I knew that this was the Prince, the child born of God and Woman, that the Lady had told me about. I had the maids fetch the child and bring him to me. And I claimed him as my own. It was easy to get the confidence of the maids and my daughters, for I only had to tell them the story. For the King this was more difficult. I could not tell him the truth—why, I do not know—but I am able to convince him that I had kept the pregnancy a secret. Since I am large boned and have always carried my pregnancies in a way that hardly shows, and since the King was overjoyed to have a new heir in his older age, it was not so difficult to convince him.

"So we rejoiced in the Prince, and adored him. And he grew well in our hands. Then one day you appeared, little Mother, just as the Lady had promised. I was left breathless when you appeared at the Well, when my daughters told me of it. I almost fainted when I saw you and your likeness to the image of the Lady in my dream. I was both overjoyed and frightened. For I was, indeed, threatened by the fact that my loving care as a mother was to be taken over by another. And you, even you, appeared human and limited like myself, but the mantle of the Goddess came with you, and I submitted.

"My submission was greeted with value, for the Prince grew in your hands and seemed to flow up and out and around like a young God. But I was jealous, I must confess, and did not trust. Then, last night I could bear it no longer for I knew that you were doing something with the Prince in the night—and I came out to see what it was. The rest you know. I weep in shame and contrition. Forgive me little Mother, and seek forgiveness for me from the Lady."

Thus ended the brief tale of the Queen. I felt sorry for her and tried to comfort her as best I could. She seemed frail and vulnerable and mortal, like myself, and I felt for her despair. I prayed to the Lady, but the only message that came to me—and even this was not clear—was the speech that she had delivered to us all earlier. She seemed to demand the construction of the Temple before anything else was forthcoming.

At the grey of dawn we awakened the King, and the Queen told him the entire story. It is to his credit that the King did not grow wroth but immediately felt compassion for his wife. He understood at once that a great and rich temple to the Lady had to be built, and he so commanded it. A large and shining temple was build, above the Well of the Virgin on the spur of a hill. It was built quickly and well. The labor was completed in a matter of days for the temple arose by the will of the Goddess.

When the temple was completed, in its great and shiny wonder, we thought that the Goddess would relent. But She did not. That same night She appeared in a dream of the Queen, the four daughters and myself, and to each of us gave the same message: the Prince was to be returned to the Well from which he came.

Hard it was, for us all. Hard and impossible. Saved from the fire, returned unto the water? Hard. But implacable. For had not the Lady appeared to us all?

The hardest of hard tasks was accomplished. The Prince was returned to the well, just three years old. Drowned, was he? None could know.

I returned to my mourning, and now, I was joined by the Queen and by her daughters. I sat in the Temple, clothed in dark raiment, and mourned for the Prince–lost. I mourned for my own husband and son–lost. And I mourned once again, as if it were all afresh and from the beginning, my daughter–lost. The Queen and her daughters mourned too, for the Prince, for the loss, and for the horror.

We mourned together quietly and alone.

MOURNING AND THE KNIGHT: MOTHER RESTS

We, we poor women. We mourned. We fasted. We took no food and little water. We grew weak in our mourning and then ate enough only to keep us alive. And so we sat in that gorgeous temple on the spur of the hill. And so we mourned in that great temple to the Lady built above the Well in Her name. And so we mourned the loss of Daughter, the loss of Son, the loss of Husband, the loss of loved ones. Our mourning was deep.

Then the world around us began to change. A dreadful time was upon the land. The crops ceased to grow. The sun shone only dimly and rarely. Dark clouds and dreary sky were upon us all day, every day. The animals grew thin and misery was upon the people.

Famine. Despair. Emptiness. Death. Mourning.

So we sat, day after day, night after night, unyielding in our hard and bitter mourning.

One day the eldest of the three sons of the King, who was the one in charge of the cattle, came to me and whispered that he must speak to me.

He, the Cattleherder, as the eldest of the sons of the King, had been approached by his two youngest brothers, a Swineherd and a Shepherd, who had had a remarkable experience. This experience was a visitation of a divine nature; it was of such import that these two had come straightaway to him, the eldest, who would, perhaps, know what to do. The eldest decided that the experience should be told at once to me, the Mother, the Visitor and the Searcher after Daughter. He felt that I would know what to do. Would I then listen to the experience? I would indeed.

Forthwith the Cattleherder, handsome and strong, brought before me his two brothers, who looked far different. The Cattleherder was strong and handsome. His Swineherd brother was small, dark, like a wiry, tough and wizened wild pig. The Swineherd was mute but was able to communicate with his brother, the Shepherd.

The Shepherd was like Shepherds are–or ought to be–slight, but well built, fine featured, and sensitive. His Pan-like ears were softened by dark, tender eyes, he played his flute like some creature out of nature. Only he could understand the Swineherd, his brother, who was said to have the gift of prophecy.

I looked at these three sons of the King and Queen, the strong and good hearted Cattleherder, the beautiful and poetic Shepherd, and the dark and uncanny Swineherd. No wonder the Queen longed for another son in her old age, no wonder she felt a little awed herself by these three, who were more like Gods or Demons than ordinary men. No wonder she was doubtful if she herself had been an adequate mother to have produced such a strange brood. Yet all three were good and true; all three were fine sons. No monsters had she but each had a strange divine spark.

I looked to the Queen who wordlessly shared my experience. It must have been strange for her, I thought, to have her sons come to me, a stranger, and to bypass her. Yet she seemed accepting of this. She seemed even friendly and grateful. She was not wroth, nor sad. So I accepted the three sons. I embraced each in turn as if he were something of my own lost son, and something, even, of the little Prince we women had nursed with the Goddess and whom we had had to sacrifice back into the Well.

We all sat down; the Shepherd played a few notes on his pipes as if in introduction, and then began to speak:

"As you all know, my brother, the Swineherd, is mute and cannot tell you of his remarkable experience. He has asked, though, to use my pipes and my tongue to convey the vision of his dark and dreary eyes. For so it was ordered, he says, by the Goddess, She whose service he is in, and whose gifts go deeper than my own. I also serve the same Goddess through my words and tune. But I, like my pipes, will be only a vehicle for my brother's experience, and I will tell the experience through his wordless words. So hear me, Shepherd for Swineherd for Goddess, and listen to me as you would to the pipes which are only a vehicle for the breath.

"Listen, my friends, to the song of the Swineherd,
For the Swineherd, though lowly, has seen God.
Listen, my friends, to the words of the Wordless,
For these words come from guts and from sod.

I sat with my swine one day, and counted my blessings,
For visions come to me, and prophesies and peace.
I sat with my swine, as I say,
For pigs and mud are as good as sheep and fleece.

So I sat and held my head and looked at my navel
And I worried about food and comfort and women.
So I sat and was inside myself and my desire
And I worried about what to do with my semen.

As I sat and worried, as I was inside myself,
I heard a thunder break, I heard a rolling fire.
As I sat inside myself and closed myself in,
I heard a thunder roll, with noised dire.

I looked up and saw the ground crack open
And earthquake jolted me awake.

I looked up and saw the swine fall in,
A chasm split open and them did take.

But I could do nothing but look,
As the swine fell in and cried in pain,
But I could do nothing but cry, nothing but cry,
As the pigs were swallowed, and went instance.

And then I saw another sight, another sight,
Which made me cry, which made me cry even more.
And then I saw a chariot bright
Which, though golden, had blood on it, and gore.

This chariot, my friends, was something to see,
Was as large as a house and heavy as lead.
This chariot, I saw, golden and weighty,
Was drawn by a horse, winged and black with dread.

As great was this horse, winged and black,
Greater yet was the charioteer,
As golden and black was the horse,
Brighter and blacker was his peer.

Horse and Chariot, Chariot and Charioteer,
All arose from the chasm, as though weightless
Horse and Chariot, Charioteer arising,
All arose like a God, and mateless.

For He rose and leaped forward to a maiden
And the Maiden was astonished and dismayed.
Yes, he rose and leaped onward to this maiden,
And the maiden trembled and swayed.

The maiden screamed and called to her mother,
But the mother was taken as well.
The maiden screamed and longed to be free,
But the mother was raped, as she fell.

The Quest

The mother was soon loosened to wander,
Of grief she would nave no end.
But the daughter was kept in the Yonder
Of dark pain, iron will, black end.

And God the Father knew of it,
His Eye, the Sun, did see it,
And God the Father approved of it,
His Eye did wink at the pall.

Why, ask me not, for I am a Swineherd, not a Wise Man
Why, ask me not, for I am a prophet, not a saint,
But I, though a Swineherd, saw God,
Why then, does God have a taint?

The maiden wept in horror, the mother wept in pain,
But God did not assuage it, He did it.
The maiden's heart was broken, the mother too, I say,
But God did not mend it, He caused it.

My friends, all this I saw, I, a Swineherd low,
I saw the rape by God below, a wink from God above.
My friends, I saw two faced of God
I saw rape and wink, no love.

But I was dumb and could not speak
And I feared God and pain
But I was dumb and something of a freak
And I feared to go insane.

For who can see the darkness of God
And keep in mind in one whole?
Who can feel both rape and wink
And cling, in love, to his soul?

So I wept and was raped, like Mother and Daughter, too,
I prayed and I pained, I held my sides together.
So I strained and was torn, like a woman, old or young,
I was splayed and I was trained, 'til supple and strong as leather.

But I was not alone in what I saw, the Goddess saw it too.
But though I thought I was alone, I wasn't,
The goddess suffered it through.

She, She came to me, in dream and fantasy.
She, She spoke to me, The Goddess spoke.
She, She touched me, soft and hard, did She,
She, She chose me, me did She yoke.

Left hand is She, said She, of God above and below.
Knowing does She, said She, when Right hand does not.
Loving hand is She, said She, of God blind and violent,
Loving is She, said She, beyond violence and greed and rot.

She told me to tell, dumb Swineherd that I am,
To tell that which I have seen.
She told me to tell my brothers and the mothers,
To tell the vision, oh so keen.

So I "told" my brother Shepherd, with looks I told him so,
With looks I told my brother, with words he tells you so.
So I tell my story to you, from Goddess do I speak,
With looks I told my brother, with words he is no foe.

So, listen my friends, to the song of a Swineherd,
For the Swineherd, though lowly, has seen God.
So, Listen my friend, to words of the Wordless,
For God and Goddess are two peas in a pod."

With that final, homely analogy, the Shepherd ended his song and looked to us all with a smile. He clearly felt that he had indeed been a vessel, a reed, a pipe, for his inarticulate Swineherd Brother, and had done only that which had come top him. Strange, how the brothers marvelled–each a vessel for another; God to Goddess to Swineherd to Shepherd to Cattleherd to us all. But I did not marvel for I knew what the Goddess could do and feel. I knew too her two-faced nature, for had I not seen it? Why then did the men marvel that God too should have a two-faced nature? Why should He not rape and wink?

Why not? Was this duality easier for a woman to comprehend than for a man? It did not matter anyway, now did it? For pain is what mattered right now. It was pain that mattered and not theology.

And we women, we knew what to do. We remained with the Goddess. We knew how and what the God had done. We knew that He, in heaven, with his eagle and sun-eye, had blinked upon his Son below. We knew that my daughter had been taken, not only by mortal man, but by the dark God the Pegasus-like animal was a wild and passionate one, and that we could do nothing, but wait and mourn and be rigid and stubborn as any woman can be.

So we waited, and were stubborn. And we waited with the Goddess. We would not eat, nor drink nor let anything grow. We waited and were stubborn.

One night, I dreamed that God the Father, in heaven, was trying desperately to woo back His Goddess. He sent her the warm, colorful pigment around his Eye of Heaven, called Iris, which was as a flower, with the intense light of the Sun, and, at the same time was a rainbow-like Goddess with golden wings.

This same flower-eye-rainbow-goddess implored the Goddess to relent, to let up on Her sorrow and wrath and mourning so that life could flow once more. But the Goddess did not relent; She looked only to me, a mother who had been raped and had had her daughter taken from her. She looked to me, who had been there at an earlier Crucifixion and had seen both what Men can do and what Gods can do. She, this Great Goddess, stayed there adamant, on behalf of Man, of Woman, of me, her poor suffering human follower. She supported me at the expense of Her own union. And I saw. I saw that God was supporting me at the expense of God. This I saw. Goddess and woman, God and Man, continuous interaction.

At last, God the Father relented. He said that God the Son, in the Underworld must surely be appeased. He had been given the gift of a human girl and must be appeased. Who could approach him? That was the end of my dream.

I awakened in a highly numinous state. I went straightaway to the Queen and told her my dream. She too marveled at it, and said at once that she knew who could be the mediator into the Underworld. It had to be a man since we were human, but it had to be a man who had seen the faces of God, just as I had seen the faces of the Goddess.

It had to be a man who had wrestled with both. There was only one in the Kingdom, and that was the Knight. He, it was, the Knight, who had been called on a quest; he, it was, who had been summoned by an Angel; he it was who had wrestled with God Above and Below.

And so straightaway the Queen summoned the Knight, and set him about the task of finding my Daughter in the Underworld and bringing her back to me.

Now I must pause in my story and let Daughter tell how it was with her, how it was that she lived below in the Underworld, and how it was that she returned to me, and how it was that the Knight did aid us both. So now my story rests. Let Daughter speak.

A SECOND BEGINNING IN AGONY

Let me begin where mother and I were together, where we waited outside the Cave of our Lord, hoping for His Resurrection. And let me begin, as she did, with sweeping wind, the noises, wild and demonic, which were upon us as we peacefully sat before the Cave.

There, before I was thirteen years old, there, in my wild-eyed innocence, even though I had already seen God crucified, there it was that my adult life of pain and horror and opening of eyes began. I was peacefully, joyfully gathering wild-flowers, and was about to pluck a gorgeous narcissus when there was a wind as of a tempest and a rumbling as of thunder. Then there was no wind and no thunder. There was a rustling only, of men's feet, and the faces of wild and demonic and lustful men. They were upon us, and unearthly, and all over us before we could even make out who or what they were.

They took us. In every way, they took us. Twenty or thirty men took us. They raped us and whipped us, and lined us up against poles and tied us there while they used us in every way that their cruelty, viciousness, and lust for their own pleasure and our pain could combine. They repeatedly used us–outside the cave and inside. And it was not just with their desire of the flesh, no. They cut us with blades, and they burned us on our fingernails. Some of these things are so horrible Mother probably does not remember them–I hope.

I cried out but I could not look at Mother. I could not look at her, not because I was afraid of seeing her pain, or of having her see my own. No, not that. That would have been a fellow-suffering, an understanding, a sharing that I could bear. I did not look because I was so ashamed, so deeply ashamed. I was so ashamed that I could not bear to either live nor die.

Why was I ashamed, you might ask? I was ashamed for two reasons. First, I was ashamed because, in the midst of my pain and fear and anguish and hurt and horror, I was getting pleasure. The pleasure was not only the pleasure of the physical stimulation to the organs. No. There was that, of course, but not only that. There was, I am ashamed to say, even pleasure from the infliction of pain itself; no, I do not think so. Rather, I think that there was pleasure in having all my centers touched, awakened, and even desired by so many men and in so many ways. For even in the horror there was some kind of union, and a kind of bestial recognition of my being. Now this recognition was bad enough for me, for I was only thirteen, after all, and a good Christian as well! Imagine what such recognition of one's pleasure in pain can do to a thirteen year old and to a Christian!

But even that was not all. Despite their interest in me, using me, devouring me, hurting me, I was after all only an object to them, and hence did not exist at all as a person. I became therefore an object to myself. This, I am sure, women can understand, but I wonder if males can. I found that when I was treated like a "thing", I became a "thing". I was and had my being directly in terms of how I was treated.

These two states–the pleasure-pain of the intensity of awakening and being desired, plus the nullity of being an object–together produced the most excruciating state imaginable. It was a crucifixion of my essence which was different from but, in my opinion, no less than that suffered by Our Lord on His Cross. For I felt that I was on the Cross. I was torn apart in my innermost being, by nullity and totality, all at once. No mere post, no mere rape, or burning of nails, or cutting of me; no. Rather a total and horrible inner crucifixion of a wordless kind that made only pain. It was a pain in my belly and a pain in my chest. It was a wrenching pain and an unceasing one. And it was deep, not in the muscles, not in the organs, but in the depths of my being both as a female and as a human being.

The agony produced shame and I could not look. I was cut off from one person in the world who might understand at that moment, my Mother. I was alone, utterly, and in agony. I cried out for relief. I cried out that I die. I cried out.

But days went by without relief. I vomited. I gasped. I could not cry, for tears, blessed tears would mean that I was once again having feelings which would cleanse me, let me feel pure pain, and my pain of opposites was beyond that. After some time–when I no longer knew if there were days or nights–when pain and pleasure and totality and nullity combined into one blur of silent agony, then it was that I called out and cursed God. Like my Mother who had done the same–although I did not know it at the time–I cursed men and I cursed all maleness. And most of all I cursed myself. I cursed my own nature for its ability to be both awakened and to be a nullity. I cursed my being and wanted only death. I called out to Death to take me.

But it seemed that Death did not take me at that time. Not at least in the form in which I expected it. In a way Death did come, but in a strange way. After my combination curse-prayer was uttered, I caught a glimpse of the face of a–what? Shall I say a creature, a Goddess? A Medusa, or Gorgon? I cannot say. I can only describe what I saw. I saw a face of a feminine being, but it was contorted in both agony and in sneering. Its hair was wild and alive as of snakes. But this was no ordinary Medusa with snakes for hair, no. The hair was hair, but it was alive and moving in a slimy and horrible way. The eyes were fierce and filled with the greatest pain that I have ever seen in a creature. There was a living death in them, and in the redness which inflamed the whiteness there seemed to be hell upon hell of suffering and agony. The mouth was open, and silently shouting a horrendous cry of pain. It was a witch-goddess-medusa-gorgon-woman. I saw her for an instant, then went limp. At that moment, too, I began to smell the odor of both flowers and hellish scents of sulfur. The narcissus was at work, the thought came. I became so drugged with odors that I gradually felt no more pain. Nor did I feel pleasure. There was only the surcease of sensation, and the cessation of bright consciousness, into a cloud.

I was drugged. I was in a limbo state and felt and was treated like a rag doll. The men continued to use me but I felt nothing. Sweet limbo of limp nothingness. Sweet only because there was an end to the belly-crucifixion of total awakening–total nothingness. Drugged. No awareness. Blessed limbo. Into–nothingness–sleep.

Some time later I found myself outside the Cave. All was overcast and dreary. Where light and flowers had been, there was now darkness and barrenness. Mother was not there. No sound was there. Silence. I went back into the Cave and found–nothing. I went outside once again, and sat down amidst the barrenness. I sat in loneliness and aloneness. There was no more pain but now there was a conscious nothingness. The nothingness, however, was no longer inside me; it was outside. But this was better than where I had been.

I knelt and prayed, in thanksgiving, to the medusa-witch-goddess for She it was gave me peace. And as I prayed, she appeared once again, not in such agony, not with the living snake-hair, but with the same dark, black eyes which reflected an abyss of suffering and a chasm of experience. She opened her mouth, the mouth which previously uttered a silent scream of agony. But this time the mouth let forth words, quiet words which came slowly and as if weighted down with earth. Indeed it was as if the earth itself were speaking. She spoke:

"I am the Cross, I am that Tree of Life upon which the God was crucified. I am the pain. I am the agony. I am the awakening. I am the nullity. I am the totality. I am–" (There was a long silence)–"Female am I. Goddess am I. Life am I.–(Another silence.) No more words."

I drank in these few poor words of the Goddess. I seemed to understand them, though they had a certain ambiguity about them which seemed to claim all and everything and nothing. But the words also reached a wordless place in me that silenced me. I knew that I was not alone. I knew that the Goddess was with me. I knew that She must also have been with the Madonna at the moments of her greatest suffering. I felt, suddenly, that I was blessed above other women, and honored. And that I had experienced the pain which was different from, but on par with that which the Madonna had suffered. But for me, it was not that my Son was crucified, no. For me, I was both crucified and experiencing that which crucifies. I was in the hand of the Goddess. I did not know what that meant. But I knew that I was in Her hand. And now at thirteen, I was brought to a womanhood far deeper than anything that I might have imagined. And I was open to destiny. For the Goddess was with me.

BLACK TREES, ABOVE AND BELOW:
THE CHARIOTEER

What did it mean, "To be in the hand of the Goddess?" I did not know. I felt that it meant to accept my fate, as it approached me. I felt that it meant to accept awakening and pleasure, pain and agony, totality and nullity. I felt it meant to accept the pain of life. But was that all? There was, too, the pain of Death, was there not? But Death had been longed for by me, it was no pain at all. It was more likely a surcease from the pain of life. Was I confused?

Now I saw, suddenly, quite near me, a number of black trees. Had they been there before? I did not know, but I had not noticed them. They were poplars and looked very black, not only because night had fallen, but because they were indeed a strange species of poplar, totally black. I was drawn to them, and in the moonlight, approached them. They were in a circle around a pool of black, black water. The reflected its light into this pool; suddenly, within this white circle of light of the full moon, reflected in the black waters of the pool, I saw, once again, the face of the Goddess. She spoke:

"You have accepted Life. But you have not accepted Death. You have plunged toward Death as an escape from Life. But now you will accept Death. And I will help you. For you will help me redeem the Life in Death. Life, more life, even in Death. My words confuse, but you will understand."

The Goddess vanished. Again her confusing words. But again they left me with a certain peace. It was clear enough about my accepting Death as I had Life, rather than running from it. But "redeeming Life in Death?" That was perplexing. It sounded like the Goddess had a task for me. And I was ready to be in Her service. I thought of Mother, and how I missed her. For a moment I felt that I was being a traitor to Mother by being almost too quick to serve the Goddess, and ready to abandon Mother altogether. But it was true. This was how I felt.

I missed Mother, but longed to serve the Goddess. In this mood I quietly fell asleep and had the most peaceful night that I had experienced in a very long time. Toward dawn, however, a dream invaded my peace, and it harkened back to pain. In it I had glimpses of shades, of ghosts, those wandering in only half-states, with no bodies at all.

And they were clamoring for life. It was as if they wanted my blood and my vomit and my urine. They wanted anything of my bodily fluids for this would give them life. It was uncanny and dark. Somehow the Goddess was in the background and I was protected by Her; but the whole atmosphere was eerie and frightening. It was good to awaken and find that I had only been dreaming.

The day was, once again, sunny and bright. The ground was not fertile with growing things, but the warmth of the sun was good again. Here and there were some wildflowers which seemed to have survived the cold, the change, or whatever it was that had caused a pall in the region. Strangely there was no sign of either the black poplars or the pool which I had seen the previous night.

I meditatively picked a pleasant little wild-flower, when suddenly the earth opened up with a roar. From deep within the earth, from under the very land upon which the Cave rested, there appeared a huge Chariot, all in gold, drawn by a magnificent black horse. The horse was winged for an instant I wondered if the horse was the same as the black poplars, and at the same moment thought, "How mad of me!" It is strange, is it not, that one will have such enquiring thoughts in the midst of what seems to be a great upheaval?

Hardly had I taken in the sight of the green golden Chariot and its great black Horse, when I saw the Charioteer. He was huge and dark and like a God. He was, I suppose, really of human size though he seemed far more vast and powerful to me. In an instant he picked me up and drew me to him. He kissed me and I felt drugged once more. But this time I was drugged by sweet smelling flowers and perfumes. If this was a drug it was one of a paradisiacal kind.

He placed me in his Chariot and took me into the Earth. I cried out as I was taken but I felt strangely at peace. Though I feared this great figure, Whether God or Demon, I felt the protective hand of the Goddess at my side.

In the depths of the earth, I was brought to a place which defied my imagination. For here, deep beneath the earth was an underground palace, but of a kind that I had never seen. Was it Oriental or Persian? I did not know these regions. But here was an open sort of palace with rooms facing upon gardens, with jewelled and grilled gates instead of walls. There were walls too, of course, with all sorts of nooks and crannies, and corners for statues, for boxes, for little things which a woman would like. And the gardens! The gardens! They contained all manner of flower and radiated a great perfume; but most of all they had the black trees! So many varieties of tree, and all black. I knew now that I had seen, above, a replica of these black trees, but it was only now here, in the Underworld, that they grew in such profusion.

As gorgeous as was the Castle, as gorgeous as were the rooms, as marvellous as we the Gardens, as exciting as were the black trees, there was upon each of the trees a sight which alarmed and sickened me. For on each tree I saw a person hanging. On each tree there was a man or a woman hanging as if crucified, though there was no sign of nail or anything to hold them there.

I turned to my host, the Charioteer, and asked in a shocked voice what this meant. I was able to look into his face. It was a remarkable face; it was strong and handsome and masculine, but the eyes were filled with deep compassion and looked as if they had suffered great agony. I was shocked to see in those eyes a great resemblance to the eyes of the Goddess. Was this Her Son, I thought? And the thought shocked me. For I was used to thinking of Our Lord Jesus Christ as the Son of God, and now I was thinking of this great Lord as a Son of the Goddess!

The Charioteer noticed my shock and, a seeming to know what I was thinking waited a long time. He chose to answer the question that I put to him rather than take up what else was going on in my mind. He spoke:

"The people you see are effigies, copies of the living above. Every time someone above takes on the task of the Goddess, every time someone above is possessed with Her work, whether man or woman–then an effigy, and image, an icon, is shown here. It is not what you think. These images are honors, they are notes, statements in the Underworld, in the Land of the Dead, in the Land of the Unknown, that someone is taking on the suffering of the Goddess. These are like amulets, or the crucifixes worn by those above. But here we have the amulets below, while the living crucifixion goes on above. In short they become Gods or more accurately, God-men and God-women; or more accurately still, Goddess-men and Goddess-women. Thus, Daughter, were you also chosen, for look there!"

And there, to my astonishment, was an image of myself on a black poplar! I was astounded. The Charioteer laughed at my astonishment. Then he picked me up in his arms, and I felt him both as a Father an as a Lover, and I was astonished. He held me gently but strongly and kissed me tenderly. I looked at him with great compassion, for his eyes showed much pain. He smiled and spoke once again:

"I too have suffered, Daughter. I am spoken of as the Dark Son, or the Dark Sun, in the Land of the Dead, in the Underworld. It is true, in a way, but I am, in deeper truth, the Brother of the God in Heaven, that God on high, whose Eye, the Sun, looks down in apparent benevolence upon all creatures. It is I who misunderstood, and I suffer for it. It is true that I am lustful; it is true that I can be aggressive, and cruel. It is true that I am passionate. But all that is because I serve the Goddess, my Sister-Mother, as well as the God, my Father-Brother. And for this I am banned, I am in the Underworld. But I too am a God. I too wish to become human. I too wish to be in more perfect union with mankind. Our Fates are the same–the humanizing of God, the deification of Man. But enough, Daughter. My words are too many, and I am a creature of touch, of emotion; even if in the Land of the Dead and among the shades, I am to be felt and experienced."

His speech ended, this great Charioteer took me and loved me. And it was a healing and a union and a passion. I was loved by a God, and was made whole–a woman and in touch with the divine.

THE TASK OF REDEMPTION BEGINS: SEX CRIMINALS

The ecstasy of my union with the Charioteer did not last long. I was soon left alone to pine, once again, for my lonely and lost Mother. I was once again left alone in this dark and sacred castle with its strange gardens.

I was not left alone for long, however. Soon I beheld the face of the Goddess, that Bringer of Destruction, that Persephonic creature who had been both raped and maligned, but was not understood, just as the Charioteer had not been understood. The Dark Goddess looked at me with deep and pain-pleasure dark eyes and told me that my task in this Underworld was, as She had said, to redeem the Life in Death. Had I not gotten ready, she gently rebuked me, to be about Her business?

I had, hastened to assure her. Was I to have Labors, like Hercules? Or to fight some dragon, like the Heroes? The Goddess gave me a wan smile which was both amused and compassionate. She said gently that a woman's path of redemption was not like that of a man, and that I would both know what to do or have help with it when the time came. But now, she said, I should be prepared to meet two great criminals, both of whom had committed sexual crimes, and who were doomed to remain in the Underworld, in pain for Eternity. The first man was called "The Attempter." The second man was named "Strong-Moon-Man." That was all the information which the dark Goddess gave me before She vanished from my sight.

I accepted the tasks as given by the Goddess and looked to see how I might go about fulfilling whatever it was to "redeem the life in death." I walked away from the castle, beyond the rooms, beyond the gardens of black trees with their strange fruit, beyond the precincts of the Charioteer. I walked, letting an inner instinct from the Goddess guide my way. It was mysterious to walk in the half-darkness, the inner light blue, sunless sky, illuminating–God knows how–a sunless and moonless black landscape. But walk I did. And I saw, dimly, ahead of me another dread sight.

There, securely pegged to the ground, was a giant of a man. He was spread-eagled and held still by four small posts to each of which a limb was tied. That might seem horrible enough a painful torment but added to that was a repulsive and sickening addition–two large vultures were busily eating of the poor man's insides.

I looked on horrified, yet fascinated. You know how strange that is; one is sickened by the sight of an accident or violent event in which someone is killed or mutilated, yet there is equally strong interest in seeing what happened, and in seeing the horribleness. Are we worse than beasts, who take secret pleasure in torn flesh, diseased bodies and agonizing souls? I hope not. Perhaps we only need to see, in outer reality, the darknesses which lurk in the depths of our own tormented souls. In any case, I was both horrified and fascinated. I was fascinated, I must really conclude, because I knew that "a God was present." That which fascinates us, compels us, terrifies us, mystifies us, always has a God in it, does it not?

I crept forward to the poor man, carefully avoiding the great vultures, those ugly creatures who frightened me. I need not have been frightened, incidentally, for these sickening birds merely went on with their eating and paid no attention whatsoever. I spoke softly to the man, who lay in continuing pain, eyes closed. I told him who I was and that I was sent by the Goddess on a mission to redeem Life in Death here in the Underworld. The huge man opened his eyes and looked at me vacantly. "Redemption?" he said. "Me?" "Perhaps," I replied, for I did not know for certain that he was "Who" or "What" the Goddess meant with Her strange task.

"But I will remain in such agony for eternity!" said the Giant-Man. "Such is my Fate, and such is the punishment given me by my Father in Heaven."

"Given you by your Father in Heave!" I exclaimed, and I grew furious at the Sun-Eagle-Eye who gives judgments and punishments of such horror. "But what happened?" I asked, when I calmed down a little.

The large, suffering man told me his story. He was called the Attempter" and he was doomed to eternal punishment in the Underworld in this way for a very heinous sexual crime. He was wandering one day and chanced upon a grove of sacred black trees. He had never seen such black poplars and was drawn to them. There in the center of the circle of trees was a small lake in which was reflected both the crescent moon and the great evening star. And then he saw there in the evening light, augmented by the two heavenly lights, a very lovely woman. She knelt there praying. "The Attempter" was filled with a tender and sensitive appreciation for the beauty of the scene and of its divine goodness, and in the next he was swept by an overpowering desire to possess this woman.

Before he realized what he was doing the poor man had rushed into the clearing, grabbed the woman and thrown her to the ground. At first, she was startled and easily succumbed. Then when she knew what was happening she started to fight. As she fought the Attempter became aware of the horrible thing he was doing and started to relent. He heard, for the first time, the woman's screams. But in the next instant he felt the blows of many arrows upon him, head and chest and back and legs, and he felt the pain all over him. In another instant, the Giant-Man continued, he was dead.

When he awakened, hardly knowing that he was dead, he found himself here in the Underworld, just as I found him, pegged to the ground by all four limbs, with vultures devouring his intestines. He knew that it was for Eternity, and he knew that his agony was great. There had been no trial, no defense. It was just so. He had cried out for explanation and was told by a cold, hard voice that this was the punishment for his heinous deed. He had attempted and nearly accomplished the rape of a fine motherly woman. The woman, under the protection of the God on high, and in the service of the Goddess above, Mary-Demeter, had already given birth to the brother-sister pair as a consequence of her union with God. The Attempter had tried to rape her; luckily he was stopped in time by the brother-sister pair of the Virgin and Youth-Son-God, but he had been condemned by the Father in Heaven to his present punishment. He was to suffer thus, forever.

As the Attempter told me this story he wept. He had been agonized by the horrible chewing of the vultures, but he did not weep. Now he wept. I soothed him and gently asked, why does he weep now? "Because–the one who judged me, the one who tortures me, is the God in Heaven, and He–and He–and He is my Father."

I breathed deeply myself when I became aware that this punishment was given by that same Eye of Heaven, that Father, who was notorious for his rape of the soul of those who served Him. I thought of Our Lord Jesus, whose soul was raped, who was abandoned at the last moment by this same Father in Heaven. As I thought of Our Lord, I looked upon this poor giant of a man and realized that his Crucifixion, lying pegged to the earth was much like that of Our Lord. The Attempter was experiencing, horizontally and under the earth, what Our Lord experienced vertically and above it.

The symbolism of it sank into me. Here was a man, though a giant and the son of God, suffering the fate of a God-Man; but he was doing it, dishonored and disdained, here under the Earth. And he was suffering the agony of two vultures devouring him! Prometheus, that Hero who stole consciousness and fire for Mankind, suffered only one vulture! This poor Attempter was suffering two! Was he suffering the pain of being eaten up from within, by the two children of the mother he had attempted to rape! Were these two pains the agonies of the Virgin and of the Youth-Son-God? It seemed to me, and it seemed unjust that the Father, notoriously a rapist, was making his son suffer a punishment which properly belonged to the Father.

I soothed the Attempter as best I could, but I cried out to the Dark Goddess to rectify this wrong. I shouted loud and with a shrieking and eerie sound which surprised even me as it came out of me. The vultures heard it, looked startled, and immediately left off their gruesome feast. At the same moment, I saw the Face of the Goddess nodding and the poor Attempter, mercifully, died. For him Eternity was over–at least the Eternity of suffering. I sank to my knees in thanksgiving, and was sure that I saw the shade of this shade–if one can call it thusly–float away and go directly to the Charioteer. And I knew that this new Son-God, Sun-God, dark-God, would take on the soul-substance of this giant man who suffered unjustly. Our poor giant man, called The Attempter, tried to reconcile God and Goddess, Son and Virgin, Sun and Moon, but had not been able to contain all these pairs. Now was his spirit entering into that new God, the Charioteer. Enough. I cannot say more.

Hardly had I completed this adventure, which practically put me on a level with a Hero like Hercules–although all I did was scream out to the Dark Goddess in agony and in anger at this injustice–when I was quickly pushed on once more. The words of the Goddess, "Strong Moon Man," came back and I walked on.

I had not gone far when I saw in the blue-light of the Underworld sky what looked like a fiery wheel coursing through the Under-Heaven like a Sun. It came by quickly and rotated rapidly, but I could make out a figure of a man bound to this fiery wheel. He turned and rotated as the wheel revolved and rotated. As he turned I heard him call out the words, "Benefactors deserve thankfulness", repeatedly.

At this strange sight I stood dumbfounded. The fiery comet-like apparition continued on its way and vanished, to return within a few minutes as if it were itself a moon in this Underworld, orbiting around a small but thickly gravitied body of earth. I did not know how to reach this figure or if I should. Could I fly? I had not thought of that until now. Could one fly in the sky of the Underworld? Was gravity the same? I did not know but I resolved to try. I did not flap my arms or imitate a bird–I knew that would be foolish. Instead, I concentrated strongly, felt sure that such a thing as magic existed, and willed myself to fly alongside the poor creature who rode so painfully and spoke his peculiar words. In an instant I was borne into the air of the Underworld and found myself flying effortlessly alongside the wheel-bonded man.

I asked him, "Are you the Strong Moon Man?" He was revolving like a moon and indeed he must be strong to survive such a hellishly hot flame and dizzying rotation and still be able to recite the words "Benefactors deserve thankfulness."

The man answered with a nod, yes. So, he was the second creature whom the Goddess had enjoined me to save if I could. But what was his sexual crime? I told him, as I had The Attempter, who I was and what my mission was. But Strong Moon Man merely sighed as if he thought I did not have a chance in the world of helping him, and continued his litany. Benefactors deserve thankfulness."

I persisted, however, in demanding he tell me how he came to such a demand since the Goddess whom I served had promised to help me redeem Life in Death and that, perhaps–I could not promise– She intended to help him. My pressing him seemed to give him slight hope, so he told me the following story.

"When I was young I fell in love with a beautiful girl. She also loved me and there was no difficulty in our marrying. I was happy but annoyed at the large bride-price that her father insisted upon. I had not been especially mercenary or greedy before that. Indeed, I had sinned little, being aware that my father had been a man whom the Gods had despised, since he had no respect for Them and had burned down temples erected in Their honor. I knew that I might be punished for the sin of my father–the God being as He is. So I was especially 'good'. Furthermore, I was so happy to be able to marry the girl that I loved that I was overjoyed. And yet–and yet the exorbitant bride-price of the father of the girl enraged me.

"I took counsel with no one and conceived a dastardly plan. I dug a hole in the land in front of my house and put fiery coals in it. I covered the hole with a very thin layer of dust and wood-shavings so that the father of the bride, when he came to collect his money, fell through the trap and burned painfully on the coals.

"When I heard his cries I recovered from my diabolical scheme and tried to rescue him but it was too late. I screamed and ranted and went mad with guilt and pain. I went here and there and everywhere hoping for purification or forgiveness of my heinous act, from God or man, but it was not forthcoming.

"Finally one night I had an experience which you might call a dream, but I experienced it as reality. In this experience God in Heaven

Himself brought me up to Him. I experienced his forgiveness for my greed and destructiveness. He even, I thought, winked at me and suggested that He Himself was not without greed and destructiveness.

"I was much relieved but not thankful. This was because I did not know why I was forgiven nor did I have a high regard for God Himself. I kept my own counsel, however, since I knew that my own father had disrespected God and had burned down His temple. Nor did I know why I disrespected God. I knew only that it was so.

"I joined God in a kind of repast and saw God's wife, who was most handsome. She immediately evoked great desire in me. The Wife of God understood this at once but since She had no regard for me at all She informed Her Husband. God became jealous and sent me a cloud, looking every bit like His wife, but only an image of Her. I did not know this but when She came I immediately embraced Her, loved her, united with Her.

Now God saw the truth–that I lusted after the wife of Him who had been my benefactor. He thereupon punished me by binding me to this fiery wheel and condemning me for Eternity to circulate wit hit, saying the words, 'Benefactors deserve thankfulness.' So have I been rotating, 'Strong-Moon-Man' that I am, for ages.

"Nor am I really penitent, dear Daughter. I am in pain, it is true, and desire relief. I say the words that I am told but I do not mean them. In short I am, more than ever, a hater of God and a despiser of Him and of His Wife, just as my father was. My father burned down the temple, I did not. I made the mistake of loving the Goddess. So for the sin for which I am truly ashamed, that of greed, I am forgiven without question, that of greed, I am forgiven without question. And where I loved and felt no sin, for that I am punished.

"How can I reconcile myself with such a God and Goddess? The Goddess, loyal to her idea of monogamy and jealous of the God's infidelity, betrays me without a moment's hesitation. Where is Her love? The God, caring nothing for the real sin of my greedy misuse of another human being, punish me for loving, and loving only an image! So I speak, but mean not the "words."

So ended this Strong Moon Man, and I loved him for his truth to his inner sense of where he had sinned and where he had not. I loved him that suffered, but would not repent meaninglessly. I felt that he was a truer believer in the Divine than was God in Heaven Himself! And I told Strong Moon Man this. I told of our Lord Jesus and I told of the Charioteer. And I told him, most of all, of the Goddess. I whispered that the Goddess was with me. I turned to the Goddess and prayed that She help me now, for I could do nothing.

Then, as the Strong Moon Man and I moved through the inner space of the orbiting fiery wheel of the Underworld Heaven, the image of the Wife of God appeared. She was the same Above as Below, a Wife of God in Heaven and as Destroyer below, and She wept. As we looked at Her She wept and She spoke:

"Strong Moon Man speaks truly of me. For I have deceived him. I have spoken of love and marriage but in truth I have been only jealous and greedy. I know as he knows that the true sin is of greed and of lack of care for another. He speaks truly of me and it is for that reason that I have sent you, dear Daughter, to redeem the Life in Death. I have sent you to redeem him, the Strong Moon Man, and in so doing to redeem me. For you, Daughter, are human, like him, and have been unjustly hurt, like him, and only you can forgive him. God the Father has punished him for this infidelity when He Himself has been unfaithful. Not just to me but to his own principle of the manyness of conception. He demands thankfulness and honor, forgetting that without his awareness of the individual man He gets nothing. He forgets too that 'manyness' can be greediness."

Strong Moon Man and I were startled at Her words. They came like a healing balm. For these were words of the Godhead, asking forgiveness from Man. We were happy to render this forgiveness of the Godhead; as we did so we fell to the ground, wheel and all. The wheel changed from a burning and painful flame to a golden and shimmering coin, and one that Strong Moon Man could hold in his hand. He looked at me and said, "Benefactors deserve thankfulness, and you and the Goddess are my benefactors, You both, I thank."

And then we heard other words from the Goddess:

"Know, Strong Moon Man, that your union with my image, the cloud which was I, yet not I, has had result. From the union has resulted a horse-man. And from the horse-man has emerged a healer. Know then that you are a father of healers. Know too that even your father, who disrespected the Gods, is a father of healers, through you. Know too that the disrespector who respects at the same time, is of God and is a healer. Indeed He is a healer of God!"

With those words Strong Moon Man and myself, for many days after that. We lingered in love and in great and passionate union. And this union was different from that with The Attempter. I have said nothing about my union with The Attempter, for after our union of being swept by passion; with Strong Moon Man there was a union–slow and deliberate and stubborn, even battling. I will say no more for this is of the Goddess. Yes, I will say more, for it is also of the God. After our union the shade would unite with the God. These great men condemned to a Hellish Eternity for sexual crimes were redeemed and their souls–not their "crimes"–would continue for Eternity.

Thus did I rejoice in my service of the Goddess.

DIVINE BETRAYOR (1)

After my adventures with the men who had committed "sexual crimes", I returned to the beautiful castle with its strange trees and rejoiced in my union with the Charioteer. I felt myself to be Heaven and pondered that strange experience: for I was in Hell. And here in Hell, in the dark Underworld, I had experienced the heights of pleasure, of love, of union.

But I was not permitted to continue my speculations of Heaven-in-Hell for very long. The Goddess soon whispered in my ear. "Come, Daughter," She said, "You have rejoiced being in my service, you have pleasured yourself to find Heaven in Hell, but now you merely loll about. Are you still drugged with the scent of that narcissus flower? Are you so self-preoccupied that you will forget why you are here, and merely sink into the depths of drugged contentment?

"No, Goddess," I responded, "that is not so. I am at your service, though I must confess that you seem more like a chiding and resentful wife of the Lord Above than the deep and passionate Daughter-Goddess Persephone of the Nether-World!"

The Goddess laughed with pleasure at my ability to stand up to Her. "You must be about 'our' business. Know now that you have to meet those who have committed even greater crimes–for they have betrayed God! These, the 'Very Wise One' and the 'Adventurer' will challenge your mind and your heart and your soul. Go now and find them."

With these words the Goddess vanished and there was nothing for it but to be up and about Her business. I sweetly bade goodbye to the Charioteer and walked in the semi-darkness of the Underworld. I did not have to walk far before I saw a man whose image I had long known. It was a surprise to see him so incarnated. I suppose he has been known to one and all from stories of the past. And when I relate what it was that he was doing, one and all will know of him. I doubt, however, whether one and all will know the truth of him as I was fortunate enough to learn of it.

Strange, isn't it? I was reluctant to leave the warm embrace of the Charioteer for the adventure, just as I had been "raped" into joining him. But once I left I discovered ever renewing things. Secrets, secrets. Such was the adventure that I undertook, out of my laziness, driven out. Oh Goddess, You it is who know; You it is who drive us! You it is who want us to know the secrets! But, I get ahead of myself. Let me tell the story s it happened.

I mentioned that I saw a man whose image would be known to one and all–a man who painfully and with all his strength rolled a huge stone up a hill. He sweated and grunted in his labor until he almost reached the top. Within a hair's breath of the top however, the stone would slip away from him and roll back down to the base. And once again he would begin his task. You know him, of course. But do you know why he does this task and why he was doomed? I will tell you what I learned from him.

I came up close to the man and whispered, "Are you the Very Wise One?" In his panting he said, "Such is the translation of my name, but I am better called the Cunning One, or Trickster, I suppose. Better yet, the Cunning-Wise. But I cannot talk to you for all my energies are devoted to this great and terrible task that you see. If you wish to speak with me you must either summon a great and good poet who can stop all the horrors of Hell–at least temporarily–or else give me a hand in my labors!"

"Cunning-Wise One," I replied, "I am no poet and cannot stop the horrors of Hell. But, though woman, I am strong, and can help you in your labors. I am sent by the Goddess to hear your tale and redeem you, if I can, so let me help."

"By the Goddess you are sent?" And he laughed. "I doubt that She will wish to redeem me for I tricked even her too! But I have been lonely and I will be glad of the company and of the shared help in my labor. And I will tell my tale with pleasure. Prepare yourself, however, to be shocked a little, for, though cunning and wise, I am also a Betrayer of God!"

I merely nodded at this revelation, having known it already from the Goddess. I gave answer by putting my shoulder to the stone and pushed as my co-worker did. We worked slowly but between us, he was freed of sufficient energy to tell me his story.

"Why am I here, you will want to know, and why this punishment. There are many reasons and no reasons. First of all, I betrayed God! That same God in Heaven, that Eagle-Eye who overlooks all mankind; I saw Him one day, and I saw him carry off the Daughter of the God of Waters. It was a rape, mind you, a rape by that very moral One on high. Now I, even I knew that the Faces of God did not know one another and that they betrayed one another; yes I, mere stupid mortal that I was, saw that this they betrayed one another; yes I, mere stupid mortal that I was, saw that this was so. And when the Face of God which was that of the Waters came looking for His aggrieved and lost daughter, I told Him that I knew where she was and what had happened. I stayed, however, on my rocky crag and would not divulge what I knew until this God of Waters blessed me. And what kind of blessing did I ask? I asked, of course, for water. I asked that a spring appear among the rocks. I asked that new life flow among my people. I asked that out of a Virgin Rape among the Gods a Virgin Spring flow among men. This I asked. And this I received; this I received from the Face of God which is that of Waters, the flow of life.

"But it was not so at the time. No, not at all. For the Eagle-Eye sent forth Death to punish me. He in his fury, sent forth Death to take me then. But I was clever. Oh was I clever, for I deceived even Death! Yes, O brave girl who comes to the Underworld to spy on the dead and to redeem, ho, to redeem even the dead–it was I who deceived even Death! Perhaps you have heard the tale for I am not alone in deceiving Death–many more have done so. It was easy. Death came and asked me to hold out my hands to be cuffed in chains. And I deceived Him. For I said, 'But, good sire, I do not know how to put them on, please show me.' Even Death is deceived by good will and apparent desire to be cooperative and do the 'right thing.' He was promptly put the cuffs upon himself. And just as promptly I turned the key and popped it into my mouth. For now, even Death was at bay for me!

"From that moment no one died on earth, and there was great rejoicing, but great chagrin in the Face of God. And God, the Moralist, turned into another face, the Face of War and Destruction. That face knew that Death must be freed. For if Death is not freed, there can be no war and destruction, now can there? And so the Face of God which is War freed Death and I was consigned to accompany him to the Underworld, to Hell.

Accompany him I did, but I–trickster that I am–I had even another plot to deceived that fate. I asked to speak once more to my beloved wife, that dear creature whom all the world loved. Who would deny a dying man the chance to speak with such a dear and lovely creature? Who is so heartless as to deny that last wish? Not even the demons are so heartless, and not even is Death, when he is so approached. And so I was allowed to speak to my dear and sweet wife.

"And speak I did. But I did not moan and groan and bid her adieu. I did not thank her for our good life together and bid her think of me always. I did not even free her to live and love another. Oh no, none of that. For I am a clever one, am I not? I am called the Very Wise, am I not? And so I am. For I bade my wife pay not attention whatever to the dead. I told her to forego funerals, to forget mourning, to simply ignore the God of the Dead, or of Hell or of the Underworld. I told her to free herself of all foolishness and pretend even that these Underworld facts did not exist. And this my wife, blessed and praised be she, did.

"I was brought below, it is true, to this place. But my wife shocked the entire world and God Himself by paying no attention whatever. She neither grieved nor mourned nor paid any attention whatever to the fact that I was dead. This was a shock to all the world. For everyone knew what a good heart she had. Everyone knew how she loved me, though none could understand how she could love such a rascal. Everyone knew that she was pious and good. And here she was, having no respect whatever for either God or Death!

"Now the one most shocked all was the Goddess of the Underworld. She, dear lady, whom you serve. She it was who was most mortified that the dark passion of death, of mourning, of blood, of sacrifices, of agony, was not observed. And she was particularly mortified that a woman, one who always served the Goddess, should be totally unmoved. And I with my cunning words also deceived the Goddess! Ask Her, and you shall see."

I was, indeed, shocked by this story, but I would not ask until he finished.

"All right then, dear lady. There is little more to tell except that the Goddess let me go. She is so desirous of her blood, of her passion, that people devote themselves to Her rites and needs, that She let me go. And I was redeemed from the Dead. I lived and I deceived the Goddess! But it was not I, dear lady, it was my wife who deceived her for the sake of me. It was that great and good creature who did so. And all for the love of me. Now ask Her, dear lady, ask Her, and see if what I say is not true."

Now I turned to the Goddess, that Persephone, that Queen of the Underworld. I turned to Her to hear if what his Cunning and Wise Man said was true. Had a mere mortal, had a clever man so deceived both God and Goddess?

The Goddess appeared and nodded. Nor was She a bit mournful in this. She whispered to me: "He is a beloved of the Gods, though tormented by them. For he is clever and he challenges them. And yes, he deceived me. But it was his wife, really, who deceived me. He, it is true, knew my weakness for the libations, for the feedings of passion, of mourning, of tears and emotion. He knew that I could not survive without these. But she, his wife, she it was who gave these things up. She, who needed these things as much as I, she it was who sacrificed them not for me but for him, her husband, and her love. And that she loved him so dearly, this good person, spoke well for him. Thus is he a chosen one, and a beloved one of God and Goddess!"

I heard this and shrieked: "But you must tell him! You must not hide this from him. You must not torture him and make him think himself a criminal and a betrayor when he does in fact your bidding, even when you do not know it!" The Goddess hesitated, so I immediately told the Clever One, the Wise One, all that the Goddess, had told me. I told him with passion and with love, and I threw myself at him, forgetting even the common task of pushing the stone, and we both fell down as the stone–to heavy for us now–fell back down the hill.

We got up and looked sheepishly at each other. And the Goddess was present also and She smiled. And I knew without words, that I had gone against the Goddess too. I had gone against Her whom I worshipped and treasured and with whom I had agreed. I had gone against Her both for truth and for care of a man and his wife. I had indeed repeated the act of his loving and devoted wife. The man knew it, I knew it, and the Goddess knew it.

A miracle happened. The stone which we were pushing grew much smaller. It became half the size, and a good deal smoother. It was still large, however, and heavy, and difficult to push. We started our labor up the hill once again without enquiring about this miracle. For the Cunning-Wise One had more stores of himself to tell.

"Now, dear lady, now that our task grows a little lighter, I will relate another adventure of mine. But this adventure is not with God. Himself or Herself. It is a rascal like myself. This rascal is the product of the union of the God of Thieves with a mortal woman, the attractive Snow-Maiden. But this rascal son of God and mortal was called 'Wolf-Himself' and had a talent for theft and perjury beyond anything that mortals can do.

"It is true I was rather clever along these lines but nothing like the Wolf-Himself. I had escaped Death twice, but I was rather more clever than talented as a thief. All the same, this Wolf-Himself, having heard how I cheated Death, thought that perhaps I was an even greater cheat than he and this he could not abide. And so he came at night to my farm where I once again lived peacefully, with my wife and animals.

"He came to my farm, as I say, and stole my cattle. And there was nothing I could do to stop it. For this son of God and woman was a magician. He knew how to make white beasts black and black beasts white; he could exchange horns from bull to cow and back. Such a trickster was greater by far than me. And I knew it. For I could not change the truth. I could not make black-white, nor could I make male-female. I could only live by my wits and by my love. And my herds grew smaller and smaller.

"But I was clever, was I not? I had cheated Death–let me then use my cleverness, thought I. I can read and write. That is my cleverness, isn't it? Yes. So I carved my initials into the hooves of my cattle, thinking that I would pick them out of Wolf-Himself's cattle. But Wolf-Himself was cleverer than I for he could change the letters. And this he did.

"But I was cleverer, still. When he changed the letter, I put new letters on the hooves saying 'Wolf-Himself has stolen me' and poured lead into the hollows. And I followed the trail of the footsteps which led right to his barn. And there it was that I found my cattle and confronted Wolf-Himself with the fact of the trail.

"It is to the ever-redounding credit of Wolf-Himself that he acknowledged my cleverness. The master-thief owned himself defeated. And, good man this rascal was, he immediately concluded an agreement of friendship and hospitality with me. This perhaps is not known to the world. For this son of God and mortal woman, this magician of changes, this patron of thieves and rascals, acknowledged me. He told me that my wits were good but his were better. But when I used the lead, when I turned to the mercurial substance which is changeable and tricky and volatile and turns hard and makes its mark–then he knew that I knew his Father. And his Father? That volatile and quick and clever Supreme Trickster Himself!

"Thus it was that I lived long, having cheated Death and been aligned with the Trickster. For those aligned with the Trickster live long. It is only the good who die young, do they not? But upon my death, I was consigned below to the Underworld. And the Judges of the Dead, those emissaries of that Father in Heaven whose moral Eagle-Eye shines on all but Himself, those Judges gave me the exemplary punishment of rolling this stone forever and ever.

"And thus do I do it. I do it in sweat, and in effort. But I know, in sooth, that the Eagle-Eye is punishing me for His own sin. I know that I am loved by my wife and by the Trickster. And in truth, I am glad to be in the company of the Charioteer, that Great God who dwells here below and will, one day, come up and dwell above. And thus am I content."

The Cunning-Wise One completed his story and I looked at him in awe. Indeed he was a great one. And he was unjustly maligned for he hurt no one, and his sin was in seeing too much.

I looked to the Goddess to help me. How redeem this man? After all, She had sent me on this errand. No word came. But I knew that I would stay with him in his task. I moved with him as we patiently plodded up the hill with the stone until we reached the top. I plodded back down with him when it fell. And I did so with good cheer and no complaint. I laughed, for I was no longer lazy, nor did I need a reward. Indeed I was content with my task.

Cunning-Wise One and I worked hard at our task but it was good work and, if foolish, was a great good joke on us, and we laughed. He was condemned and laughed, and I did it voluntarily and laughed.

This went on for ever so long, but in the Underworld one does not know time, really. Perhaps it was less than it seemed. Then one day the Goddess appeared.

She looked lovingly at us. She spoke: "Daughter," she said, "You have done as asked. You have loved, you have joined, you have volunteered the difficult task. In this, like his wife, you once again redeem him from Death.

"And you, Cunning-Wise One, you are a hero. Know that the Stone which you have rolled is the same as that which God-Himself became when He, on high, raped and plundered His own girlish and tender Face. Know that the task that you have faced and have done in all Eternity is the never-ending raising of God-Himself. You know the Stone as the mercurial Trickster. Know it now as God Himself. For all Faces are One."

As the Goddess spoke these words the huge stone became smaller and smaller. It finally became a little stone of hand size. The Cunning-Wise One looked gently at me and smiled. He made as if to throw the burden over the hill, but merely pretended. Instead, he wordlessly put it into my hand, closed my palm and faded like a ghost in the being of the Charioteer. For he too would be born again in Life, I knew. I blew him a kiss and carried the God in my hand.

I then went on to find the second betrayer of God and His divine secrets, the "Adventurer."

BETRAYOR OF GOD (2)

I did not have far to wander to come to my second criminal, a betrayor of God, and I knew it as soon as I saw him. For there in the perennial twilight of the Underworld stood a lone fruit tree from which hung a sad and tormented creature. This unhappy man, unlike the human fruit of the poplar trees in the gardens of the Charioteer, was no emblem, symbol, or shade. No, he was a suffering, fleshly creature whose torments seemed terrible as I watched them.

No doubt you have heard of such a one, for I too had always known of the torments of such a being long before I came to see and know him with my own eyes. There he swung, with dry thirsty lips and hungry panting breath, suspended between luscious fruit and delicious water. Above him the tree contained every manner of gorgeous fruit–pears, sweet figs, shining apples, ripe olives, and even luscious pomegranates. Whenever he would reach for the luscious, bursting, eye-dazzling mouthfuls, a gust of wind would whirl them out of reach. Below, there lapped at him refreshing waters of an ever-fresh, ever-cool pool, whose waters came to his chin. Whenever he would try to sip this liquid-better-than-wine, the waters would dry away and all that would be left would be the black mud at his feet.

Nor were these torments all. For there above his head hung an enormous stone which dangled precariously and threatened to crush his skull at any moment.

I knew that this must be the second of the Divine Betrayors whom the Goddess had sent me to redeem. So it was that I addressed the poor creature. "Ho, sir, are you not 'Adventurer', Betrayor of God?"

He looked at me mournfully, emptily, with eyes full of pain. The look in them told me that he was, like Charioteer and myself, also touched by the Goddess. "I am, I am," he responded, as if he could only ruefully acknowledge the horribleness of who he was. All the world knew him and reviled him, he seemed to say, and there was nothing to do but suffer it.

"But I am here," I said, "to help redeem you, to free you from your horrible punishment and I am sent on this mission by the Goddess Herself!"

"You, a young girl?" he said. "It is hard to believe."

"Tell me your tale in any case," I asked him, waving aside his incredulity as not worthy of my patience. I noticed that I was becoming rather sure of myself and of my capacity to bring redemption and wondered if this were a hubris of mine. I resolved to keep my own feet fully in contact with the earthy reality of dark rock and muck, even though this was the relative "unreality" of the underworld, for pride in my being sent by the Goddess could of course quite undo me and my task. So I repeated, but more gently and less peremptorily, with even a note of pleading in my voice, "Please tell me your tale."

"I was born, some say," began the Adventurer, "as a son of God-in-Heaven Himself. I do not know that for certain and I am, I must say, rather rueful about such things for God-in-Heaven did not treat me as one would expect a father to treat a son. But you will soon hear about that. My Mother was called 'The Rich' and she was very favored by the Goddess. If you, dear Daughter, are sent by the Goddess, it would be no doubt because of the intervention of my loving Mother who was a nymph and favored by the Goddess. Even my son, the dull-witted but talented sculptor, was among the first to honor the Great Earth Mother in stone.

"But I do not wish to dwell upon my genealogy nor upon my descendants. Suffice it to say that I am not sure of who my father was, though he was said to be God. I was invited to feast with God and felt myself chosen by Him. Indeed if not God's Son I was, at least, an intimate friend. As such I could taste the nectar and ambrosia, I could participate in the 'secrets' as they are known to men. And I was singled out, chosen, among mortal men, though it was uncertain if I was mortal or not.

"I must tell you right away of my first 'sin'. For this sin I feel no guilt at all though it was accounted by God Most High as a betrayal. Do you know what I did to be accounted 'Betrayor'? I shared what I received from God with my fellow man. The sweet and good food which I attained from God I took to my friends and gave it to them. The secrets from God, these too I shared with my fellows. This was my first sin, and why I was called a 'Betrayor of Divine Secrets.' Would you like to know what this food was and what these secrets were? I would be glad to tell you for I felt no betrayal in the Betrayal; what good are divine ambrosia and divine secrets unless they are shared with man? And what good is it to be Chosen unless one uses one's Chosenness to improve the lot of one's fellows, as well?"

The Adventurer seemed to be really asking me this question, and not just being rhetorical about it, so I nodded in agreement with him. It was only a moment before that I had been aware of my own hubris, my own arrogant pride at being singled out by the Goddess; now I was impressed by this poor sufferer, this poor tormented one who used his Chosenness to share with his fellows. So I nodded. The Adventurer continued:

"I was known as one of many talents. I could speak and write and heal, and all these I used since they were given by God in the service of my fellows. I also told the secrets, those Divine Secrets–that God is envious of Man, and wants to become Man; that Man is immortal just as God is immortal; and that Man and God are in a never-ending state of evolution, of a Being-Becoming Union in which both participate, individuality and collectively. All this I told and was accounted a sinner because I told the truth of the Divine Secrets. Thus was I condemned but I do not grieve. For God did not want men to know these truths during the time that I lived and my sin was that I spoke too soon! But I am not repentant.

"But for my second sin, for that I am repentant. That, indeed, is very horrible I must admit, and it is for that horror that you see the pain in my eyes. My pain is not only that I thirst and hunger without reprieve and forever; my pain is for the horrible thing that I did.

"One day, after I had been feasted and fed by God beyond all belief, God became to me and said that He would soon come to me for feasting. He would want the best I had to offer, and hoped for some recompense for the fine fare that He had offered me.

"I was deeply honored and humbled. For what could I, poor mortal that I was, have to offer God that He did not have? Nothing. I had already offered myself, and was already in His full service. All that I had, my talents and being were from Him and they were in His service. I had had the apparent hubris to think that in serving my fellow man that I was serving Him. Obviously I was not correct. But now, I thought, I had already offered myself; what more could I offer? I could offer only the apple of my eye, the most treasured thing of my life–my son. My son was the fruit of my entire being for he was more talented than I, more loving, more joyous. He was the best that I had to offer. And so in a madness, I offered my son to my Lord, and I offered him as a meal, as a repast, as a nourishment to that God-in-Heaven who asked me for that which I had.

"So God came to dine with me, but suspected what I had roasted and cut up and put into the kettle, and ate not. But the Goddess, His wife, that Demeter-Mary-Mother creature, mourning as she did for Her lost daughter, did not know what she was doing or eating, and She ate absentmindedly of the dish, devouring the shoulder of my sweet son."

When I, Daughter, heard of the mourning-sorrow of the Mother-Goddess-Demeter-Mary, I heaved a sigh. I was reminded of my own sweet Mother and I yearned for her. I missed and longed for her and felt guilty that I had not thought of her during these anxious and inspired journeys in the Underworld. Adventurer's painful tale brought this back to me, and I said a silent prayer asking forgiveness of the Mother-Goddess, and of my own poor mother for having forgotten her in my absentminded devotion to that other Goddess, Her Daughter. But The Adventurer was not aware of my reaction and went on with his own story.

"When God found out for certain what I done, He was horrified. God was able to reconstitute my son as a reborn whole, and he emerged from the cauldron in radiant beauty, bearing only a mark like ivory and a white star on his shoulder. This indicated his chosenness by the Mother-Goddess. I was secretly told that his fate was that of the God to come, but I did not understand just then.

"I was punished by what you see and I have had many years to think about the punishment and the crime. But before I tell you what I have thought and what I learned, let me get beyond the horror of this crime for which I am being punished. For this third crime, you see that great stone hanging there above me, ready to crush my skull at any moment. That cruel punishment of fear is in recompense for having been a thief and a perjurer before God. There was a great statue of a dog made in gold which had a mysterious relationship to God Himself. This golden dog was of the days when God Himself preferred to be worshipped as an idol and it was this Dog that had been worshipped in his place. Now this golden idol was brought to me by a friend, do not ask who, and I was asked to keep it safe and to tell no one, not even God Himself, that I had it. I loved my friend dearly and I agreed, for I knew that he would not ask such a favor of me unless it was of great importance and essential.

"But God Himself came enquiring after the golden statue. I lied and said that I did not have it. For this, God grew furious and gave the third cruel punishment: for lying to God I am doomed to fear the great stone crushing my skull.

"So here have I existed for endless time, in an agony of my punishments. I am suspended in the Underworld between the upper and lower, never enjoying the fruits from above nor the waters from below. And I hang in fear of being crushed at any moment. Thus, the story of my crimes and of my punishments."

I listened to the story of Adventurer with great and expectant interest, but when he stopped, I was disappointed for I wanted to learn more from him. So now, in genuine humility and far from the arrogance of wanting to "redeem" him that I had displayed earlier, I said, "But you say, Great Adventurer, that you have pondered deeply over the meaning of your crimes and of your punishment. How do you understand it all now?"

"It is hard for me to answer in words, lovely Daughter of a mortal, but I shall do my best. I have already told you my views about having shared my talents, the food of the Lord with my fellow man; I do not think it a crime. For I was ready to serve my fellow man, the creation of God, before God was ready to do so. I was guilty only of the hubris of anticipating God.

"And so for the horrible crime of offering up my son to the Lord. Did I not do that which God Himself would do at another time? Has He not offered up His Son for Mankind? And do not mankind cut up and eat this offering of the Most High Himself? And do they not count themselves blessed thereby? And is not this great communion between God and Man, this great sharing of the God-Man, is this not just like the secret which I shared with my fellow man? That God wishes to become Man? That Man is immortal, and all of that I said to you before? It is so. And again, my crime was of anticipating God, of doing something that He would do only later on. And again this is the arrogance, of being greater that God. But I was at my most abject when I did so.

"And the third crime? Of lying and perjuring for the sake of a friend and against God? Does God not lie and perjure Himself before Man, withholding His secrets until it is convenient for Him? And is there not a secret connection between that which was 'worshipped in the past' in God's name and that which comes? That is a mystery, for God Himself has told me that. And so I stand, between Heaven and Hell, above and below, suspended, neither enjoying the fruits of above nor the waters of below, and in fear of being crushed by God Himself.

"Am I not then like a God? Do I not suffer the torments inflicted by God the Father, making me serve Him and anticipating Him and being His experimental object, as he suspends me between the opposites? Am I not then a God-Man? Whether my actual Father was God or not? Well, that is what I think. That perhaps is why I am kept here in the Underworld, For God cannot permit that His creature anticipate Him. God cannot permit Himself to see what He Himself does, until He is ready, and God, though He wants it, cannot bear to have His creature know more than He does. And so I see, and so, I suffer."

At this point, the Goddess Herself appeared and spoke:

"The Adventurer speaks truly for He is of God. He, though mortal, is of God. And He speaks truly of God. For God has forgotten His compassion. God has forgotten his own creatureliness. And the Adventurer speaks truly. Redeem him, Oh Daughter, if you can."

These words came from my own authority, the Goddess, and I must obey them. But I did not know how. I could not share this man's suffering as I had shared the torments of the Cunning-Wise One. For I could not hang suspended as he did. My fate was different though I understood, only too well, what it meant to have the hanging in the tree as one's image! But how then could I redeem him?

I thought: he is thirsty and hungry and cannot nourish himself. He is fearful of being crushed and cannot help himself. But I am under no such barrier. And I am not afraid. Perhaps I can give him the things that he needs. Perhaps these things will not be withheld from me! So without further reflection, I ran forward and climbed the tree. It was easily climbed and a beautiful tree and, to my delight, the fruit did not turn away from me as I tried to pluck it. The great wind of the forbidding spirit did not blow the branches away. On the contrary the fruit seemed to bend toward me as I reached for it. Sweet figs, shining apples, ripe olives, lush pomegranates, all of these leaned toward me as I picked them, as if saying, "Take me! Take me! So I plucked them, and so I gave them, one by one into the hungry and yearning mouth of the Adventurer. And he ate them as the repeated and new ambrosia of God. He ate them and gave me a look that told me that once again he was tasting the nectar and food of God as he had of old. Now he was feasting as he once had feasted and as he had once shared his feast with this fellow man.

I leaped down and cupped my hands with the fresh water of the pool and I rested my toes in the rich, black mud of its depths, feeling its softness and richness like the lap of my mother, and the richness of Mother-Earth Herself. I cupped my hands and held the water up for the Adventurer to drink. And drink he did, greedily and thirstily and in ecstasy. For the waters of life coming from the Underworld, from the world of The Great Mother, nourished him and sustained him, and made him feel joy once again.

I placed myself between the great stone which I could not move and the Adventurer, knowing that if it were to fall that it would crush me. And I cried out to the stone, a prayer and a threat, which came through me:

"Oh Great Stone! Oh, Symbol of God Himself. Whether you are rock or gold you are threat to man! And You do not even know it. You, Oh Stone, You need us, You use us, You devour us, yet You threaten us.

We do not mind but only know it. And, Oh Stone, love us too for we are as immortal as you!"

With that rather impudent and girlish prayer-threat, I jumped down and embraced the Adventurer and closed my eyes. We would die together perhaps. I knew that I was endangering the existence of Adventurer with my girlish taunt of God; but we were already in the Underworld, the Land of the Dead–what more could happen to us? We were not afraid of death, had suffered pain; let us take our stand, tell our truth and be done with it. So hug him I did.

Then I heard a roaring of laughter. I looked up and saw the Stone transform into Golden Hue and on it appeared a great Eye. It was as if the Stone were both rock and gold, both inert matter and living substance, both eye and mouth. The Eye looked and the Mouth laughed. A thunderous, but playful sound–if one can combine such strange and opposite things together and be understood–came out and spoke:

"You have spoken truly, O Daughter of Man and Daughter of Woman, You have spoken truly!"

That was all. But now I saw a smiling face of the Goddess, and I could not tell if it was Persephone or Demeter, Mary or her chthonic sister, for it was a benevolent, smiling, somewhat amused, but very earthly woman, though the Goddess.

And best of all was the Adventurer. He was smiling too. He looked at me with eyes that had been longing, empty, marked with pain, and now they were loving, full, and shining with the lights of sun and moon. Adventurer, the Betrayor of God, was redeemed and I shared in the event and had done my task in it.

THE WOMEN, THE WOMEN

I returned to the Castle of the Charioteer to await the next bidding of the Goddess, She of the trim ankles and dark mien. I had hardly made my way back to my pleasant bed-chamber when the Goddess appeared, but not as a head, nor a dark Medusa or Gordon, nor as a benevolent sister. No. Now she appeared as a human being, looking much like myself. I was surprised but happy at the change and raised no question.

The Goddess summoned me with a gesture of her fingers. "Come, Daughter," said She, and we walked along the floor of the Underworld.

There was a mist of blue rising like a gentle fog from the hard surface beneath us. The "sky" of hell, which had always had a bluish hue like it does just after sunset or before sunrise in the land above where the sun shines and the Eye of Heaven has full sway–that "sky" of hell had changed its hue. No longer blue or azure, now it was a purplish color. I had never seen a sky quite like that except at sunsets or sunrises. It was, I think, a pomegranate sky. I made no comment but followed my guide wordlessly.

We came in time to a scene of quiet beauty and meaningless despair, both at once. There before us were some forty or fifty woman walking in single file each carrying a jar filled with water. They walked from a well where they filled their jars, over to a parched land which had many seared and browned flowers, dying from lack of wet care. The women walked rapidly but the jars had holes in them which made them like sieves. Not one of them was able to get the least bit of water to the parched earth in time. But they carried on in an endless circle–filling their jars, hurrying to bring the water, having it all drain out before they arrived, dejectedly returning for a further refilling. It had the beauty of a dance, but the despair in their faces was worsened by the seemingly foolish expectation, with each round, that "This time it would be different."

The Goddess spoke to me sadly. "There you see the Daughters of the Judge," She began. "Those Daughters, like you, were good and true, Daughters of their Father. Their story is sad. Watch them, see their despair in being endlessly hopeful and endlessly disappointed, never being fulfilled; see them and mourn as I tell you their tale."

"I will, O Daughter Goddess," I replied.

The Goddess continued her tale. "These Daughters were the seed of a man called Judge. He was a fraternal twin of another man who was the father of fifty sons, as many as there were daughters of Judge. The twins were given the lands to the east and west of the Holy Region. The Sons of the West longed after the Daughters of the East, to wed and to have them. But Judge did not trust his brother and his sons, thinking that they only wished to kill his daughters and take the land. He was confirmed in his suspicions by the wisest oracle of the region. Judge, therefore, went off in a fifty-oared ship with his fifty daughters to return to the Holy Region. But when they arrived, the inhabitants were suspicious and wanted to reject the Judge and his daughters. Then a sign from heaven appeared and showed that the land was meant to be governed by the Judge and to be lived in by his daughters.

"But the Egyptian was not to be denied, and he brought his many sons to conquer the Holy Region and to possess the daughters of Judge. Though the daughters were tough and spoke with mannish voices, they were no match for the sons and Judge knew it. But he was crafty. He surrendered to his brother and agreed that a marriage ceremony be performed the following day. Secretly, however, he gave each daughter a dagger with which to stab her unwanted husband in the night.

"And so it was. The daughters slew their spouses in the night and became murderesses. All of them, that is, but two. One, called 'Lover-in-Excess,' fell in love with the Son of Egypt assigned to her. She told him of the plot and he ran away to escape harm. Next day she joined him far away. Their story too is great. But she was adjudged a guilty one, not for murder–for she committed none–but for having betrayed both father and sisters. But my Sister, the Goddess-with-the-Face-of-Love, became the attorney for the defense of Lover-in-Excess, and informed all the Judges of Her powers. Pure heaven, said She, longs to fill the Earth with Love and Earth desires it as it longs for rain. This love water from Heaven makes Earth fruitful with plants and animals who nourish men and themselves. Thus is the great round of Love in Life fulfilled. The round of Living-Dying, Loving-Fulfilling, that is the round of Love in Life. Thus did my Sister speak of the Eternal Law of Love which is higher than all laws of Man or God alike. Thus, with this impassioned speech of the Goddess-with-the-Face-of-Love, were both Lover-in-Excess and the Son of Egypt spared. He became a King and she the ancestress of Heroes. Thus does the Goddess reward love and devotion.

But a second Daughter was also spared. She was called 'The Blameless one.' Now Blameless was sent out by Father Judge, the day before the Sons of Egypt arrived, to get water for a sacrifice to the God in Heaven and Under the Sea. Blameless One was pleased to do her father's bidding, but in gathering the water she was assaulted by a devilish little being who wished to rape her. She cried out to God in Heaven and Under the Sea to help her and thus did He appear. And He Himself did mate with Blameless, for she cried out to Him. She was given a three-pronged magic sword which could bring water from the rocks, and she too was ancestress of heroes.

"So these two, Lover-in-Excess and Blameless, were of all the fifty daughters, spared. So it is that the woman who gives all for love is spared and protected by the Goddess-with-the-Face-of-Love. So it is with the woman who is loyal to the Father, to the Spirit which governs, thus she too can bring water of life like magic, but only if she is loyal and loving at once.

"But these, these forty-eight, these murderesses–they, poor souls, were loyal to the Father, but they were not loving. Thus they pine in Hell and thus are they doomed to unfulfillment."

So spoke the Goddess and I listened beyond the words. I was a woman, a Daughter like them and I understood. What a task have women, have we not, to be loyal and loving. But I had been disloyal, unloving and raped, and I was a Daughter of the Mother. I knew not perhaps what it meant to be a fulfillment. Doomed to waste the Water of life. Doomed to be hard and combative and loveless. Forgiven by God the Father but doomed to exist in the Underworld forever and ever.

I stood and looked at these forty-eight, daughters like myself, doomed to lack of consummation in marriage, in love, in initiation. I stood and sighed. But the Goddess went on.

"Do not assume, O Daughter, that these daughters were unfulfilled in marriage. For they were. The same Judge, their father, later married off his daughters to those men who competed in a race. He married them as a convenience, a game, and a bargain. And he cared not for love nor for devotion to the spirit. But he was not a bad man, just typical of the laws of the day. So you see the daughters were fulfilled in marriage, the ritual of the law, but unfulfilled in love or spirit. Thus do they live in despair and in an eternal fruitless round."

So ended the words of the Goddess and I looked at the daughters with compassion. Oh my God, I thought, thus are we all, in our endless repetitions of our lovelessness and our lack of devotion to the spirit, thus do we repeatedly waste the water of life. Thus do we endlessly repeat the round of our stupidities. Oh daughters like myself, how can I help? I thought these words and spoke them out but the daughters heard them not. It was as if they were behind an invisible shield which prevented me from reaching them.

I called out to the Goddess to help me help them. But She simply stood there in despair like myself, unable, it seemed, to move from the spot. I cried out to the God in Heaven to help me help them, but I knew that even if He could hear me He could do nothing, for He had already forgiven them. They had in truth been loyal to the Father. There was no one to call out to.

Except the Charioteer. I thought of Him, the God of the Depths, and I cried out to Him, Him whom I had feared and despised and grew to love to excess. And I cried out in love and compassion and in hope.

The Charioteer came.

He came upon his Chariot like the day that I had first seen Him. He came with a roar and a flame and a fire. And he broke through the invisible wall which blocked me from the daughters. He broke through it like a rape. But it was a transparent shield which he raped. And he broke in upon the despair of the daughters.

Now each of them did he take and hold. Each of them He loved and solaced and enquired of and invaded and molded. Each of them He took. Each of them in turn and together. And He did so like the God that he was. For He loved them and penetrated them and softened their hardnesses. He molded them and petted them and listened to them so that the hardness of the body became strength of spirit and the aggression of murder became the passion of love. And He did this to all, to each, before my eyes. And He did this in an aeon or an instant. By this act I was purged of my jealousy and my possessiveness for such was the power of the Charioteer, and thus was the help of the Goddess at my side.

So, then were the unfulfilled filled and the incomplete completed. And so was the power of love and spirit made manifest in the Hell of the Underworld. Thus were the daughters of the Judge redeemed. Not by me, not by the Goddess, but by the Charioteer.

THE LAST TASK BUT ONE: THE CHAIR

"There is one more task of redemption," the Goddess said to me some time later, "before you will be allowed to return to your Mother and the Upper World where the light of day shines.

My pulse quickened when she mentioned my Mother. I once again was filled with longing to see and hold her. So long and endless is time here in the Underworld, I thought. How often have I been caught up with my adventures and my tasks in the service of the Goddess. In that time, I confessed to myself, I had often forgotten my mother, forgotten her who loved me and bore me, forgotten her who suffered as I did from our separation. But she no doubt had suffered more, even though it is I in Hell, and not she. For I had secretly found the Charioteer. But these thoughts I kept to myself and if the Goddess knew them She neither commented upon them nor enquired of me. She merely went on with her words.

"Once again I set out from the Palace of the Charioteer. I walked in the sunless light of the sky which since my last adventure was more and more magenta, reddish-purple in color. A pomegranate sky, I had called it, and so it was thought parts were still of the many-shaded blues I had known earlier.

Now I walked slowly and gently in a quiet, reflective mood. This would be my last task and journey, the Goddess had said, and perhaps my most difficult. Then I would see my Mother once more. Would that mean that I would never see the Charioteer again? At this thought my heart sank. Could I leave and never see Him again? It would be too much. Rather never see Mother than forever be cut off from Charioteer!

Lost in these thoughts I almost ran into a block of stone. There, seated in a large, stone-hewed chair, sat a man as if glued to it. He seemed lost in dreaminess and forgetfulness. But it was not pleasant or ecstatic, apparently, for his eyes had that look of pain in them with which I had become so accustomed to seeing ever since that day, long ago, when I was raped out of my innocence and brought to live and experience the creatures of the Underworld. I had learned that these eyes were the mark of the Goddess and the Charioteer and that they were beautiful when filled with loving, but horrible when filled with pain. And this man's eyes were filled with pain.

I spoke gently to him. "Who are you? And why are you sitting there in a chair carved from stone? You look to be in pain."

The man stared at me, but as if from far, far away. He spoke to me. "I am called the Turn-Around. And I sit here because I must, not from choice. This stone chair, hewn from the rocks of the Underworld, has me in its grip and I cannot move for fear of leaving parts of me behind. I am in pain, even though dreamy, and that upon which I sit is called the Chair of Forgetfulness. But who are you and why are you here?"

"I am called Daughter and I am here at the behest of the Goddess who sent me here to redeem you, if I could."

The man looked rueful and continued his story. "The Goddess, yes. I know of Her. She who rules in the Underworld. I know of Her but have never seen Her. The Charioteer, yes. Him have I seen–to my regret. But the Goddess, She whom I came to find, She who was to be the betrothed of my good friend, She has never shown Herself to me."

"Tell me your tale, O Turn-Around." I said, "and perhaps a way will present itself so that the Goddess, Blessed be She, will manifest Herself to you."

"Blessed be She, say you? Well, that is something! Blessed? That dark Goddess of the wild locks and loathsome mien for whose sake I now sit on my horrible seat, cut off from human kind! Blessed, is it? I doubt it.

"But I will tell you my tale, all the same, and you can draw your own conclusions.

"When I was young, I was a gadabout and a joyous one. I was strong and brave and comely and used to both loves and fights. Though only mortal and no hero I carried my weight in the world and was well thought of. One day I met a man in battle who was more handsome and braver and more magnanimous than I, and I loved him. We did not battle each other, for we felt an immediate attraction and embraced as brothers. But he, I learned, was a Chosen one of God and a Hero. He, it turned out, was not so mortal and limited like myself but had God as a father! It is good to have such a one as a friend!

"We played and caroused and fought and did tricks. Even after we found wives and married and settled down we still had many good times together. And even when tragedy struck and we lost our wives and had many setbacks from God, even then we were good friends. But it came to pass that I, in jest, had said that my friend should have no one less that a Goddess of the Underworld as his wife, for such a Hero was he. He took the jest as nothing more than that, but it was not so taken by God. He above, through His oracle on earth, bade us descend into Hell and find the Goddess below. His son, his Chosen One, He said, should have no one less than the Daughter of the God should he not? Little did we know that God too was jesting, but His jest becomes a joke on the Universe, does it not? When God jokes the Universe is created in play. And so we had to make our way to Hell. What began as my jest became God's joke and bought us to Hell.

"We could not come the usual way since we were alive and did not plan to die to find the route to the Land of the Dead. So we went around. We went through the Land of the Golden People as they were called and entered their sacred place of a Cave. We wandered long and had many adventures but ultimately came to the Land of the Dead, the place of the Underworld, the Hell that we had long feared, wondered about, and–it must be confessed–even scoffed at.

"Once in the Land of the Dead we presented our request to the Lord of the Palace, the King of this realm, one known only as Charioteer. He heard us out, bade us welcome and be seated. We sat upon chairs, such as that upon which my mortal flesh now rots. We sat and could not move.

Well, thus we sat for a very long time. Four years it was before we saw another soul. I know this–not from any calendar or sense of time that one has in this dreary place–but because we were told this by our visitor and hoped-for redeemer. Four years later there came another Hero, to redeem us from our glued-in position. My friend and brother who was a Hero, like himself, he was able to lift up after having made peace with both the Charioteer and the Goddess. My friend lost a bit of his flesh but was freed. As the Hero attempted to free me, however, an earthquake shook his place. It was as if God Himself were decreeing that my sins were too heinous, that I must remain forever enthralled as a passive victim to a chair. And thus it has been. I sit here, trapped, glued, bound. And what is my sin? I do not even know. Is that the Hell of it? To sit in pain and unmoving paralysis, without even knowing why? I often think so.

"At other times, however, in the vast clock clicks of eternity that I spend in periods of forgetfulness–in these periods of quiet contemplation and periods of agony–I reflect that my sin is in having been a mere mortal and included myself with Heroes. I have embraced a Hero's life, I have even jested with God! That, I suspect, is a grievous sin in God's eyes, and so I sit nailed to a seat in the eternity of Hell, unable to redeem oneself from death? That is being mortal, isn't it? Being unable to redeem oneself from death? I hurt, however, and feel the pain and soreness of my backside. For if even a Hero like my friend can feel the pain and fleshy limitation in his own backside, how much more so for me, a mere mortal, who cannot even move without feeling pain!

"But why, I ask myself, was God so ready to let me go with the Hero on his quest and why did He let me come to Hell? Why did He send his angry earthquake only when I stood a chance of being redeemed? Would that make me a Hero, to return from the dead? Would that make me, an ordinary mortal, a God-Man too? Well, Daughter, that is what I think and what I have come to after all these years, glued to a chair, and being forced to both endure pain, to sink into swamps of nothingness, and to reflect. And this is what my great insight, out of my pain and passivity, has been: God does not want me, a mere mortal, to be a God-Man, though he has jokingly followed my joke, allied me with Heroes, led me on adventures, and now leaves me to suffer my mortality. So you see I am not very impressed with His 'leading me on' as they say, and leaving me in the lurch. And why did he bother? And where, indeed, is the Goddess He allowed us to seek? Such are my thoughts and reflections, O Daughter. I ask not for an answer, but since you ask for my tale I have told it. I am sorry to have complained, for you like me are mortal, apparently, and have stumbled or been sent like me, to this dreary Land of the Dead; so perhaps I tell you nothing that you have not thought of for yourself."

The man, Turn-Around, seemed to have thought more deeply on some things than I, and I had to acknowledge it to myself at least. Why indeed, I thought, does God, or the Goddess for that matter, "lead men on" as he said, and leave us "in the lurch" with our mortality? Turn-Around was right. But why was he called Turn-Around?

I turned to look at him and he gazed back. As I looked I saw him smile. His smile was very beautiful and I was charmed. But as he looked at me I saw his face change. His features gradually shifted and molded themselves so that before I knew it I was staring at Charioteer Himself! I was shocked and bedazzled. But, just as I was about to point to him, open-mouthed, to shriek out that he looked just like Charioteer, I saw his face look back at me in shock and disbelief. But I knew now what he saw.

Before he could tell me what he saw in my face, there appeared above us a giant figure whom I knew, without having to be told, was the friend of Turn-Around. Here was the Hero whom he had loved, had befriended, and been befriended by. Here was the Hero who had been to the Land of the Dead and returned to the world of sunlight. And here he was, as if coming back to free his friend from bondage.

But what was the instrument by which we were to be freed of our bondage in the Land of the Dead, in the Underworld, in Hell? Was it a sword? Or a pen? Or a salve? Or a drug? None of these. The Hero held in his hand two mirrors, two shiny looking-glasses, two silvered reflectors! He held one up to Turn-Around and one to myself. For an instant I remembered the task of Hero who had held a mirror up to the face of the Goddess of the Underworld in Her horrible form and turned Her to stone; and for that same instant, I wondered if I, too, would see a horrible face. What did I see? What did Turn-Around see? Can you guess? Yea, I will tell it, and shriek it and proclaim it! I will shout it until all Mankind knows it! And what must I shriek and proclaim and shout? Turn-Around's face was the face of the Charioteer and proclaim and shout? Turn-Around's face was the face of the Charioteer and my face was the face of the Goddess! God had become man and mortal and God's face was our face! Need I not shout it? Need I not proclaim it? Need we not know it! For, Mankind's face is the face of God!

Now the great stone seat upon which Turn-Around had been glued changed to gold and was a throne. And we both knew that this was a throne of reflection, the golden light of self-knowledge, when man knows God. It is hell if one is forced there and glued, and heaven if one knows and sees God. Turn-Around knew his name, for it was God become Man and Man become God, the greatest Turn-Around of all time. And now the Hell of the Underworld was bathed in the pomegranate light of purple Heaven and Hell was Heaven.

In the next moment Turn-Around ascended and rose in the air of the Underworld until he vanished. He rose and was reborn into the Land of the Living and I knew it. And I knew that image of God was living again and that one day I would see him again. And not him alone but others too, all created in the image of God. And I knew that I too was a God–or rather–a Goddess, and that my face and the Goddess' were one. For I, too, like Turn-Around, was totally mortal, yet I was a God-Man–or rather–a Goddess-Woman too.

Thus was my final task, in the service of the Goddess, completed. My last task but one. So be patient and learn what I learned after this last task, the last task but one was completed.

THE KNIGHT, THE RETURN, AND THE "LAST TASK"

"The last task but one," I have told you. I imagine that you are wondering what the last task was. Well indeed it was hardly a task–and yet it was. It had to do with my return to the Upperworld, the world of light and air and sunshine, the world in which my Mother, poor sorrowing one that she was, awaited me in continuing gloom. So then let me tell how it happened that I could return and what my adventures were. For I did not return to the upper world with Turn-Around, as much as I might have liked.

I returned to the Palace of the Charioteer and spent many wondrous day and night with him. The was no time, out of place. But lo, one day, there came to our door–and how he managed to find his way to the Underworld I still, to this day, do not know–a handsome Knight. This Knight said that he had come from the Upper World, the land where the Mother wept for her lost Daughter, the land where the Eye of Heaven looked down upon mortals, the land of pain and barrenness since Daughter had "gone away"–as he delicately put it. Knight had come, he said, to beg the return of Daughter, who no doubt was herself wasting away with grief for her Mother, would He permit that Knight return her to the Upper World? This would be a great boon and would allow life to be green once more.

Thus tactfully spoke the Knight, and thus did we, the Charioteer and myself, receive him. Charioteer and I both looked at each other and grinned. We knew that though I missed mother I did not grieve for her. We both knew that thought I would enjoy the sunlight and light above I was very happy to be below among the Dead and those waiting to be redeemed, as long as I was in the company of Charioteer. But we both knew that I was not supposed to have such feelings nor show such sentiments. Who, after all, would prefer Death to Life, or Hell to Earth? No one of course. No one of course, except me. So I knew that I must keep silent about my true feelings.

The Knight went on to say that he hoped, for the sake of my Mother and the Upper World, that I had eaten nothing of the special foods of the Nether World; if I had, then I would be obliged to return to the Land of the Dead and spend part of the year there as well as above. And would you believe, Knight told me this information with a wink! Yes with a wink, as if he already could read my mind or know my feelings and was helping me follow them.

Without further hesitation I leaned forward to my gorgeous and redoubted Charioteer and ate of the seeds of pomegranate which he put into my mouth. Seven seeds he fed me and with each seed I felt as if I were impregnated with a wonder of Heaven rather that a pain of Hell. The taste was sensual and tart and sweet at once. I closed my eyes and imagined that I was devouring the splendid pomegranate sky of the Underworld in which I had lived for I knew not how long. With each seed my internal vision grew greater and I saw things which I cannot divulge. Suffice it to say it had to do with the Mysteries of Life and Death, of growth, and rebirth. I do not withhold; I simply cannot speak, for these are wordless, they are mysteries. Secrets can be revealed for they contain words; Mysteries cannot for they are wordless.

When I had devoured the sixth seed I suddenly saw a great tree growing from the base of Hell. It grew straight up beyond the vault of the sky of Hell, into the arches of unseen Heaven. At the same time it seemed that the branches were also roots, and that this same tree was growing downwards, with its roots in heaven as well! Can you imagine it? I beheld this tree in the presence of the Charioteer. And then, with the seventh seed the image vanished, something was at an end. Life was begun anew, I understood. So the Knight placed me upon the borrowed vehicle of the Charioteer and we climbed right up out of Hell into the upper light. We climbed I know not how, but once again I found myself on the solid ground of Earth.

There before me, at a temple with other ladies, was Mother, overjoyed to see me. Despite my love and my shock, my pain and my adventure, I was deeply moved to see Mother. She was older, as was I, but deeper and wiser and sadder and more beautiful than ever.

We embraced, Mother and I, in a warm and delicate and enfolding way which encompassed all, and told all. All day long we embraced and loved and made each other whole. And we knew that Mother and Daughter were One. For the Goddess was there in Her upper form and lower form, and She was two and one, just as we were two–and one.

At last I was asked if I had eaten below in the Netherworld and I admitted that I had. There was grief, for now it would be known that I could not remain in the world of light, but would have to spend part of the year below, with the Charioteer. I feigned sorrow but it was hard to conceal my delight.

So it was settled; three months of the year I would stay below in the Netherworld, apart from Mother and Mankind. Six months I would live above with my fellow mortals and in the sunlight and green of this great and beautiful world. And the three final months I would stay below in the company of the Charioteer but with my Mother as well. For she too had earned the right to be with me. She, too. She was no ordinary mother, simply pining and waiting. She too had served the Goddess. She too had loved. She too knew what it was to be a God-Woman. She too could face the God of the Underworld.

These remains only one final thing to relate to you, which I will in a moment. But this is the delicate matter, and a deeper question which you have raised, O Son of the Knight; I must rest a bit before I can tell you of it. Strange, I have related that which would embarrass another woman perhaps, but not me. Yet, this final revelation is the most delicate of all...

Ah, now I understand. I have said to you that I told you of my "last task but one." Now I understand that my telling you my tale is indeed my "last task." And this last word of this last task is, I confess, the most difficult of all. Rest, now, and allow me to rest, before I tell my last word and finish my last task.

LYSIS

Now Son of the Knight, now Dog, and now Mother, I prepare myself for my final task which is to related this last part of my tale. Mother, you already know it; but be patient as you have until now and let me tell my story and my shame without protecting me from it or from the painful revelation. You are indeed a good mother, but like many a mother you have difficulty accepting the pain of a child. And it is natural that a parent suffers when the child suffers, and wants to relieve the pain.

During my long stay in the Underworld I gave birth to a child. Yes, even in Hell one can be pregnant. Even in Hell one can go on and live the life of the flesh. Even in Death there is Life. This child that was born was a delightful boy. I treasured him. But I did not know who his father was. That is the shameful thing. It could have been any of the number of men who raped me originally. It could have been any of a number of the men who were ghosts in the Underworld with whom

I had union. It could have been–and this I both believe and want to believe–the Lord of the Underworld Himself. He looked like Him after all with his dark curly hair, his deep brown eyes with passion and tenderness glowing therein, with his husky frame. I was confident that the Lord of the Underworld was his Father but I could not assert it with certainty. In any case though Life can exist in Death, though a child can be born in Hell, though flesh exists below, I could not keep the child. I sent him above and he was cared for by the very people whom I would have wished that he be nourished by–my Mother and the Goddess.

Now you know the story for Mother has related it. You also know that the child was returned by the route of the Holy Well. What you do not know is that when I returned to Life I could take the child with me. I could come back to the world of the living as a Mother and with a child. But it would be scandalous to bring a child who is the product of Death. It is scandalous, unbelievable. For could the father be a ghost? Or a God? Nonsense, all would say. But I must have my child. Who would be the father?

The Knight, blessed man that he was, said that he would claim fathership. We had been gone long and besides that it was known that in the Land of the Dead there was timelessness. There would be quizzical looks but the Knight was so upright, so well thought of, who would raise any questions? And I would raise the boy as his son.

And yet–and yet–I had in truth been in the Underworld. And the Charioteer, who in truth believed himself to be the Father of the boy, could not permit that he be known always as the Son of the Knight. The Charioteer therefore decreed that the lad would stay in the Underworld or on that brink thereof, between Life and Death until he was eight or nine, until he could go out on his own. The Charioteer would teach him and he would not know his father was). Then at eight or nine the lad would go abroad and wander among the living to find out who he was. He would have his own adventures and come to himself. Until he was thirty. And he would have thirty stones, thirty jewels which would serve as a talisman to guide him. And when he returned he would then know his full identity. Until then, he would be known as the Son of the Knight.

Now, good lad, good Son of the Knight, I have told you the whole truth. Now you know why, during your early childhood you did not receive the care of your mother. For we were gone in the Upper World much of the time. Know too, that we could not care for you. And know that my sorrow was that I could not acknowledge my motherhood to you because of my sin. My sin was not knowing who your father was, and having to lie about it.

For I, good Son of the Knight, I am your mother. I proclaim it! And the lady who seemed so motherly but could not acknowledge that she was your mother–for she was not–was, in sooth, your grandmother. But she too mothered you. And know, O Son of the Knight, that you are indeed a Son of the Knight, for he was good enough to acknowledge you and support you and stand for you in the world when it was unpopular. He was indeed your God-Father.

And know furthermore, O Son of the Knight, that you are a Son of the Underworld, the Netherworld. In short, you are a Son of the Night! O, then, Son of the Night, know that your Father was a God! He it was who taught you. He it was who sat remote in the cave, not because He did not love you but because you had to find out for yourself. And you have. Your God-Father is a mortal, and your Father is a God. You are indeed a God-Man. You are indeed a mortal, and your Father is a God. You are indeed a God-Man. You are indeed a mortal.

You did not know who your mother was and now you know. You thought you knew who your father was and you did not. Yet you did. Come my son, let me embrace you, and let your grandmother embrace you. We have longed to do so for an eternity!

Now, praise God, we are united–Mother and Daughter, Mother and Son. And you too, O Dog, for you are the friend of my Son, just as the friend of below befriended me. Embrace us. And we will be your Mother as well.

We four will be as one!

PART THREE

The VESSEL

INTERLUDE

It is night and the four sit quietly in the cave. The four: Son of the Knight and Dog. Mother and Daughter. The four: Christian, Pagan and Jew, Animal and Human, Divine and Mortal. They sit together in silence. They are strangely sad. They have grown, they have developed, they have become individuals, they have become sanctified and god-like, and at last they are all together. But they are sad. Why? They will speak and other voices will join them.

"Sad am I," said the Son of the Knight. "Is it because my father is not here? My father, where is he? He who taught me, who counselled me, he who was a God. Or was it he who was my father? Or is my father my God-Father? No matter, both are my father. But is that why I am sad? Because neither are here? I'm not sure. Why, then? I have found my mother and she is kind. Indeed as with my father I found I have two mothers. Where there were none, now there are two. Still I am sad. Perhaps, as I found out before, I have no need of mothering and fathering, for I am more than thirty. Why, then, am I sad? I do not know—Yes, I do know. I am sad because I have nowhere to go. My quest is fulfilled: I have found my mother and I have found myself. So now shall I sit, like the God, here in this cave, knowing of men and of the times, looking out over Eternity? No, I need somewhere to go. I need adventure. What say you, Brother Dog?

"Dog am I and Man," said Dog. "For so I became. From the tales of Mother and from the story of Daughter I know two who were there when I was there. They too saw the pain of God becoming Man. And that I know. Now I miss not the Father, whether two or one, whether

Charioteer or Knight, whether Eye of Heaven or Phallous of Hell, but the Son. I miss that God-Man, who suffered so. Do I miss the God-Man so much that I am sad? Is it because, like you, Son of the Knight, that I long for new adventures? I think not. I do not need somewhere to go, I need somewhere to be. Here between Heaven and Hell; here between the Upper World and the Lower World, here is Non-being. I would go to Heaven, I would go to Hell. I would seek the Father, I would seek the Son. Most of all I would need to live, to be. Now that I know what it is to be Man, to know that I live and that God lives through me, I want to live, and to be. That is what I seek. So, Son of the Knight, I want to leave this place and be. With you I will go, for it gives me pleasure to be with you. What say you, Mother?"

"Son of the Knight, Adventure need you," Mother said, "something to go. Dog, Being need you, someplace to live. And I? It is simple. I need someone to serve. Not some place but some one. But who needs my service? None. Son of the Knight, you have found your Mother–and need her not. And you, Daughter, we have found each other but we are separate and free. And you, Dog, you need me not. Who then can I serve? The God? Which? The Goddess? How? So I too am sad. I have served and been served. I have been with God and Goddess. I have sought and I have found. But I am sad. Whom can I serve? Thus am I. What say you, Daughter, the glow of my life?"

"Sad am I, Mother of my soul," Daughter said. "Sad am I, Dog; sad am I, Son of the Knight. Son of the Knight, you have your 'some place to go,' your searching, becoming. You, Dog, have Being. And you, Mother of mine, you have your devoted Serving. But I? What have I? I have only loving. Loving need I, loving must I. My son has no need of mother-love and the Charioteer is not here. How then can I live without loving? Thus am I sad."

"So here are the four," said another voice. "Becoming, Being, Serving, Loving–developed, independent, free, united, whole. But alone. What then can they serve together? Alone, they are empty and sad. Together, they can–what? Serve a God? Find a God? Be a God? Love a God? Yes, all that. And who is it, then, who speaks? Who is it who comments upon the four? Is it the fifth? Is it the quintessence of the four which unites them? No. It is I, the Voice of Silence. It is I, that Vessel which can unite them all. It is I who will illumine and guide them. Listen, now, for they shall see me...

"Time passes. How long? Hard to tell. For the four sit and wait. The four sit and wait for that which will illumine and guide them. Is it years that pass? Is it months or days? Again, hard to say. For they sit in the cave of Eternity. They sit in the cave in which Son of the Knight was raised, where Mother and Daughter came and went. They sit where Dog was brought, and where the Charioteer made his presence known.

"But they sit in the Limbo of a quiet reality, far from the precincts of Hell, far from the Charioteer and where He roams; far from the precincts of Heaven, far from almighty Eagle Eye of God, the thunder-bearer and lightning thrower, far from God the Father, and far from God the Son, He who lives in the empyrean above. They sit, these four, quietly, in abnegation and in sorrow. They have achieved all, but they have achieved nothing–or so they feel. But I shall illumine them and guide them. Not I alone, but through the Father, and through the Son, for I am–need I say? Nay, one shall see who I am. Listen now and they shall see me..."

"Look there, my friends," said the Son of the Knight. "Is that not a light which gathers and pulls and shines? It flows in through the cave but I am not sure if it comes from before us or behind us. Look! Do you see that same strange light that I see?"

"Yea, brother, I do!" said Dog. "I see the light. It is green and yellow, and has an eerie shine which I have never seen before, not even among the Golden People!"

"I too see the light," said the Mother. "But I see it as red, glowing in vermillion and pink, and sometimes blue perhaps. Or is it just the walls of the cave which make it seem so? I cannot say. But look how it shines and glows!"

"I too see the light," said the Daughter. "But to me it looks like a vessel; it looks like a cup, a brilliant cup of jewels. Yes, now I see! Can you not see it so? It is a cup, a cup or glass for wine! It looks much like the wine glasses we used when I was a child for Passover Feast. Remember, Mother, before the Lord came, before the blood and the sacrifice? But this one has jewels, strange jewels which give off lights. Those are the lights you see, of blue and gold and red and green. Oh, how they shine! I cannot tell–is it Grandfather's glass for wine for the Passover, or is it a jeweled beaker, a cup beyond compare?"

"Now hear me," said a quiet voice, "for I am here, the Voice of Silence. Listen clearly, you four, for you are privileged to see and to hear. To hear the Voice of Silence, to hear the voice of the grave, from under the earth, and from the sky, from that which is beyond. And to see; to see that which the Voice refers to, and speaks out of. What is it that speaks? What is it that calls and glistens and shines? Look, ye, for it is the Grail. It is that vessel longed after by men, that vessel which was used for the last Passover. This is the vessel which received the blood of that poor God-Man as He stretched on that cross, the vessel that caught the blood of the Holy One as it flowed from the lance wound in his side.

"That vessel was cup and glass, that which received. It was lance and sword, that which inflicted. And it was plate and dish; for that vessel is the plate of holy lamb, of the paschal sacrifice, that dish; for that vessel is the plate of holy lamb, of the paschal sacrifice, that dish where God sits and is eaten. For God is a cornucopia of good things. That vessel, of sword and lance, of cup and dish–all these am I, for I am the Grail. Do ye know me? Do ye know my hallows? You, Son of the Knight, speak, for you are said to know much. You have studied much, you have read much, you have traveled much, you have suffered much, do you know me? You who know? You who lust for adventure? You, Son of the Night, and of the Knight, yet Son of a God, do you know?

"Oh, Grail, oh Spirit of God made manifest unto us," said the Son of a God, do you know? Knight, "I know little. I know of the Hallows but I know little. But I am a Knight and a Son of a Knight and I would seek adventure. I would seek as my father sought, and I have sought and I long to become. I long to become that which I was meant to be. So guide me, O Grail, Guide me in my ignorance. Show me that way. And take me for I am a Knight. But take me to become, and take my friends, for I love them."

"Yea, O Knight, I will take thee," said the Grail. "As to thy friends, they must speak in turn. For you, O Dog, you creature of the great animal world who has suffered and been torn and been a God, who has learned to know what it is to be man, You, O Dog, what say you? You, who have seen the Crowning of Thorns; you, who have seen the anger and horror and betrayal of men; you, who have seen the goodness and badness of men, you who have become man; but you, you who long to be, and to be with the Son of the Knight, will you come too? Will you seek and be guided and be illuminated? Will you suffer that which I send to you? Will you follow and search, as well as be?"

"Yes, O Grail," said Dog. "I will go. I will go where my friend, the Son of the Knight, goes for I love him and will follow and serve him, as he serves me. I will go for those reasons. But I will go, too, for myself. Yea, for myself, too, will I go. The Crowning of Thorns have I seen, but I long for more. I long for that Grail, that horn plenty, that vessel of the Lord, which you are. Yes I will go if you will have me."

"I will indeed, O Dog. I will indeed," said the Grail. "For you are the stuff from which the bones and flesh and heart and spleen of our Lord has come. You know it. You live it. You sanctify it. I will indeed have you, O Dog. And you, Mother of all; you, Mother of the Universe, and Mother of Daughter; you who long to serve, who is happy only in serving; you, who have nothing more to serve, will you serve that which I present?"

"Grail, I would be honored," said Mother. "To merely see that vessel, to merely sense its majesty and greatness, to merely be dazzled by the beauty that you present to us, the vessel of the Lord–all this is more than I could have hoped for. To serve, to go beyond that and to serve the Lord, that God who passed by my life, that is beyond all that I wished. I will serve and I will go."

"And you, Daughter," said the Grail. "You who profess to love, and be loving; you who suffered–like your Mother suffered–the pain of distance, of separation; you who suffered Hell and darkness, the rape of flesh and soul, the vision of torment, you who speak of love, will you go?"

"Grail, majesty and beauty, I will go, and gladly," said Daughter. "For I would seek that vessel, that way of love beyond which I have seen. I would seek and find or only seek–if that is my fate–if I could be with Mother and Son and Dog. We four needed something and we knew not what. We four needed to be and become, to serve and to love, but together. Without this we are nothing. Without this we are sad and mournful and sit in our cave, knowing nothing. Yea, I will go and gladly."

"You all accept, and gladly," said the Grail. "You may regret having agreed so easily–but, again, you may not. It does not matter. I do not seek you for your sake. I do not choose you for your sake. I choose you for God's sake, and for the sake of the God in you which speaks. Now look and see that which you seek and will serve. Look and see!

There it is, a crucifixion. God standing upon His Cross, filled with pain and agony! That is the grail and vessel and servant and demander. Look at it! You, Dog, you have seen the Crowning of Thorns, but you have not seen the Crucifixion. Do you know what it means to be crucified? Do you know what it means to be torn between opposites? To be nailed upon that cross of yourself which demands all of you?

"And you, Son of the Knight, who have known the God in the cave, do you know this crucifixion? And you, Mother and Daughter, Christians by experience, by conversion in the beginning, and having gone beyond into pagan begin, do you know?

"You look and you do not speak. It is good. It is meet that you do not speak, for your words would be as nothing. I will tell you what your task will be. I will explain as a flaming angel would explain, as that Angel of God explained to your Father, oh Son of the Knight, I will explain. Now hear.

"You see before you the God of Love! Is that what Love is? Is that horrible sight of pain, of torture, of humiliation, of never-ending sorrow, of serving the highest and being torn apart, of God suffering the fullest, is that what Love is? Do you know it? Do you believe it?

What I ask, O Son of the Knight, O Dog, O Mother, O Daughter, is that you follow what I present, that you serve this. But not in the ways of old, not with pain and sacrifice, horror and martyrdom, no, not any of these. I ask that you find the secret words of understanding. I ask that you, because you have lived and suffered and found, that you answer the questions posed to you. For that is what the Grail is to those that seek, they must answer the unanswered questions. But the Grail is not like that great Sphinx who posed riddles and devoured those who could not answer. Nay, the words must be four, and the mystery must appear. The secret Mystery must be made manifest but without destruction. You will see as I present to you words and scenes of great import. You must voyage and sit and meditate, and be together. I will help you. I do not wish to devour you, nor test you, nor exalt you. I wish to help you, so you may help others, for such is the destiny of a God-Man, and a God-Woman, and a God-Animal. Such is the destiny of those who have sought and found, and seek more.

"What is it I seek? What is it that I ask? Think again. The God of Love! Look at Him! What is it then, this love? How will you live it? How will you solve it? Can you be a knight, can you be a seeker?

"You all nod. It is good. For you will be Knights and Seekers, as before. But this anew; seekers for the Grail, a Son of the Knight, a Dog, a Mother, a Daughter. It is well. For the seekers of old were knights and brave. No women did seek, no animals did seek. And thus did few find! But you Four, together you shall find for you have found. It is not just to find, but to help, to answer questions, to serve. Together shall we find.

"Prepare then, for the visions and the questions.

"Prepare then, to face love."

THE VESSEL PRESENTS THE THREE

"I present to you the vision of the three," said the Grail. "You four, who have achieved a measure of solace, of fulfillment, of grace, look at a vision of three. These three are not trinity of divinity, no triangle of love fulfilled, but a triumvarate of pain, doubt, dismay. They are a three of guilt, of passion, of destruction. Look at them. Do you know who they are? They are King Arthur, he the master of the Table Round, Queen Guinevere, his great and beautiful wife, and Sir Lancelot, he of France, of charm and quick wit, of skill and strength. Yes, you know them. Who does not?

"Who does not know the fame and grace of the great King Arthur, whose wife fell in love with the good Knight Sir Lancelot. Who is not familiar with their struggle, of how Lancelot could not wean himself of his love, nay, did not want to; of how Guinevere suffered greatly from her betrayal, and of King Arthur, who knew nothing of this, except that he loved and trusted his favorite Knight and impeccable wife. Everyone is aware that in the end Arthur did know, and war took place. Men bled and Guinevere became a nun. All know, in short, the miserable end to the marvelous tale of the Round Table. They all sought the Grail but found it not. Only Sir Galahad, Lancelot's son, was worthy, though many glimpsed it. The end was sad and dark.

"But now look you, you four. The three, Guinevere, Arthur and Lancelot, though dead, have not vanished from time and space. Here they are, first as a vision, then as a living reality to occupy space with you here in the limbo of your cave. Look, you, and see. Note that in their day they sought the Grail; paleness, in their agony of suffering. I bring them here for your answer, your solution. I bring them here for your healing word. Listen first to the brave and handsome Sir Lancelot."

"Lancelot is my name," said the knight, "and you know my fame. Brave was I indeed and handsome enough to be sure, for I had many loves in my life. More loves I suppose than are right for a man, but my main perversity was my greatest love, Guinevere. Oh, how I loved that woman! How my passion waxed at the sight of her! But wait, I leap ahead of my story. I came to King Arthur and his Round Table because I wanted fellowship and to serve a great and goodly King. I had traveled much, and studied much, and was, in my fashion, saintly and virtuous. I longed only to serve the great King as the son of a spiritual father, as a brother to a brother in adventure, in service, and in pursuit of the highest aims of Our Lord. I was arrogant, I suppose, and immodest–perhaps those were my greatest sins. If so, they have been deeply crushed by the pain of my life, of my conflict, of my suffering.

"Despite my aims and goals and real successes in the spiritual life of quest and service, of masculine prowess and strength, chivalry and devotion, despite these aims and goals and my achievements, I fell totally and completely and passionately in love with Guinevere. She of the queenly manner, she of the gorgeous lips and fiery eyes, she of the golden-red hair, she who laughed at me and taunted me. Perhaps I fell because she taunted; perhaps I saw her as a challenge; perhaps I was blinded by her greatness; perhaps of all of these. But I fell. Did I say fall? Nay, I did not fall in love, I rose. I rose to the heights of passion and desire; I rose to an intensity of feeling and sensation which surpassed itself each time I returned anew. After time spent in repenting, in withdrawing, or away on adventure, I returned only to love more deeply than before.

"But fall I did as well. Not in love, but in grace. I fell in my own eyes, for I betrayed the love and service of my friend and spiritual father. I betrayed the best man in the world, King Arthur. And not just once and with remorse and petition for forgiveness did I betray this man, but many times. I spent a life in betrayal and a life in remorse and guilt. It was a rack of guilt that I suffered–the unlawful love of a woman and the betrayal of a man. Passion and devotion, split. Love and friendship, split. Desire and duty, split. Service and fulfillment, split. Spirit and flesh, split. Split was I, and rent asunder. Like our Lord on His cross, I was split and rendered and felt my life blood drain out.

"And more. In order to protect the good name of Guinevere and to protect the secret of our love, I had to challenge those who claimed that I was treasonous I had to smite those who gossiped and caused mischief. Many did I kill for lying. But it was I who lied. So to my sins did I added lying, unjust violence–that which I never done before.

"In the end our secret was found out. I returned Guinevere–as if I could do so–and retreated to my castle in France from whence I came. I retreated to become a recluse and to spend the remainder of my life in the search of inner peace. But Arthur, the proud, was wroth and sought me out to do a battle and kill me. You know the story, how he died, how Guinevere became a nun, how I too took the cloth; but it matters not, for we all died unredeemed. Our love was unredeemed and here I am, suffering. I suffer it yet though dead, and live in neither heave nor hell but in this limbo of deadness. I no longer feel the full pain of it nor the ecstasies of the love with Guinevere, but I suffer. I suffer the lack of redemption. What is the answer to my question, my search, my quest? I sought the Grail, glimpsed it, but have no answer, have no peace. Can you four release me from my purgatory? What say you, Grail?"

"I can add that good Sir Lancelot–so much I call him, though he suffers in badness–good Sir Lancelot lived in the sign of one of my hallows, the Lance. He, the lance, the little lance, was a great lance, indeed! For he fought and slew and wounded, and was fought and wounded and slain. Just as the great sacred lance with body of wood and head of white metal, was that same weapon which the Roman soldier Longinus used to pierce the side of Christ, as He suffered on the cross. Now know that Lance is Lancelot. Lancelot's wound of suffering is the suffering of the God of Love, the agony of being strung up between opposites so that only pain comes from any movement. Know that Lancelot's suffering is a Godly one; it is a suffering inflicted upon the God of Love and suffered by Him. Your answer then must be to Christ as well as to Lancelot! Speak then, you four! Speak to Lancelot and help him in his wounds! Speak–if your adventures have brought you to being God-men–then speak the words of healing! Speak the sacred silent words which will heal! You, son of the Knight, you begin!"

"Oh, great Grail, and Sir Lancelot," said the Son of the Knight, "I will speak because demanded to. But my words are frail and small compared with a task so big. It is true that I am a Son of the Knight, and a God-Man, but to me your task seems so great that I bow in reverence to your suffering. I will speak from where I am, Sir Knight, Sir Lancelot, and trust that my words will give you some solace. Whether or not they will heal is more than I can say.

"I can speak, for I too have been a knight, have had many loves, much as you, have never married, much as you, have quested, much as you. What I see in you is not deep sin as you feel it, but a process of change, of becoming. I too never rest, always change, always search, always become. And so did you. But you suffer so from guilt that you bleed. Sir Lancelot, you may have been arrogant and greedy, but not now. For I see deep suffering and deep modesty in your eyes.

"What is your guilt? Is it guilt toward Jesus Christ, that you sinned? I can say nay to that! I can say nay because I have been neither Christian nor Pagan, and have had two fathers, one a God, one a man! My natural father was a God of the nether regions, and my God-Father a man, a Knight like yourself, who was a Jew with Christian heart and pagan longings. I can say to you what neither father could say: What did Jesus know of the love which you suffer? Nothing! Did he love a woman? No! Did he carnally take on the passion of union? No! When He, the God, became man, did he become so carnal as to copulate? No! Well then, good Knight, Sir Lancelot, I salute you. For the conflict between your love of a woman and your love of a spiritual father-brother was a cross which Jesus the Christ never had to bear. Your cross of suffering of love was great and just as great, I think, even though you are human and not a God-man. Let the God of Love feel what it is to be human and to suffer a love which betrays another love, let the God of love feel that! I, a Knight and a Son of a Knight, stand with you! I tell you that your guilt is lack of being true enough to your love, true enough to your humanity, true enough to your god-likeness of suffering the cross of love. It is not arrogance and greed from which you suffer but guilt, and a guilt which is erroneous. Hold your head high and be proud of how you have carried your love! Be a Knight, and proud to be the father of a Knight who held the Grail. And be a man, a man proud to have borne the pain of his love! Thus do I speak, O Lancelot, the Lance."

Well said, Son of the Knight, well said" said the Grail. "Thus would Jesus the Christ have Himself spoken if asked. See now, Sir Lancelot's eyes brighten. They change from the dark moroseness of guilt and take on the sparkle of joy. What was said of Longinus may be true of Lancelot. When Longinus pierced the side of Jesus he suffered from inflammation of the eyes–only his poor vision hindered him from striking a mortal blow. The blood which issued from the wound fell upon Longinus and flooded his eyes. The inflammation was healed on the spot. It is so with you, Lancelot? Are your eyes, inflamed with pain and guilt, healed by the words of the good Son of the Knight? Is he indeed a healer?"

"Grail, I, Sir Lancelot, can better understand, and am soothed. If this is healing then I am healed–but not altogether. I can see–and perhaps this indicated a healing of the eyes–that my guilt has been excessive, I can even see that I can heap more upon Jesus the Lord, just as the Son of the Knight said, for has not our church and our religion called upon us to heap our sins upon Jesus Christ who suffered to become Man for our sakes? So, what he says is not a blasphemy upon our religion. What he says, too, about the man Jesus cannot be gainsaid.

My guilt is not to Christ, but is a sin toward my friend, King Arthur. And that sin can be dealt with only with him, only if he forgives me. But I am grateful, Son of the Knight, for your warmth, for your respect for me and for your true words about Our Lord. I am hastened thereby toward healing and see more deeply."

"It is well," said the Grail. "Now, Sir Dog, who was there at the Crowning of Thorns, who has himself undergone transformation from Dog into Man, who is indeed himself a God-Man, now you speak to Sir Lancelot. You speak to this man who has suffered his passions, who has suffered his guilt, who has suffered his love. Speak to his condition, if you can.

DOG AND MOTHER FOLLOW SON OF KNIGHT IN THE HEALING OF LANCELOT

"Oh, Grail, you ask me to speak. I, a poor Dog-Man before I was a God-Man. What have I to say to such suffering? Have I known love such as Sir Lancelot? Have I had many loves like him or like my friend, the Son of the Knight? I have loved, and I have experienced woman but not like that. I have not suffered my fate as a man in that way. What then can I say?

"You, Sir Lancelot, I look at you and I weep for you. Just as I wept for my brother, the Son of the Knight. You have suffered at the hands of men, have suffered in life. You speak of betraying, of having lied, but you too have been betrayed, have been lied to. There has been so little compassion for you. I know your story, I know the tale. Who does not?

"I weep for you. I recall the condition of the Son of the Knight when I found him in the desert, alone and weeping, sad like you. I recall the vision of the Christ, crowned with thorns, in pain and humiliation, like you. I recall them both, simply seeking, painfully loving, not understood. Thus do I feel for you. Thus was it that I did understand men who tortured their Gods, and tortured themselves. And you too torture yourself for being an animal, like me. What is so horrible to men about that? Why is it so terrible that one lusts, hungers, and goes away from the spirits above to the spirits below? Think you that animals have no God? Think you that God Himself is not an animal? Think you that your sin and guilt is beyond repair? Abandon it, love yourself! Abandon it, be an animal! Abandon it, be a man!

"I, the Dog-Man, I, Sir Dog, I speak to you, Sir Lancelot. I tell you to be. Live and be. Accept pain, accept joy, and accept–what?

Accept that you too can be loved. Yes you, the great Sir Lancelot, the charming, clever, strong, able Sir Lancelot. The one who aids all, whose strong arm can be relied upon, whose chivalry and charity are as great as his fury and his love. Yes you, Sir Lancelot, you need the loving and compassion as much as any. Nay, more! For you give more and have suffered more. But can you accept it from the Dog-Man? Are you as plain and simple as my friend the Son of the Knight? Are you able to accept my love and my care?

"I have been a friend, loyal and true, like you. I have been a guide and spiritual brother, like you. I have been a companion, just as you. Son of the Knight and I are much like you and King Arthur. I can forgive you, understand you. Can you forgive and understand yourself? Can you let me assuage your wounds, soften the pain and hold you like a brother? For that too you have lost, Sir Lancelot, Lancelot the Love-Man, you have lost your brother. Perhaps he suffers too, but you are alone. Let me embrace you. Let me love you, as I loved Son of the Knight. You, Sir Lancelot, a father and a son, you who have known the love of a woman, accept the love of a Dog-Man, accept the love of a brother. You who lost the love of a father-brother, have had little of the love of a son, accept the love of a Dog-Man, who can be Father-Brother-Son!"

"Well spoken, Dog-Man, friend of the Son of the Knight, well spoken!" said the Grail. "See there, the sad Sir Lancelot looks up! His sad eye forlornly allows it pain to show, Embrace him, Dog, and show him what the love of an animal can be! Embrace him, Dog-Man, and show him what the love of a brother can be! Embrace him, Dog become Man become God always was God, show him what a father can be! Embrace him, Sir Dog, and show him what a male love can be!"

"Thee I embrace, Sir Lancelot, I the Dog, and Son of the Dog, Friend of the Knight, and Son of God. I embrace thee, brother and man. Accept my love, my tears and my compassion. Even God, on the cross, needed my love and so now do you. And love me, Sir Lancelot, for I have known the love of woman as you have known love such as yours. I have not known the love of woman as you have known it, so have compassion for me, poor Dog, who has not loved as you have loved."

"Sir Dog, I, Sir Lancelot, weep under your embrace. When have I wept before? I can hardly remember. My eyes weep and my eyes clear. And they clear not only in vision as they did with the words of your friend, Son of the Knight, but with a healing, as did Longinus who felt the blood of God in his eyes. For with your tears, which awaken mine, I feel the blood of God in his eyes. For with your tears, which awaken mine, I feel the blood of god in his eyes. For with your tears, which awaken mine, I feel the blood of God in my heart. I weep and my heart is racked. Before I was torn in pain with passion and guilt; now I am torn in my heart, with the pain of love. I feel it, Sir Dog, and I know what our Lord felt. True, He did not experience what I have–as you have not, Sir Dog–but neither have I felt his Crowning of Thorns! But I feel the cross of love, I feel the pain, and I feel the need for compassion and to be loved. I thank you, O Dog, and I embrace you."

"Sir Lancelot feels relief of guilt and softening of pain, thanks to the brothers, Son of the Knight and Dog," said the Grail. "What now, O Mother and Daughter? What will you have to say to a man such as this? What will you, as women, say to such a one? Speak, Mother!"

"I, a Mother, speak. But I will speak in my way, with my way of serving. My way is a question. My way is a seeking for an answer, an enquiring of how it is with one. So, Sir Lancelot, Knight of the Lake, Knight of the Suffering Love, how is it with you? What is it that you need, that you long after and pine for? What is it that you feel and how can I help you?"

"Well said, Mother of the Daughter, well said. A new way of helping. Enquiring!" said the Grail. "Would that the many who would help, who would serve the Lord, serve Love, or serve even another, would be so bold and so modest and so true as to simply enquire of another how it goes with him, what he doth require, what it is that he feels! Well said, Mother. So now, Sir Lancelot, Knight of the Lake, Knight of the Sorrowing Tears, do you hearken to the Lady's entreaty? For she entreats of you, of your state, and not of herself!"

"Remarkable, Oh Grail, I know it well! Remarkable, for usually it is the Lady in need, the Lady who wants to be served, who is in need of my knightly task and my hero's service. I rarely recall a lady enquiring after my need. Even Guinevere, the love of my life, even she–did she enquire? Was I blind? I do not know. But you, Mother, I thank, for your asking of me. I am grateful for such an entreaty, rare in my life. That one should care, should search for after–that alone softens my pain. But if I tell you of my pain, of how it is with me, it may not go so well with you. If I tell the truth of my images, of my hurt and rage, you may not like to hear it."

"Nay, Sir Lancelot, speak! I can hear of suffering, I can hear of pain. Did I not endure a long and painful search after my Daughter? Do I not also understand the feeling of our Mother and Sister, Mary, who knelt at the cross watching the pain and agony of her Son, unable to cry out, and worse; unable to ease his pain? I understand that these things and I am ready to face where you are. Only one thing is too much for me–where I have caused the pain, where I am guilty of bringing the tears and, most painfully, am unable to assuage them. This I cannot bear; with this I am a coward. Here, O Lancelot, Knight brave and good, you are greater in love than I, for you have borne such pain and guilt, you have continued in an agony which my Daughter can understand better than I. But speak to me of where you hurt, and I shall listen."

"Listen, then Mother. Listen to my fantasy, and to my feeling, and see if this does reach your tender heart. I sit, O Mother, with an image before me of another Mother, one that I have never seen. She is dark, with deep black eyes, thin, long-nosed and gaunt. Her hair is dark, in ringlets, her face is bony and hollow. But her eyes, her eyes! Sometimes they are flat and impenetrable, like those of a cat. Sometimes they send out sparks of pain and hurt. Sometimes they reach out to find exactly where the hurt of another is, where his pain is; to hear, to soften? No. To touch the wound is all, to drink the blood, to open the gash of pain further, that is how those eyes go out. And they do so in the name of love, mind you, in the name of love.

"But these eyes do not love, that heart does not love, it only speaks of love. Yet those same eyes can be merry, they can laugh and be gay, but they are gay for themselves, not for another. Those are the eyes in the face that I see. That is the face that I see. She is the mother for she sits and worries about her son. She sits and speaks of him, hounds him when he is there, goads him on, tells of her suffering and her love. Is she a witch? A Goddess? Tell me of her, Mother, for you are a Mother. Tell me of her. Does she dwell in me? Does she dwell in women? Does she live in life as a parasite in the cells of one's being? I feel her in my bones and am unable to cope with her. I feel her destroying me and cannot divest myself of her curse. That is what lives in me, Mother, that is what lives with your Knight of the Lake!"

"I feel her, O Knight, Sir Lancelot of the Lake. I feel her and I know her, and I am honored that you trust me enough to speak of her. Yes, I know her, I know her in women, I know her in men, I know her in the cells of being, as you say. I know her in myself. For she is the 'other' side of woman, the lying, deceiving, spiteful, hateful side which is just as real as the goodness and love which you see. She speaks of love but she loves not; she looks deep but she is shallow. She is cruelty and hurt and madness itself. Yes, I know her. I know her in myself and, worse, I know her in the Goddess! I wish I could tell you my story, of how I burned a child in the name of love! It was true, although horrible. I know whereof you speak. But it is not enough that I know, it is not enough that I recognize. It is not enough that I acknowledge that women have this more than men, that it is part of the Goddess and in the cells of being. For I would help you with it if I could, I would aid you to cope with it. How can I? Oh, Goodness, aid me to aid the suffering Knight. Aid me here as you aided me with my Daughter! Help me to help him. My Daughter has succored men and lovers and sufferers, more than I. I would help, if I could. Help me to help him and thus help myself. For we know, Goddess, that when we help we also help ourselves. All service and giving is also a giving to oneself, or it is a painful and hollow gift indeed. We know that, but men do not. So help me, Goddess, to help him."

"Silence. I, the Grail, speak. I understand. For that which speaks in the agony of Sir Lancelot is self-destruction itself. That which undermines and reduces him, that which deprives him of joy, and causes him pain and sorrow without result in suicide of the soul. Mother knows this, the Goddess knows this, but will She Speak" Can She Speak?

"I can speak. And I will speak through the Mother, who understands me. For I am a Goddess, and human, as she well knows. I will speak, Sir Lancelot, for I have already been speaking to you. Yes, you have my image, you have felt my horrible darts, from within yourself as worry without result, as fear, as recurring doubt and rumination, as grinding guilt and pain, as lovelessness, as death, as a blind purgatory of lifelessness. All these do I bring, with flat eyes, as you say, and penetrating horror of blaming another for one's own fault. All this, yes–and do you know how this is?

"Sometimes I speak as a fierce Mother Tigress protecting her cubs, absolutely ruthless and fearless. Should you come between a woman and her cubs, look out! Sometimes I speak like a child, or a girl who is needing and demanding and will do all to get her way. But these you know. These everyone knows of women, and also of men, when they are open to me. What you do not understand is where the masks the other, where the one parades as the other, that is the hell you feel! The agony is when the man sees the woman and gets the child. For the woman will claw him for the child in herself, and there he is helpless!

"That is the secret, Sir Lancelot, that is the secret of that image which haunts and plagues you, for it is the image of madness, of deceit, of a mother who cares not for you, but for herself alone. And it is also the image of daughter masquerading as mother, of a child behind the apparent woman, of needing and demanding, deceitfully posing as giving. Most deeply it is the Universe as love not caring a fig for you, Sir Lancelot, but ready to use you, abuse you, and devour you for its own ends! Know this, Sir Lancelot, and you will be saved. Know this and your self-destruction will change from horror to self-service. For, in serving yourself, in caring for yourself, in loving yourself, you will in truth, as every woman knows, be serving the Goddess! Can you understand it? Can you take it in?"

"Oh Mother, I can understand it with my ears and with my mind but it does not penetrate my heart. I hear one, Mother, and I hear you, Mother-Goddess, but I am dense and slow when it comes to these things. I know of love, but I am chary of self-love–but perhaps I love myself too much! Perhaps that simple animal love of one's being is more modest than my own self-love of ever-seeking perfection!"

"It is so, O Knight, it is so, O Lancelot of the Lake," said Mother. "You have ever sought perfection. You have ever sought to improve, to change, to purify, to go beyond. You have ever pursued the religion of the fathers and the sons, a masculine love of understanding. Know now that the fathers and the sons, to a masculine love of understanding. Know now that the religion of the mothers and daughters–the love of the females–is caring. It is caring for another, but also love of self, acceptance of self, care of self, and tender indulgence of the child within! Know this, O Lancelot, and be saved from self-destruction."

"I know this, O Goddess, I know this, O Mother. I know this and will be saved. But help me to know it. Help me to live it. For I need you. I need Your service and Your love."

"Now you know it, O Lancelot. Now you know it for you have asked. You have asked and begged and acknowledged your need. Now you will be human and imperfect, but God-like and whole! Now I will serve you and in so serving will serve myself!"

While all watched, Sir Lancelot took the Lance and put it into his mouth. He fed upon the blood on its crimson-stained point, upon the emotion, upon the need, and he tasted his own feelings.

"Now," said the quiet voice of the Grail, "You have tasted the fulfillment of love, the fulfillment of love in need. For that too is Motherlove and Mother-child love. Accept it, Sir Knight, accept it, Oh Lancelot, and drink of the blood of the Lord.

"For on his cross He cried out, 'Eli, Eli.' 'Do not forsake me,' he cried out. He cried out in need and His Mother held Him in her arms and daubed his wounds. He suffered her to hold Him, to hold God like a child in her arms. This Man, this God, this God-Man, He suffered His mortal mother to hold Him as a child and weep over Him and succor Him.

"He who was only 'about His Father's business,' He who was alone and unmarried, without wife and children, alone on His mountain, He allowed Himself to be held in His Mother's arms like a child. For even God needs love and to be held and to weep and to cry out and to be contained. And, Sir Lancelot, so do men."

DAUGHTER SPEAKS–AND GOD

"I, Lancelot, Knight of the Lake, have heard the Grail; I have heard the Son of the Knight, I have heard the Dog, I have heard the Mother, and I have felt their care, their love, their understanding. I know now, more deeply, the feeling of the Crowning of Thorns, the feeling of the Crucifixion, the feeling of the Deposition, and I have taken it in. But of the Eli, Eli, of the statement, 'Why has thou forsaken me, O Lord,' I have hardly spoken. I know in my bones that Jesus was enraged at the cynical Romans and the rigid Jewish elders as He suffered His pain and humiliation without cause, How do I know this? Because I, too, have felt rage and fury at this abandonment by God. Not only have I felt this rage at the Lord, who abandoned us–all of us, Guinevere, Arthur, and myself–in our suffering and despair, but also at Arthur.

"In the end, he died himself. He was a fool. Though I despise his needing to punish me, I understand him, for that is human. He felt humiliated and needed his revenge. He felt cheated and wanted satisfaction. Even though I loved him, tried to spare him, acknowledged my sin against him, he needed more for his Kingly ego. So be it! I understand. But I am overcome with rage, at times, with a sense of injustice, with an awareness of having had no support in the conflict, of having carried a huge burden and then to be punished as well. And to whom shall I complain for this? To whose door shall I bring my rage and my complaint and my grievance?

"I believe that I know how Jesus felt when He said 'Eli, Eli,' and 'Why–forsake?' Not even the gospels speak of His being enraged at the Father, but I know it. I know it because I too have borne a cross of love without support and have been abandoned. I know how it feels. So then, you three, Son of Knight, Dog, and Mother, can you speak to me of rage? Can you tell me, and cure me of my own fury at the injustice, heal me of my wound of pain at the lovelessness, aid me in my important rage at God?

"You, Knight and Dog, you merely nod, sympathetically. As if you know, as men, what I mean and what I feel. Yet you seem to be as important to deal with such a rage as I–at least you say nothing about it. And you, Mother, you looked only aggrieved. You look at me with compassion. That is pleasant, but does nothing for my pain and my wrath. So you three, you say nothing. What then, Daughter, will you speak? You, a woman like Guinevere, who have loved, and suffered love, can you speak to me of my pain and wrath at God? You who have gone into the Underworld, I am told, and have redeemed the suffering of dean men–can you redeem the suffering of a man in limbo? A knight who sits in a pool of frustrated rage and pain? What say you?"

"Oh Knight, Oh Lancelot, handsome prince who has suffered so deeply for love, I can say little but I can act. I would relieve your pain, not like a mother, who sits impotently below and watches in horror, but I would love you physically, I would love you passionately. I would curl my lips about your wounds and lick the pain away. I would suck upon your manhood, draw it out, to bring you back to life from pain. I would suck upon your manhood, draw it out, to bring you back to life from pain. I would touch your lips tenderly as I would your eyelashes and ears. I would take in your spittle. All this I would do. If you say that this does not assuage pain, I would agree. But I can change the passion of pain and the passion of rage into the passion of love. I can love you like an animal, I can take the charge of your fire, I can hold the strength of your squeeze, your bite and your scream, and transform it into the ecstasy of love! This can I do!"

"Oh Lady, Oh Daughter, you are as Guinevere to me, and you excite my lust and my pleasure, as well as my admiration and my love. For this is what she said, too, this is what I felt, and it is true–the passion of pain and rage, transformed into the ecstasies of love. This, the Son of God did not have, It is true. But what of the rage, what of the fury that does not transform thusly? What of the pain, dear Lady? What say you to it? What say you to my tears of frustration? What say you to my hurt and teeth-grinding?"

"Oh Knight, Lance of the Lake, impetuous dashing searching man, I say speak it, give it, open it out unto me. Display it–whether it be the fiery semen of vicious words or the bitter complaint of urinous flow. Let it come, let it show itself as the natural flow of fluids from within. Even be they full of pus and venomous, let it flow out and be gathered. We will take the fluid words and harden them into threads. We will sew the strands together and made of them a garment of the Lord. For was not the cloth, the purple robe which He wore not just such a garment? Were not his wounds covered with the pain and hurt and fury of humiliation? Of being hung, of being strung, of being lanced? Sit it out then, Oh Lancelot, and we will make such a cloth of words for the Lord!"

"You speak well, Daughter. Would that I could speak words that would transform into such a cloth, into such a purple robe of mystic color and shape that would warm and heal the God of Love. In truth, my words feel more like urine and feces and blood and semen and sweat which have no spiritual shape. They are only wordless tears of frustration, rage and pain. Can you form these, Oh Daughter? Can you speak for me? Can you cry out to the Lord? Can you in your love not only assuage and copulate, but speak out and complain? Can you beseech? Can you cry out? Can you, in short, say the 'Eli, Eli' that Jesus said? Or is woman forever doomed to sit passively by? To weep for her man, to assuage his wounds, to copulate with him, but never to cry out to the Lord, never to complain to the Most High about Man's suffering, his state, the injustice of his agony?"

"You are right, Lancelot. It is true. We women wait, we endure, we have compassion, we unite, but we do not cry out to God. We hardly cry out to our men, for they must do what they must do, so we say. Men must express and give forth their substance and juices, which we take in and mold, and from which we make new life. But for you I will cry out unto the Lord. For you I will speak, and complain, and say 'Eli, Eli'. I will do this for a man, for a Knight who has borne his cross; for you, this I will do. But for such a task I must retire. Words are deep with me. It is easier to love, to assuage, to express with the flesh, than with the spirit of words. But I will try; I will speak the words of prayer and entreaty, I will speak the words of complaint. And perhaps, most strange for my sex, I will speak the words of outrage at God.

"This is hard for me. It goes against my nature. Better to heal with a touch, to embrace, rather than with words. Words to me, yes. Words, even to God. But words of challenge to God? And words of challenge to God about the suffering of a man? Hard, every hard. We women complain enough, it is true. We complain about our lot, about our suffering, how we are abused, or tired, or burdened–that is not hard for us. But to complain about the suffering of men? About the pain of man who has suffered for love? That is so hard. Do you know why? Because that is natural for us. That is a natural cross for woman, to suffer for love. That seems right and true, and not something to complain excessively about. Just as a man who must 'be about his Father's business' feels that natural–he must serve his spirit, and his dedication to God; that is natural to him. But for a man to serve Love? And to serve it in a way that a woman does naturally? Well!

"Lord. Father in Heaven. Eye of the highest eagle and judge of mankind. Father of Him who died on the cross. Do you hear me? I must ask if you hear me, Lord. I am sorry. Usually we women are content to say our few words of petition, and quietly bear our suffering. But now I must know if you hear me, for I would speak and pray and complain in a way that is foreign to us. So I must speak, not into the blue and to some absent and far-flung Father, but to a living God who will hear and attend to what I say. Do you hear?"

"I hear."

"Hear me then, Oh Father, and hear my complaint. For I speak about a worthy man, a Knight, who has served You. He has served not only You but Your Son as well. For he has borne a cross of suffering of love which is borne by few men. Indeed I know of none, though there have surely been many in history, in the course of time, who quietly and unknown by others, suffer the cross of loving a woman in the flesh and being, while at the same time they are a betrayer of another loved one, be it friend or spouse. Yea, there have been many such. But do you know of them, Oh Lord? Do You know? For I am speaking of Love different from that suffered by your Son. I am speaking of the love of a man for a woman, incarnating totally in the flesh. I am claiming that such a love is as divine as He who bore Your cross! Do You hear it, Lord, does it reach Your ears?"

"I hear."

"If You hear, Oh Lord, then speak. Nay, do not speak, for You speak enough, being a Father-God and full of words. Being one who begins with the Word and is the Word become flesh, do not speak but act! Be like a woman! Be like myself! Help to assuage pain, help to fulfill love! Help to take off the cross agony! Can you do that?–

"You do not answer. I can understand that, for I have challenged You to love like a mortal, or at least, to understand it. I know Oh Lord, that You incarnated Yourself in Your Son, and You know what it means to be a Man! I know that! I know how You suffered and died, through your Son! But do You know what it is to love like a man! Or worse, to love like a woman! That you do not answer–Nor should You for, I think, You cannot. And why not? Because You have not experienced that kind of love?–But no. Oh Lord, forgive me! I have forgotten my own experience! I, Daughter, have forgotten Your Other Son, who is really Son-Brother to You! The Charioteer! He of the dark mien and great passion! He who is totally devoted to Love! He who taught me everything about Love and lives love totally! He whose crosses of agony are multitudinous in the Underworld!

"Oh, God the Father in Heaven, forgive me! I understand. I have that flash of insight which releases me. For You know about your Son-Brother in the Underworld. And You know the many men and the many women who have borne the cross of love! You know it even though they live in the Underworld!

"But do You know the pain of the rape? Of the agony? Of having one's belly torn open? Of living that cross which is the hangman's noose of pain? Of being misunderstood? Of having the world put its own meaning onto you and then punishing you for it? Of being a cuckold, or a producer of cuckolds?

"Ah, now I feel the pain of the rage of Sir Lancelot! I feel his pain and rage at You. I feel it in my belly, just as he felt it in his heart, his eyes. I feel it. And now I see you, Lord, as the vicious, Son-sacrificing Being that You are! You let man suffer for Your mistakes, Your misunderstandings! Lord, You are not omniscient, I know! And You know that! Ever since Job! But then You bragged of Your power, of all that You had created, etcetera, etcetera! While poor Job was crushed in his pain! You bragged about Your power! Yes, we know. The consequence of that was the Sacrifice of Your Son! But that was using someone else as a scapegoat for Your own failings! Wake up, Oh Lord! Wake up!...

"Perhaps I misjudge You. Maybe You are not omnipotent as well. You talked endlessly to Job about Your power. Perhaps that was like a little boy who brags about his power when, in reality, he is unsure of it. Can that be true? Are You Lord, the Father, like a little boy who likes to think of himself as powerful but is aware that there are limits to it? Perhaps so. I had not thought of that. God is not omniscient, perhaps He is not omnipotent; perhaps he cannot free man from the horror of the suffering of love. Perhaps He cannot do anything about it–The Charioteer would know. I must ask Him!"

"I and the Charioteer are One!"

"Words, Lord. Words. Is it true? That you suffer Love, as Lancelot did? Then tell him so! Show him! Support him. I entreat you, Lord. I beg of You. I pray to You."

A long silence.

"The Lord of Heaven does not answer. I, the Grail, have noted it. Daughter, you have done well. You have all done well for Lancelot, the Knight. And he feels it. You can do no more this time. It is in the hands, finally, of that God who dwells in Heaven. Let us wait for His response."

A voice thunders into the pregnant silence.

"Grail, You are wrong. It is not in the hands of that 'Father who dwells in Heaven'. Rather, it is I who speak. It is I. And do you know who that 'I' is? Listen, Sir Lancelot; listen Knight of the Lake; listen to me. I am the Charioteer. I am the God of Loving of which Daughter speaks! I am He. And she speaks truly of me for she has lived with me, around me, and of me, for a very long time. You, Lancelot, listen too. For you have lived me. You know full well what it is to love. It is I whose fate you have lived; it is I whom you have served when you thought you were serving love. It is true. But do not repent it, for you have served that which I also serve! For I am the Son and the Brother of God who serves love in the flesh, in life, in suffering, in agony, in passion. I know whereof you speak, how you have lived. I know it. Yes, Sir Lancelot, it is known. Not known in life, in the world, among men, but it is known by me, in the Underworld. And, it is also known by that Father in Heaven who is rendered speechless by it. Know, too, that it is known by the other son, Jesus, whom you have also served. You have served the cause of the Chariot and the Charioteer; you have served the totality, as a living reality, as a reality of love. Stand and hold your head high, Sir Lancelot! Stand up, for I count you a servant of Love. And, in love, a servant of God!"

KING ARTHUR TELL HIS PAIN AND SHOWS A POSSIBLE WAY OUT

"Thus is Lancelot, Knight of the Lake, healed of his pain," said the Grail. "The thrust in the thigh, the wound of the lance are healed by Chariot and Charioteer, container and contained. Look now, oh four, look now, Son of the Knight and Dog, Mother and Daughter, for the Knight of the Lake and the Charioteer embrace. In that embrace, in the brotherly union of God and Man, in love, there is healing. So you four, look and be not dismayed, for you have participated therein.

"Turn now, to another corner of the Limboid World, the Purgatorial Place of Pain. See you there another figure, another man lost in thought. See now, Arthur, King of the Round Table."

"Welcome, Grail, and welcome friends," said King Arthur. "I have been forewarned of your coming. Forewarned? A strange word to use for those who presume to be of help to me. Be not offended at my language nor at my expectation. They are as habit to me, having lived so long in fear and anger and suspicion. Lived? Yes, I can say it, for even though I am dead and pass my lifeless time in the Limbo of loveless thought, I feel the same as I did when alive. For so did I live for years. So did I live, keeping my fear and wrath and suspicion to myself while pretending to be the wise and kind King of the Table Round.

"The word 'pretending' may startle you. For none knew that I knew. Yes, I knew for many years of the betrayal by my wife and my favorite Knight, the son-brother of my dreams and plans. I knew and I pretended not to know. For to know would have meant to take action. It would have been demanded. And, with action comes death or pain, or worse. Death and pain were required of me when the time came. Everyone knows the story. I behaved as the situation demanded, not according to my heart. My heart said otherwise. For my heart concerned itself with pain and love for both Guinevere and Lancelot.

"My heart concerned itself, too, with guilt, for being a poor King and leader and not the true leader of the Knights and the Round Table. My heart spoke of sadness and my own pain and cross–for whatever I did would be wrong. To act would be to remain a cuckold, a poltroon, a fool, and worse–to allow injustice to reign in my land. To allow gossip and horrible slander to issue forth from every knave in the Kingdom and in Christiandom as well. To be humiliated, scorned, laughed at, from afar, from behind my back. Ah, that was the worst–to allow injustice to reign in my land. To allow gossip and horrible slander to issue forth from every knave in the Kingdom and in Christiandom as well. To be humiliated, scorned, laughed at, from afar, from behind my back. Ah, that was the worst–to be laughed at and to be betrayed, behind my back. Never to be confronted directly, never to do battle and die. Awful agony. Awful pain of a cross.

"But with all, these feelings are those of a martyr. These carryings of conflict, of pain, and of service, selfless and caring, are like those of our Lord, Jesus Christ. In this I performed the *imitatio Christi*, in this I was a saint. This too I knew, and in this, and in my pleasure and pride in such a carrying of a cross, I despised myself. For I hated the very idea of such a martyr. Was I not the King? Was it not I who pulled the sword from the stone? Did I not wield that sword? The power and authority? The discrimination? The capacity to wrest, with either gentle or deft touch, the power from the depths of nature to see what was needed? Did I not have the consciousness to see the state of the world?

"Was it not I who had the vision of the Round Table? Oh Knights bent upon the service of God? Of Gentlement? Of those in the service of love as well as passion? Of integrity as well as courage? Of strength as well as gentleness? Was I not a carrier of an image of a man serving God in the deepest Christian way? 'Within you' and 'Among you' as a private quest and community service? Did I not originate these things? And was I not chosen by birth and by example to be the leader? Not a martyr, by God!

"Such feelings of mine led not to guilt, nor to carrying the cross of Christ! No! They led to wrath! The led to anger, rebellion and rage! They led to frustrated desire to scream, to lash out in righteous and powerful words and deeds of revenge, of proclamation s to what I knew it and admitted it. Yet I was used and abused, laughed at and made a fool of. Rage! Rage. Revenge. Righteous boiling of anger. It consumed me. It consumes me still. I understand. I am compassionate. I treasure Lancelot and know his suffering and truth. But I long to kill him again and again throughout Eternity. I shall always treasure and adore Guinevere, the most remarkable and beautiful woman I have ever known; but I long to slap her, kick her and taunt her with hard words for ever and ever. And most of all, I long to strike at my enemies, those who scorned me, laughed at me, those who chortled and judged me behind my back. Then I long to slice up in small pieces and serve the pieces to each other and slice them up once again. This I long to do. My wrath and my righteous indignation consume me, and I cannot free myself of it.

"Thus do I sit here in Purgatory, unable to move, unable to free myself of my bondage to wrath, to righteous indignation, to frustrated longing for revenge, to redemption of my spirit and my good name. This is the man to whom you come. This is the poor yet powerful creature that the Grail brings you to aid. Thus am I. If you think that you can aid me, please do. I must add that I am doubtful of it. Not because I doubt your capacities–no. I doubt, rather, both friendship and care. For these have been ruined for me.

"My friends have turned out to be my worst enemies. And those I have cared for have proved to care only for themselves. So the wounds to my soul leave me doubting and suspicious. I doubt friendship, I doubt love, I doubt caring. I doubt, even, healing. Knowing this of me, and accepting this from me, I welcome you to my kingdom of emptiness. I welcome you to my barren cell of conflict. I welcome you to the vision of a man once King, now nothing. I welcome you to the sight of pain and rage.

"One thing more. I am not utterly barren of a way out. Or, that is no more. Just lately, at the time the Grail forewarned me of your arrival, Son of the Knight and Dog, Mother and Daughter, there came to me, I know not how, the spirit of Merlin. That magic man, that companion of deeds of the spirit and thought, the wondrous gentlemen whom I admired more than any other in the world, even Lancelot, I hasten to add–that Magic man presented me with the little packets you see here. Three packets he gave me, each with a title–Anger, Rebellion, Metamorphosis. Within each packet he said, are two pictures, two images from magical cards which tell fortunes, which portray life, which do other wondrous things. But I am not to use them for these purposes. I am to reflect.

"I am to think and meditate, he said, upon the contents of these packets. I am to look at these pictures within each packet and reconcile in my thinking what they purport, what they suggest, what they convey. This may be a way out of my purgatory, out of my burden and painful state of rage and suspicion and fear. Strange, isn't it, that my good friend and companion of the spiritual world should offer me, as a way redemption, that which I do best, to reflect and ponder? To reflect and ponder my way out of the evils of emotion, the agonies of feeling? Hard to believe. But because Merlin offers it, I will try.

"This is my task. This came to me at the same moment that the Grail informed me that you were coming. Perhaps you can help me. Perhaps you can listen to my meditation, take in what I say in my struggling reflections about Anger, Rebellion, and Metamorphosis, and give me the benefit of your reaction, your criticism, your support. Eh? In truth I want not criticism; I have had so much of it, mostly destructive. In truth I want not criticism; I have had so much of it, mostly destructive. In truth I want not support; it too has been of no use. In truth I want not reaction; few have helped me. In truth I am suspicious, but I will try to listen to you, as well as to myself and the pictures, if you will accompany me, for this, it seems, both Merlin and the Grail intend. And these two I trust, no others. What say you?

"You all nod agreement. You accept. Let us, then, begin."

THE MEDITATION BEGINS AND ARTHUR IS CONFRONTED

"Here is the first card, The Tower. Look at it," said King Arthur. "A large tower, being hit by lightning, and having its top blown off. Fire comes out of the windows and smoke and clouds billow out. A great Crown, as if it were at the top of the tower, is blown off. Two people are falling from the tower, one with a crown. The tower stands alone upon a high and desolate mountain. So does the picture represent itself. What does this mean, where to begin?

"Ah Merlin, I hear your voice, you speak. It sounds as if you are reading from a book. Are you mumbling? Speak up, please!"

"The Tower–of Babel–of speech," said Merlin. "The mouth as organ of speech, the power of utterance. Out of it comes the issues of life. The Tower–The Tower of Babel. The Lightning-struck Tower. This is the Lightning-struck tower, the House of God, where human speech was confounded–the lightning is the power, the destructive iconoclastic force which tears down the structures of ancient custom and tradition. It breaks down existing forms in order to make room for new ones."

"So, Merlin, so do you speak. So this is the Tower of Babel. This is the Tower of Tradition, of a House of God where Tradition lives. And it is struck, it is hit by lightning, by another force of God; a lightning flash of emotion, of new truth, of inspiration. Does it knock down ignorance, old beliefs, or does it destroy that which is valuable and good? I do not know.

"But I see; I understand what it means. Man wills, he builds, he uses his ambition and his knowledge to build great structures. Nor is he just ambitious and self-willed: he builds houses to God, churches, and great monuments. And these are confounded by a stroke of lightning, by wrath, by inspiration, by power, beyond good and evil. Thus perhaps was my own Tower, my own Round Table. Did I not build a structure, even ones of the Church, so that a man could imitate Christ in a manly, spiritual way, as a gentleman, and still love, still serve, still be a warrior-priest of God, a ruler and battler, as much as could priests and monks? Did I not initiate this? And did not Lancelot follow me? Was I not such a Lancelot, with my vision, in the beginning? And it was all confounded. The Round Table was broken by horses, by the passion of my wife and friend, by violence. My wrath continues. I am wrathful at them, at those who seemed to follow my vision but destroyed it, at those of enemies who laughed at me, who gave only lip service.

"All right. Yes, Merlin, and yes, you four, I understand this picture, this symbol, I see the transitoriness of structures of ambition, of the building up of towers of speech or deed, and having them broken by nature in raw form. I see it. But how reflect, how meditate? What was it that ruined the structure? My wife and Lancelot? No, it was their passion, their love, which could not be contained in my structure, in my petty vision! Yes, now I comprehend it! I envisioned men of spirit and men of courage who would go forth to seek and serve the Lord and find the Grail; but I reckoned only on their capacity for chastity, for self-denial, for serving women, serving love, without having the fulfillment of love in the instinctual, sexual way. The image was almost priestly. I saw that men could love and marry, but my vision did not include, did not sanctify, sexual love, and sexual love outside marriage. In this I was as much priest as any clergyman, any vicar of the Church.

"And the lightning of passion, the virility of Lancelot, the diverse lusts of Guinevere–these broke my structure, my vessel of willful holding of the passions, of keeping them enchained. They loved me, it is true, but they could not contain their own lightning. Thus did they fall like these two figures in the picture. And thus did I fall as well. And thus is the crown torn away. I see it, Merlin, I see it, God! Was it You who tore down the structure I built for Your sake? Was it You who sent this lightning, this powerful natural force of sexual passion to break the structure which I built? No answer. I suspect it is true, nonetheless.

"But wrath, and anger–these are fiery passions as well. How do these enter in? How do these tears down the structures of man? Of course, in the same way. By man shrieking out in rage, by stabbing and fighting and attacking whatever institution exists. But I was clever with my institution, was I not? I built it without tearing down Church, or Marriage, or Priesthood. Chivalry there was, Knights and Manhood, without destroying the structures. Except for the fires of Mars, of War! And the fires of Venus, of Love! These united to destroy my structure. These fires I sought to quell, to spiritualize–but they would not permit it. They would not be contained as I insisted upon it. So Mars and Venus came like lightning.

"Violence and sex, the passions of struggle and love broke in. They came from outside did they not? The sex and love from my closest ones, Lancelot and Guinevere. The violence from my other Knights and from enemies, when they learned of my being betrayed, or suspected it. And what did I do about it? I chose violence. I chose to fight, hoping to thrust my sword into the body of Lancelot! At that same moment, I lost my true Kingship.

"But, what to do with this wrath? How to find again the love and sexuality in myself? These I must take back into myself and create a new vision! I must be as I once was, as a young Lancelot myself, and forge a new sword, a new vessel, a new Tower, but not of Babel. I must build a vessel where the lightning would come as a passionate fire, but gentle, too.

"The fire must touch the Tower, enlivening it with light and warmth, or if too powerful, then touch a lightning rod and safely find its way into Mother Earth, fertilizing her thick substance. Then my words would be as rich and thick and full of passion and earth as nature itself, not dry and ambitious, not built upon slave labor, not built upon an effort of will and ambition, not a mere conquest of nature, not just the subduing of Mars and Venus!

"Yes, I see it, oh Merlin. Yes I see it, oh friends. I should, in truth, go to Lancelot and to Guinevere and embrace them. I should bow to them as an incarnation of Mars and Venus whose love for me and my vision was great, but whose fiery and healthy passions could not be contained in the willful scheme of Church and Man which I built!

"My anger subsides–Merlin, you were right. Let me now look at the other card, Justice.

"Wait, Arthur, King of the Round Table! I, Daughter, will speak. But my speech will not have the loving kindness of Dog or Son of the

Knight. My words will not bow to your arrogant and pompous self-reflection! For though I am called loving and it is true, though I am called caring and that is true, I do not like what I see of you nor your love, and I am angry. I am angry for the sake of Lancelot and for myself! I prefer Lancelot with his pain and conflict, with his impotent efforts to change the situation, with his love, to all your concerns about your vision, your beliefs, your Tower, your rage. You sit upon the mountain, just like your Tower and you continue with a Babel of words! Where is the longing for that beauteous woman who was your wife and consort? Where can I hear a word of love for that queen? Where is the longing for that beauteous woman who was your wife and consort? Where can I hear a word of praise and deep sorrow for the loss of your friend? Where, in short, do I hear you, Arthur the man, and you, Arthur the King? Where can I hear about your need, your hurt, your longing, your personal love, and not about a great impersonal vision? Where, then, can I hear it?

"You are silent, Arthur. You are stilled by my words. I am glad For it is time that your words be stilled. It is time that you took in the words and pain of others. It is time that you heard and listened and not only to your own vision. Round Table and gallantry! Piety and prayer! Service and Sacrifice! Courage and integrity! My God! That is a man for you! And overly pious and churchy one at that! Where are need and love and passion in your vision? Where is the personal, the individual, the very ordinary, swampy, down-to-earth feeling, the pain? I have been in Hell and I know it, I know what it is like there. Have you? You claim to have suffered pain in the conflict over Guinevere. Where does it show? You claim to have known. But where does it show?

"You are right, Daughter. I am silenced. What you say is true. I have felt, I have longed for, I have pained, but I have kept my silence about that. Not altogether silent, it is true, but more silent than I really felt, and more than one might expect. And why? Because my vision was more important than my wife!"

"Ah, that is it, Arthur King! Now we come to it. I suspected that something was not right in it all. Your vision more important than your wife! No wonder she was attracted away from you! No wonder she let herself be enchanted and adored by Lancelot! For he loved her, he desired her, he claimed her and adored her! Not only did he not hold any vision or belief as more important than she, he violated his own vision of Christian purity, devotion and service because of her! He sacrificed his vision because of her! No wonder she loved him and stayed with him and would not give him up! He loved her while you loved your vision!"

"Daughter, you are hard. You are cruel and vicious with me. What is worse, you are right. Where was my romance, where was my love, where were the days in forest and glen, by stream and brook, with flower and tree, pebble and stone, where I could be with her, adore her, devour her, tell poems to her? Where were those days? Gone, for I was busy with my Round Table. I was busy with my plans, my Knights, my vision! No wonder the Tower broke. Now then, here was Lancelot, the man, who lived love and its pain, while I merely had a vision of it. I weep. But my coldness is not true. I wept before, many times. I wept and wept for years, but in private and before no eyes because I know of their love and I knew of their passion, but I did nothing about it. Intentionally! Was that not a suffering of love, was that not a passion and a hell? Well, Daughter, I have responded and I have admitted. Now you respond to me, and tell me if my knowing and keeping silent, of my carrying of the pain of our threesome in quiet and alone is not a passion of love as well?"

"It is, King Arthur, Knight, it is! It is the kind of love that Mother knows better than I. See there, she nods compassionately; it is a love indeed. I acknowledge it. Stand then for your love and acknowledge your passion of pain and suffering for love. For you loved both in your way, by not interfering! That is a form of love. But not enough, I say, not enough! For I, Daughter, have seen more. I have seen Lancelot and I know. I have seen the Charioteer and I know. Love is not only enduring and suffering. It is a passion fulfilled! It is not only duty and obligation and sacrifice, which is the martyr of God on the Cross, but it is also the deep swamp of underworld lust and ripping desire, of rape of spirit and flesh, of greed and thirst beyond awareness. It is being hung in a Garden of Eden in Hell. Of enjoying everything and nothing. It is agony of desire and frustration. That is love, and of this, Arthur, you know nothing! Would you like to know? Ask then of Lancelot. Ask then of Guinevere, for without that your vision is pale straw!"

"Daughter, I am silenced once again. You are right. Daughter, I love you! Your words of hard anger, of complaint and criticism are as love to me. For they come from deep, I know. They come from your love of Lancelot, they come from your own experience in Hell. Most of all, they come from a place in you which is hard on me, but loving.

Daughter, you too are like a Guinevere to me! You speak hard words but love me! Would that she had spoken those words to me! Would that she had confronted me and challenged me and brought me out of my high and mighty place, our of my foolish belief that my vision was all and right now! But no, that passion was not there. Perhaps it went to Lancelot. Probably so. Yes...Ah, that only she could have loved us both with such a passion. Then his love would be elevated to that of a God, and my vision would be that of a God!

"Oh Lord, do You hear what I say? Oh Lord, this woman, Daughter, has touched me and I have come to where the center is at last. Oh Lord, I turn to you in pain and agony. I needed love. I needed the passion and confrontation of Guinevere, I needed it! I need it to serve You! We, Lancelot and I, both needed it–he to divinize his love, I to divinize my vision! But he was truer, Lord, he was truer. For he loved Guinevere and gave up his vision, and thus deserved her love, while I stayed true to a decaying vision, one that would not serve the needs of either God or man! Lord, this woman, Daughter, the servant of love, passionate, has reached me. I thank you, Daughter, I thank you.

"And you, Mother, you hold my head as I weep, like a Mother, though not Mother to me, in age or being or spirit. You understand. For you too know my needs without words. You too know what I could not, cannot–for I too am a child and unable, though a King.

ARTHUR CRUSHED

"Merlin, you come and urge me on. You do not let me rest in the loving warmth of Mother. You do not let me take in and digest the words of Daughter. You urge me on. So be it. Amen. I will look, then, at the card of Justice, and go on.

"There, the card: Justice, in the form of a crowned woman sitting upon a throne. She wears no blindfold, but holds instead, a sword and the scales of Libra. She wears the red outer garment of Mars–action and work–and the green inner garment of Venus–imagination and love. So, Justice is a woman? And the Venus of Love? It is she who holds both Sword and Balance? Hard to take in. She wears, too, a crown with three turrets, and a square blue jewel. This crown of three–Arthur, Lancelot and Guinevere? And the jewel of four–perhaps she can help me further in my quest.

"Speak, then, Justice! Speak, woman! Tell me, if you can, what there is of Justice in this world! Tell me, if you can, of the Justice of

Love! Tell me of the Justice of rulership! Tell me of the Justice of the sword, being a leader and a discriminating guide; and of the Balance, holding a pair of opposites in careful order so that there shall be right action and right thinking. Tell me, though I believe nothing! I have had no Justice!"

"So you speak, Arthur, little King!" said Justice. "So you speak! What know you of Justice, power, of Love? What know you of right action, of weighing of principles, of the carrying of a Trinity, of a Quaternity? Nothing! You ask for Justice and you know nothing! You do not even know that in Hebrew, the language of God, there is no word for Charity, it is Justice! Justice is that which belongs!"

"You speak thus, woman? You dare? You who claim to be both Justice and Venus? How dare you! You have brought nothing but despair and destruction to me. You have brought only hard pain and worse agony. You have brought nothing! I look at you and think of Guinevere! I think of the pain and horror she has brought me. I think of the emptiness and my need for her love, her care, which was lacking for so long. I think of Love as a horrible thing. It is selfishness, it is woman who gives, but only on her own terms. Woman always takes for herself, and herself alone! Her vision is only of her own greed, her own need. I am horrified and pained and resentful. I retch in pain and horror at it! And you speak to me of Justice! You? Who are you to even come near me with such drivel?"

"Ah, you speak at last of your pain! You speak at last of your need for love. You speak at last of feeling abandoned, abused and unjustly treated! Speak then, Arthur, Oh Great King, Oh Arthur who was above and beyond everyone! Arthur who could live alone upon his mountaintop. Arthur who had a vision for all Christendom, even mankind! Oh Arthur, King of the Round Table! Now, Arthur, reduced to a sniveling, needy, pained child! Speak now Arthur, of that place!"

"I will speak! And I will weep. But my words cannot cry out enough. My need is from my belly. My need is from places where great Kings to not speak from. My need is wordless. But it is not just that of a child who needs comfort and understanding. No. It is also of a man, of a King. It is of a man who seeks understanding, of a man who has given all that he could, and is tired and frustrated, and needs so much. He needs the love of woman, deeper and greater and wider than he has ever had before.

"He needs a loving Justice, not a finger-pointing, judging Justice who can only complain and criticize and demand. He needs so much that he cannot even speak of his need. He needs, perhaps, to be silent. He needs to let his words slip into silence, and let the silent tears convey his need. To whom? To God? No. For that image of God is dead! That God who was served in the Table Round is gone. Gone is chivalry, gone is self-sacrifice, gone is service. These are all hollow and pale with me. Gone is that vision. For I am left with a feeling of emptiness, a feeling of longing, and a feeling of loathing and hatred for all those who–but enough of words. I will be silent. Let it be you who speak, Justice-Venus, if that is who you are. Speak if you can.

"So, silence is your answer! Good! Then card of Justice, card of Venus, your imperatives are reduced to silence. I am glad. I will have no more of finger-pointing. I will have no more of judgments about me, and of my inadequacies, or of my grandiosity. I will have no more of it. For I am a man, and a leader. I am a man of vision, of stature, and I have failed. But I am not to be reduced to idiocy, nor condemned, nor blamed for what is–the fault of God–?

"There, have I said it? Have I said the awful thing? Do I now blame God for the failings of love, of human warmth and compassion? For the miscarriage of justice? I do. What is that image of God that is no longer viable? Christ, Jesus, saint? People are awful, Lord. They are mean and vicious and selfish and self-seeking. They are petty and back-biting and long to reduce each other in battle for vanity and possessions. That, Lord, is how they are. And they are made in Your image! They are unjust and in Your image! God must be vain and petty and back-biting and self-seeking! All that man is, God must be. All man's virtues, and vices, come from God. It must be true. So, Goodbye Christianity, goodbye Trinity, goodbye to that vision!

"But whatever God is, man must be, too. Capable of infinite compassion, infinite love, infinite wisdom. All these, too? Yes. Not as man is in one life but in an ever-developing life of man and mankind! I can see it: God becoming Man in all men. God is not in one man alone, the Christ, but in all men and in the ever-developing all-time of all men, particular and universal! That is a place for a new vision! God omnipotent, in all men! God omniscient, in all men! God all-loving, in all men! But not at any one moment in any man! These are words, words, words. Help me, Oh Lord. Help me! Inside, outside, all around me! Help me!

"Friends, did you see, did you hear it, too? The Lord sent me a vision of Guinevere. From afar. She looked and spoke to me. She told me a strange tale. She said that she could either have been with me totally or not at all. But since she could not be with me totally, because of her love for Lancelot, she would be with me not at all. It was for that she became a nun. That, friends, is what she said. I know not if it was she or merely my imagination of her, but that is what I heard and saw–I am alone. And devastated. But quiet. I will be quiet for ten thousand more years. Thus my purgatory. Thus friends, I am back where I was when you and the Grail came to me. I am devastated. And quiet. It ends that neither Lancelot nor I have Guinevere at all. She belongs to God. So be it. Amen. I will retreat.

"I see a small light. Woman, you are Justice. Woman, you are Love. Woman, you are the power of the Sword and the Balance. For woman is fate, and life. And I, great King, great man of High Mountain, must submit. I have no vision, I have no power. I am still."

GUINEVERE ENTERS; HER TRIAL

"I, the Grail, now speak. In your stillness Arthur, you have found yet another reconciliation of Tower and Justice, of form-broken and form-harmonized, though you do not know it. For you have found strength in your wrath, firmness in your stance. And yet, you have been broken and break yourself; you give up your will. You sacrifice your arrogant claim to another force. It is enough for now. Leave off your meditation for the moment, and attend a scene in another part of the Limboid Realm.

"Come too, Mother and Daughter, Son of the Knight and Dog, come with me to a place where you might guess I would lead you. It is, of course, to the place of Guinevere, Queen. Listen now, and hear her struggle."

"Welcome, Grail, and welcome, you four," said Guinevere. "I hope to learn from you, to be healed by you. And you, Arthur, far away as behind a glass; I know you hear what I say, yet you cannot come close to me. So strange is this, in the Purgatorial Place. We both know and don't know. We both experience each other and do not. Would that the blood of life and emotion could course among us here! But it cannot. We must either provide that for ourselves, within ourselves, or get it from the spirits of those brave mortals, like you four, who can come to us and participate with us. God bless you!

"Arthur was right; he did hear me, even through a glass. It was true, as I tried to tell him–I could be with him altogether or not at all. Since I could not be with him altogether, because of my love for Lancelot, I chose to be with neither. And so I became a nun. So here I am in Purgatory, thinking, reflecting, meditating. I am doomed to chew, to understand, to redeem, before I can move out into life or death, into heaven or hell. Doomed, because, unlike with Arthur or even with Lancelot the Lover, such reflection is the death of me! A man can think, reflect, ponder and feel that he is still in life. It even makes his life meaningful. For me it is a death, and worse than death, for it is a place of no contact, of aloneness.

Yes my aloneness has meant much to me, I must confess. My thinking has calmed me, has made me less torn with the pain and agony of loving two men and destroying both of them with it. Yes, destroying both of them! That is how is resulted, is it not? Even though I would like to think otherwise, I am forced to conclude that both I and my love have been destructive. A great man of love, Lancelot, has lost his esteem, his friend, his vision, and his life. A great man of vision, Arthur, has lost his Kingdom, his esteem, his friend, his vision, and his life. And both because of me. I think of myself at times, as a witch. More accurately, I feel as if a witch inside me is crucifying me or is herself being crucified. In other words, I feel that it is I who am being torn apart, rather than that I have torn apart others. These have been my thoughts.

"Do you know what else I have thought? I have been undergoing a perpetual trial. Every day, in one form or another, there comes to me a judge, an interrogator, and group of jurors. I am continually interrogated, demanded of, judged and condemned. Then I am tried anew. Daily. But there has been no one to defend me. It goes on endlessly. That is Justice as it has come to me. Venus-Justice, with a sword and balance? Love as justice, weeding out that which is decayed and providing harmony and right action in the new? Not my experience! Love as Justice, maybe, hard and relentless, saying that my love is destructive, but only that, only that. That is where I am, my friends, that is where I am–continual trial, continual condemnation, continual agony. Yet withall, time to think, to reflect. For even a trial cannot go on all day long and all night long as well! Even in Purgatory, it is as if Judge, Prosecutor, and Jurors need rest, too!

"Let me tell how it has been, if I can. The trials have been complicated and my thinking has been confused at times. Thinking, after all, has not been my main activity–I have left that to Arthur, I fear–so when it has emerged it has been muddy, unclear, judgmental, agonized, emotional. But enough of apology, here is how it has appeared.

"First there is the Judge as a snake. He is big and black with one large red eye. He keeps saying 'Choose, choose!' What he is asking me to choose is more complicated than you might imagine. It is, of course, for me to choose between Arthur and Lancelot, my husband or my lover; my warmth, cozy security and friendship with Arthur versus the passion, intensity and romance with Lancelot–between these the Snake-Judge asks me to choose. That is obvious–as if I cannot have both.

"But there is another way this Snake-Judge makes me choose. Do you know how? It is between two forms of being a woman, that is how! I see myself, on the one hand, as a mother, warm and tender, caring for a little child. On the other hand, I see myself as a passionate woman, with a flaming jewel upon my chest. In that image I am intense, involved, vibrant with inner sensations and passions, ecstatic. The first mother-state is care for others, for the child in others, and, in truth, in myself as well. The second ecstatic state is not just that of a daughter; it also involves caring but it originates from within, is centered within. The one is outward flowing and caring (even martyring); the other is inward-flowing and passionate (even selfish). The Snake-Judge says that I must choose between them or be utterly guilty.

"You might think that these two states are parallel with my relationship and feelings toward Arthur and Lancelot. To a certain degree that is true. Lancelot does fire my passions more than Arthur, and I do feel more secure and tender with Arthur–much of the time. But it is not entirely true. For I have had great romance and tenderness with Arthur and, in the early years of our marriage, there was great passion as well. He was as father and son to me while I was daughter and mother, too. But I have also been tender with Lancelot, cared for and adored his boyishness. And I have been daughter to Lancelot as well, enjoying my awakening feelings with him and his tender caring. So, the pairing is not perfect. No.

"What I have concluded in my reflection and suffering is that the Snake-Judge will not let me be whole. He insists upon my being separated, split, dual. He seems to be like the snake of Paradise who always opted for the two, the two trees of the Garden of Eden, rather than the One that the Lord allowed our first parents. So, this Snake-Judge will not let me be whole. He will not let me be Mother and Daughter, tender and passionate for another and for myself. He keeps me forever divided...No, not true. He wants me to choose one or the other, to be only half. And that is the Snake-Judge who to me is a devil saying 'Choose, choose!"

"The other judge who comes to me is that figure of Venus-Justice whom you already know. She comes and shakes her head saying I have not loved enough. I am a bad wife, not loving my husband enough. I am a bad mistress, not loving my lover enough. I am destructive and it is obvious to all. Did not my love lead to death and destruction? I have betrayed two great men, a man of vision and a man of love. In truth, I am the devil himself. Thus speaks the second judge, your Venus-Justice!

"There is my trial every day. Snake-Judge and Venus-Judge alternate as judge and prosecutor. Sometimes in my trial, these two come together. To be prosecuted is to be found guilty. To have a list of charges, of blames against me, is to be found guilty. 'J'accuse' and 'guilty' occur at the same moment. Yes, I know that this is unfair, a miscarriage of justice even, but who is there to defend me? The jurors simply wait; they do nothing, but are unspokenly compliant in this judgment of me. I am condemned each time, as you can see. For here I am, condemned to Purgatory. The life of the three of us is over and my wickedness has brought us all here! Blame and guilt take me.

"So friends, you four, you see my trial, you see my guilt, you see my punishment. Perhaps you can be a more responsive jury. Perhaps you can break into my agony of continual trial and judgment and guilt. Perhaps you can finally free me from this Purgatory. I must confess, I would prefer to be in Hell or Heaven or back in life. There at least I would be involved, living my love, and not forever on trial, forever punished, but never fulfilling the penalty of my crimes with my punishment. So, friends, speak to me. Tell me of our verdict of me."

"I, Dog, will speak. Quickly will I speak; even faster than the Son of the Knight. Being can speak quickly sometimes, even more quickly than Becoming. And Being can speak to Non-Being. Pardon me, Guinevere, I grow abstract and symbolic, like a man (that I am), but I speak as a Dog and for life and to get you out of this Purgatory. But I too will use my Manhood, and my capacity to abstract, so listen.

"You, Guinevere, are not guilty in my eyes. You have lived your life, borne the conflict, tried to love as best you could. You remind me indeed of Jesus on the Cross, who was also despised by all. He was blamed unjustly, had all horribleness put upon him with calumny and blame. So are you, Queen Guinevere, you are a lady Christ! I proclaim it! I, Dog, and God-Man, proclaim that I have seen God, I have seen the suffering of Jesus and that yours is every bit as great as His! But enough of my proclamations. What I want to say is that in keeping the two, the two men, the two states of feminine being, you have suffered like God, the Son, and are, thus, elevated. Ask, better, why that Snake-Son made you choose! Ask, rather, what he might be getting out of it! I can assure you, as an animal, that he is an animal too and is judging and keeping you there out of his own interests and not out of an abstract Justice!"

"But what would his interest be?"

"I, Son of the Knight, will answer that! I am in full accord with my friend, Dog, for he speaks rightly and well when he says that you are on the same level as Jesus Christ! For you serve love just as He did. I, in my becoming, can glimpse an answer to your question about the Snake-Judge. Listen.

"Is he not a creature from the Underworld? Is he not the arrogant devil who makes you one-sided? Does he not go against God the Father? And does he not torment you? Of course. But, I believe that the is in the service of the mysterious Charioteer. He serves the dark side of God, the rejected God of love and passion and dark mysteries who lives in the Underworld. He forces one-sidedness in his one-eyed animal nature. But you, with your two-eyed, two-sided feminine nature are the match of him! Don't you see? He is the Binarius, the two-faced, deceptive creature who longs for unity, at any price. He does so out of his own pain and rejection, of having been judged and cast out by God, the Father. But you, in carrying our own two-fold nature, have, in truth, been just as duplex as he, with the same duplicity and complexity! You have carried it, however, and have thus been serving the Charioteer, whether the Snake-Judge want it or not. In short, you are higher than he! Can you hear it, Guinevere! Can you accept it? Not guilty, Guinevere, I proclaim. Not guilty by reason of love, and serving a higher consciousness.

GUINEVERE CONTINUES; HER REALIZATION

"They are good to you, Queen Guinevere; Son of the Knight and Dog, they are kind. I, Mother, see it. I know that they are tender and thoughtful; they do appreciate and admire you. So they judge you 'not guilty.' But I do not so judge you. I am not so appreciative of your conflict, of your suffering, nor of your value. Perhaps that is because I am a woman, and I know how we women are. We are not so good and loving and loyal and generous and all-suffering as some men, particularly such loving men, think. We are, in fact, rather self-seeking. Indeed, what looks like our martyrdom is, in truth, only that which we must do. It goes beyond pleasure or pain, or even care and service, because we serve something much higher and that gives us pleasure. Any woman knows that the service of love is everything. So, Guinevere, I am less impressed with your suffering and service than are Dog and Son of the Knight. I too have loved and served, as has my daughter. So I will be more harsh with you.

"In truth, I find you guilty. I find you guilty of not loving enough, just as you have found yourself. I agree with your self-condemnation and I would find you guilty, as Venus-Justice says; but dear Lady Guinevere, I must also say that I admire your courage, your devotion and your attempt to love. Do you know why? Because you have tried to love as few women have. You have tried to love two men, and carnally. Not only carnally, but spiritually. Not only spiritually, but romantically. Not only romantically, but maternally. Guinevere, of course all women will judge you, for you have taken on something few can! Guinevere, you have tried to love as both Mother and Daughter, you have tried to love as a God-Woman! I salute you and bow to you for this. For even if you have failed, have not loved enough to make both men happy, or make a real change in Camelot, or bring a new religious feeling to the world, you have tried and been true to your effort. You are a great woman, and I admire you enormously! Guinevere, you can love. Be guilty, but be proud!"

"I thank you, Mother. I thank you for your kind and honest words. Your appreciation of what I have tried to do and where I have failed make my eyes moisten. More important, your words lighten my heart for I feel understood. I feel appreciated and kindly chastened at the same time. Such a vote of guilty is helpful to me. For such a condemnation I can be grateful. I thank you again, Mother."

"But I find you guilty as well, Guinevere. I, Daughter, also find you guilty, but not of lack of loving. As Mother has said, you have loved enormously, more perhaps than most women–to really love two men. She has said it and I agree. And I know, for I have loved passionately, I have loved as your rubied jewel upon your chest has told me you loved–with fiery heat. If you have failed to give enough passion to Arthur so that his vision would have flesh, and if you have failed to help Lancelot give space and, thus, freedom, to his experience of love–if you failed in these things, your guilt is one of inadequacy, not of intention or hope. For you have been pushed to be a God-Woman of love, as Mother has said, and I can see. That guilt is very forgivable, in my opinion.

"There is another guilt, however, that I can see. This guilt has not been mentioned by Dog or Son of the Knight, nor by Mother. It is a guilt of lack of consciousness. It is a guilt of lack of awareness of what you do. Shall I show you how that is? You nod, yes. All right. I shall continue. The guilt of which I speak, the lack of consciousness that I am referring to, goes back to your Snake-Judge. His one eye and demanding temperament are unjust, it is true. But he has demanded something of you and you have not been able to stand up to him. Do you not see? He has said 'Choose, Choose, Choose!' And you have said, "No, No, No!' do you know what is missing? I will tell you–your conviction. Yes, conviction. A funny word. Because it has two meanings. It, too, is a binarius. For it means you speak of your inner depths, your deepest beliefs, born out of love, of pain, of experience. It also means, when it comes from outside, a judgment against you, that you are guilty. You are convicted!

"Do you see, Guinevere! That Snake-Judge kept forcing you, making you choose one or the other, thus splitting you. But he was trying to force CONVICTION! You had to say something more than 'No.' You had to respond with something more than negativity and stubbornly continuing your struggle. You had to respond with conviction. You had to be able to say that you knew what you were doing, that you really loved both men. You had to be able to say this and mean it. You had to have conviction in what you were doing. But you did not have it. So, Guinevere, you were convicted by lack of conviction! So are you guilty. You are guilty not of a lack of love, but of a lack of conviction of your love! Therefore, Guinevere, must you become more conscious of your love and what you do."

"Oh, Daughter! Your words are a balm to me! Your words bring me another peace which I did not have. What you say is so true and so right that they go into the pores of me, into the belly of me, and my tears flow once more in appreciation. For it is true; I did not have conviction in my love. I saw such pain and suffering all around me, that I did not have conviction in what love asked of me, demanded of me, forced me to do. I did not have conviction and was, convicted. You are right.

"Look now, Venus-Justice is smiling at me. Your words, Daughter, and your words, Mother, are spoken from your hearts and therefore in service of her. I see now the balance, and I see now the sword! I see! Balance mother and daughter love, for wholeness. Balance care and concern for the other, and passion from within. Balance outward flowing and caring (even martyring) with inward-flowing and passion (even selfishness), for such is the whole love of the Goddess.

"Hold the sword of discrimination, the sword of consciousness. For if you are not aware of your love and of your task and of your conviction, then all is lost. Either evil will result or one-sidedness. They are both the same. I see this now, Daughter, I see. I see this now, Mother, I see. And I see this now, Venus, I see. I see Justice as Love–Sword of Conviction, Balance and Care. I see and I bow. I have tried, I have failed, I am guilty. But I have achieved much, for I have loved and I have served love. Thus do I hear the wordless words of Venus-Justice, Goddess of Conviction."

ALL CONFRONT THE FOOL; DIVISION ENDS

"Well said, Guinevere, well said. I, the Grail, proclaim it. You have suffered your trial, like a Knight, and come to a place of deeper conviction. For that, you not only help yourself, but you aid Arthur, King, and Lancelot, Knight. See now, all three are closer together. All three participate in our meditation, even though separated by the glass walls of Purgatory. But there is a change, wrought by the efforts of all–Son of the Knight and Dog, by Mother and Daughter, and above all, by the suffering of Lancelot, Arthur and Guinevere. So come now you all, come now you Four and you Three, come now and continue with the struggle. Continue with the meditation given by the great magician, Merlin, whom the three have respected.

"Arthur, take now the second pair of cards, called Rebellion. You have discovered, all of you, that behind the rage and anger of Tower and Justice are pain and inadequacy. Look now at the cards of Rebellion. They are the Fool and the Emperor. Meditate upon them, reconcile them to overcome Rebellion, as you have overcome Anger. Begin, Arthur the King, for you have had the vision and the hope, you have had the mind, you have had the longing for the Kingdom of Knights of the Round Table. You have suffered Rebellion, you have suffered pain, you have suffered inadequacy of vision. Begin now, Arthur, you who have been both Emperor and Fool!"

"Indeed I have been Emperor and Fool!" said Arthur. "Indeed I have been a rigid old King of rules and regulations, of justice sitting upon a stone ram. Indeed I have been a one-eyed blind one, both as Emperor and as Fool. Look at the Fool. He stands there, on the edge of the cliff, blithely oblivious of the abyss below him. He holds the white rose of pure passion in one hand, wand and wallet in the other. He is gazing off into space. All is gorgeous and yellow about him as the white sun of pure light and pure energy shines above. Even the little white dog with him smiles with joy, having been transformed in time from jackal and wolf, from wild and ravenous instinct into the pure companion of man.

"But, look, a fool indeed! For he does not see his next step, he does not see what is below his nose. He sees only the universe above him, the great Zeroed Nullity above him. Such has been my vision for the Round Table! Such a foolish beginning in the wonders of youth. Such was I, as I began my happy quest to form a community of Knights. Such was I, the leader and King of a nation of heroes, of those who would seek the Grail, who would seek the way of God. What a fool! For I did not see where it would lead. I saw only my vision, only the celestial quest, only the beckoning grail of wonder, in pure light and pure vision and pure passion. I saw nothing of the red rose, of the yellow sun, of the white dog! I saw nothing of the reality of this world, and thus did I step into the abyss! Thus was I blind and doomed to become a fool!"

"But, I too, have been a fool! Lancelot, Knight and servant of the King have been a fool more than all. Do you not see the wand? Do you not see the lance which the Fool carries? Do you not see it is the lance of will, of vitality, which holds up the wallet and one eye of vision? Was it not my vitality, my energy, my passion, in the service of that one-eyed vision of King Arthur? Was it not the many-colored coat of the Fool that I wore? Was I not a Joseph to the king? Was I not a servant who foolishly let himself be guided by a vision which could not fulfill a green bough, a deep passion, a red-feathered animal yearning toward the most high? I was that fool! I was that silly youth who devoted all his energies to serving a king and vision which would not contain it! No wonder I was the fool of all! No wonder I seduced the wife, captured the soul of the King; for I longed for a vision and a passion which one could serve totally. I was the fool! I am the fool!"

"Nay, you Arthur and Lancelot, you are not fools. No. It is I, Guinevere, who is the greatest fool of all! Look you, you see only a youth there, thinking it a male. But look at its shift, at the skirt, at the white undergarment. Look at the green hose, and soft high shoes. It is clearly a girl, and that fool who thought she could be a pure wife, and love and devote herself to her husband, and quietly have another passion with the darkness of love! I am that fool! I it was who did not see reality! It is I who fears the torn and fragmented coat of many colors. Do you not see the tornness of it? Do you not see the frayed and horrible character of it, revealing only the white garment underneath? Thus have I been frayed; thus has my youth and vitality been spent, and I am left only with the white habit of the nun. I am left to be on who failed in being Wife and Lover, who failed in being pure and passionate, and thus must abdicate and become neither. I have become neither wife nor lover, but None. I am exposed as having wanted both and concluding with neither! I am the Fool!"

"Hear, now, you three! I, Son of the Knight, must speak! I trust that my words can carry through the glass of Purgatory, for the heat of your passion seems to do so! You do, at last, hear one another, and that is good. But I, and my friends have been brought here to help if we can and, at any rate, to participate in your meditation; I must intervene without so much as a beckoning from the Grail for I feel especially close to the Fool. I feel akin to the vision and passion of this youth; I feel even identified with him, though knowing, of course, that I am not he. I will, then, speak from my inner authority of connection with this Fool and tell you all that you are right; you are each of you the Fool but you are also wrong, because you see the Fool only in part.

"The Fool is the traveller. He is the cosmic Life-Breath, the forever youthful, forever vital, forever seeking Spirit which is always in the morning of its power, always on the verge, on the edge of the abyss of falling into the concreteness of reality. He is that which was, which is, and shall be–a deathless life-principle always behind each manifestation. And He is not even a He as you, Guinevere recognize. He is a He-She, an Androgyne youth, neither male or female, but a pure and heavenly androgyne which is—and now you will see why I feel especially close to him—a principle of Becoming. Was, Is, Shall Be; Memory, Energy, Vision: Wallet, Wand, Eye.

"Do you see it, you Three? Do you grasp it? The Fool is You Three! Do you see it? Each of you has a piece of the Fool, is a part of the Fool, grasps the Fool. Guinevere, the Wallet, the keeper of the Seal, and of the bag of memory. You are the vessel, the valuable container of the good things, the female lusciousness and carrier of endings and beginnings, of holding onto the past and the future at the same time! Guinevere, rejoice!

"And you, Lancelot; you, of the Wand. You have the will, the energy, the black earthy power without which there is no carrying at all. Without you, there would have been no Camelot, no Round Table, nothing. And you, perhaps, are closer to the Fool than the other two, for you are—or have been—such a blind fool, with green joyous cap of nature, and red feather of courage and animal vitality! You too have worn the coat of many colors, of talent, of vitality, of many-eyed, but unfocused vision! You, Lancelot, be not dismayed. Be glad for you have been a Fool of God!

"And you, Arthur, King. You too are there as you have recognized. Your vision, your attempt at the all-seeing Eye, your purity, and your foolishness. But be not dismayed for look again. On that wallet, on that luscious container of Guinevere there exists not only one Eye, but a double-eyed Eagle! The eagle is a Scorpionic one. Do you know what it does? It links up the one pure eye of heavenly vision with the dark passion of nature. It redirects and sublimates and spiritualizes the lower passions into the higher.

"It takes the memory of all life-power and transforms it into every new vision. Do you understand, Arthur? With the Eagle on the Wallet of the Fool, a new totality, in a never-ending change into the Most High. So think anew, Arthur, gather the memories and understandings of each incarnation—gather the storehouse of knowledge and come to a new vision!

"Guinevere, do not despair, for you are there as much as the rest. Without the Wallet, there would be no reason for the Wand, nothing for it to carry. Without the Wallet there would be no carrier of the vision, be it One-Eye of heaven, or eagle-eyes of transformation and union.

Without the soul there would be no way for spirit and flesh to meet. Without Guinevere neither Arthur nor Lancelot would merit existence. Rejoice, Guinevere, rejoice! I, Son of the Knight, have spoken."

"Now I, Dog, must speak. I too respond to your meditation as does my friend, Son of the Knight. And just as he responds and feels close to the Fool, the ever-forward-looking principle of Life-Becoming, I respond to and love the Dog. While as he is, foolish as he is, loving as he is, loyal as he is, Dog is in the picture just as much as Fool. For Dog, like me, is at one with Being! Without Being, Becoming would have nothing to become. Son of the Knight without Dog is a descendant of jackals and wolves and has been the friend and helper and companion of man. Dog, like, me has seen all that Man has done, can do, even to the crucifixion of his God. Dog too has been transformed and humanized and, like me, is nature and life changed. Loving and loyal, full of life and joy. Once dark, now light. Do you see it, you Three? Do you see it in yourselves?–You look perplexed. Let me tell you.

"You, Arthur, have changed. Not so wrathful and resentful are you. Not so revengeful nor war-like. You have changed. The doggy, dark, damp passions have changed. Like me you have seen the crucifixion of duty and love and have suffered it. You have whitened.

"And you, Lancelot, you have changed. Not so lascivious and promiscuous as of old. Not so haughty and prideful. Your vitality and life have changed to romance and love. Your pride has been humbled. You have endured the crucifixion of love and have whitened.

"And you, Guinevere, you have changed. You have suffered the pain and transformation of your lusts of both Mother and Daughter, for both King and Knight, to be the all-carrying vessel of two men, two passions, two visions, two modes of being. You have suffered, been crucified, and been transformed. You have whitened.

"All three, you have whitened and though in Purgatory and apparently dead, you are not dead. You are like the White Dog, changed, civilized, transformed, looking to the future of Becoming, of being reborn for a new chance at Life. Rejoice, for the Being that you once had will, through a new Becoming, be had once again! Rejoice for I, Dog, do proclaim it! I, Dog, do proclaim to you life, the Life of Being, and of Being as the servant and end of Becoming! I, Dog, am both servant and friend of the Son of the Knight, as he is the servant of me. The Fool can carry all three, but I too point out the abyss, the reality of the earth to which I am so close. Rejoice, for you will be born again!"

"But I, Mother, will speak as well. And my words are not so joyful and congratulatory as those of Son of the Knight and Dog. My words are mournful. For I know, King, Queen, and Knight, how sad and mournful and painful have been the rebellious lives of you three. I know how foolish you have all been. I know what a painful, foolish, humiliating, stupid triangle you have formed. You are indeed foolish! You, Arthur, to have dared such a vision and missed the reality of men, foolish. You, Lancelot, to have followed a King, and missed your own nature, foolish. And you, Guinevere, to have believed that you could have carried it, foolish. You are all foolish, pained, human, remorseful, inadequate. Your rebellion is as nought. You are foolish. I weep for you.

"I too have known the sorrow of being foolish. I have sought and cared for, have suffered the rape of my most treasured beliefs, the abandonment of my most valued love. I, after all, have lost husband and son, have witnessed the painful tearing away of daughter. I have seen the Crucifixion. All these I have seen, and I too have been a fool. I weep at our human pretensions, our human inadequacy, our human rebellion against forces greater than ourselves. I week for you all, and your foolishness. I weep, too, for myself."

"And I, Daughter, weep for you as well. I too have know the foolishness of being broken by the life of every day. I have known the loss of father and brother. I have known Crucifixion. I have felt the rape of God! And I too have been foolish. How, you may ask, for such statements sound grand and heroic, though they are not. I have been the fool for having wanted my life different from others. I have been the fool for thinking that my will would solve, that my love could change, that my understanding would free. All were true and not true. For I reckoned without the God which always transcended me. God does transcend, you know. I, even I, who has seen God light and dark, loving and hating, freeing and chaining. I, even I, am the fool of God who always transcends myself.

"So my friends; so King, Queen, Knight, hear us. I, Daughter, speak. And Mother speaks, too. For we speak from the soft, the painful, the vulnerable, the feminine, the loving, enduring, knowing. We–and you–are fools. Fools of God. No escape. Submit."

"I, the Grail, having heard the Four, having seen the Three, can now relate what I see. I see the Four kneeling; I see the Three kneeling. They kneel in a circle. Wordless. Submissive. Fools of God.

"Rest ye, Fools of God! Kneel ye quietly! Empty yourselves, Fools of God, and wait for that which is above you, beyond you, in you and outside of you, greater than you. It will speak, that I know. For I am the Grail, the Vessel in which you can all be contained

"Look you, look! Your submission has broken away the glass. Your repentance and smallness have made you human and alive. Look you! You kneel together in a circle. You are together, in the flesh. That is the miracle of accepting your foolishness. Purgatory of division has ended. Rejoice in your sorrow! Rejoice in your repentant kneeling! Rejoice, for that which was unexpected has occurred–division has ended!"

REBELLION ENDS

"Rise, you seven, rise and give thought to the next card, The Emperor," said Arthur. "Look at this King of Kings whose ancient white beard notes him as the Nous, the Law-giver, and the letter tells us that we face "he who sets in order." Father, authority, law-giver; sun, war-marker, ruler. He sits upon his hard ram throne, stubborn, difficult, definer of situations. In the distance are rocks, mountains of yellow an d orange which are barren. Thus the barrenness and sterility of laws which are mere regulation and supervision.

"He sits on high, upon the stone, fiery in his sulphuric triangle. But clad in the armor hardness of steel. Only his purple robe shows the royalty of religion and only his golden scepter of Ankh, of Venus and life, give him the vitality and energy to make his vision other than hard and barren. Note the globe in his other hand, with a T: he, too, contained a totality, an order and definition which is a limitation allowing freedom. But the hard ruler is he, with the one-eyed vision of God. Reflect, you seven, reflect and meditate on the Laws of Man, and the Laws of God. Reflect and take thought, for you face, the Law-giver, the regulator, the Emperor!

"I will begin; I, Arthur, I must begin. For I have been a king, though now a fool. I have been a man of vision, I have been a law-giver, I have been a definer of rules. I have been a stubborn ram, a keeper of the totality of a Round Table. I have carried a breath of life, a love. I have been King and I know that hard face. I know that war-like attitude, that inflexible stubbornness and hardness which reaches down into the stone where one sits, the bones of one's being. It is mineral, dead, and hard. I know it. Perhaps more than any of you do, I know it, for I have been

King. But I am King no more. My Kingdom is dead, my Round Table broken, my love destroyed, my vision humiliated. I have been King, and am no longer. I have been harsh, narrow, a law-giver without love. Judge me and let me die."

But this is not a card of Judgment, Arthur! I, Daughter, can state it. Judgment will come soon enough. But let me soften you, Oh King! Let me soften the heart of the hard Emperor. Did you have a daughter once? Did not your eye gladden to her sight? Did you not melt at the look of her, the touch of her? Her smile and gentle glance could soften the hardest of hearts, could she not?

"I, Daughter, know. I remember my Father, the ruler of our house. I remember, too, his softness and tenderness with me–the gentlest of men. And I remember how he died and how we cried. Tears are endless. And I remember God the Father, and his hardness. I remember the pain that I saw in the Underworld inflicted by such a hardness of Emperors of light. I remember. Do you remember, Arthur? Is your heart not softened and saddened in remembrance of your daughter?"

"I, Mother, know, too. I hear you weeping, Arthur, King. Daughter has touched you, for she knows. She has been Daughter and true. But all women have been Daughters once, good and bad alike, strong and weak alike, loving and hating alike. All women have been Daughters. But look to the Daughter within you, Arthur. Look to your gentleness, to your vulnerability. And look to your hurt, your tears. Let them flow, Arthur! Let them flow! let me mother you, and your daughter within, as I once longed to mother my own daughter. Let me, who was once Daughter, who has been Mother, let me hold you in my arms. Let me succor the tender daughter who lies weeping and abashed within you. Let the tears flow, let the gentleness speak, let the tenderness live!"

"They live, Oh Mother! They live! I weep, and my tears flow. I weep for my pain of gentle soul. I weep for the loss of Daughter, within and without. I weep for the loss of the tenderness of Guinevere, my love. I weep for the softness and vulnerability of my own being. I who was King, I who would have been Emperor, weep. I weep for the loss and the hurt to the little girl of inner soul, who has been torn and raped and made old and barren by a struggle too great for her, by the progression from joy and delight to age and widowhood. I weep."

"Weep no more, Arthur, King! Weep no more. For I, Guinevere, cannot stand to look into your eyes, weeping. I see in them the depths of your grief, of your despair, of the agony of pain which is covered by the hard stone of law you had become. Yes, weep, Arthur, King and Husband! Weep! Would that I could heal the pain! Would that I could soften the heart, return the daughter of joy and innocent gentleness which was once there. O, Arthur, I have always loved you and cherished you, even if I have hurt and hardened the daughter of your inner soul. Your eyes, your eyes–I cannot bear your eyes!"

"Nor I, Arthur, King, nor I! I, Lancelot, Knight of the Lance and of that which wounded you and betrayed you. I dare to speak to you. I dare to beg your forgiveness! I too cannot stand your eyes, the eyes of pain and agony! Father betrayed by Son and Wife, Father who has lost the daughter of his soul, Father whose vision and rule and order is crumbled and destroyed from without! I, Lancelot, look into you eyes and see the agony within, and I weep for I cannot look! Forgive me, Arthur, King. Forgive me, Emperor, hard-eyed and hard-hearted ruler of the Universe. Your laws are hard but limited. Soften for human flesh and feelings. Soften in the face of desire and love!"

"I see you all weep! I, Dog, see Mother and Daughter, King, Queen and Knight, all weep in sorrow and love. I see your humanness. I see your tenderness, I see that which I did not see at the Crowning of Thorns! So weep you all and love! But I will speak to this Emperor! I will speak to this hard-hearted and ram-headed crown of the barren rule! Hear me, Oh Emperor and know. For, I, Dog, do speak! Know you that though you sit on an animal throne, though you have the whole power of words, of sight, of authority and rulership, though you have the whole power of the law, both natural and contrived, that your laws must bend to life! Your laws must bend to Being, for which I speak, and to the Animal, which am I! Your definitions are barren without life. Know Emperor, that you too must bend!"

"I too will speak. I, Son of the Knight, seeing the weeping of all of you, of Mother and Daughter, of Arthur, Guinevere and Lancelot, and the firm and forthright stance of my brother, Dog, I will speak. But gently. One does not change hardness with more hardness, unless it is stone upon stone. And that I am not. Stone softens with the continual rush of gentle water. Age changes with death and rebirth. All laws change. All rules die. All hardnesses soften in the end. In time, the flow, the grand Becoming. Not even the Emperor can stop that! Look, Emperor, look! Look at the Fool. With all his foolishness he steps into the future. With all his foolishness he is forever young! Look!"

"I, Emperor, do look. I look indeed. You all speak truly of me as you have spoken of Fool. You know the Fool is my son and I am his father. Can a father love anything more than his son–unless, of course, it be his daughter? But know, I am outside you and the rock and a hardness only because you let me be so! Don't you know that every man makes his own laws, his own definition? Don't you know that your only Emperor is inside your self? Don't you know that I am within you, making the rules of your personal world?

"Most of all, don't you know that I love my son, the Fool? Don't you know that without the Son, the Father is indeed hard and empty and barren? I know it, the Fool knows it. Do you know it, Arthur? Do you know it, Lancelot?

"Embrace, Father and Son; embrace, King and Knight; embrace Arthur and Lancelot! Embrace as Emperor and Fool embrace, as order and life embrace, as form and content, and as every pair of new and old, hard and soft, mind and heart do embrace. For they must embrace, mustn't they? If not now, then when? Sometime. I embrace my son. Emperor and Fool. Know it."

"Thus do they embrace, Emperor and Fool. Rebellion is over. One can see it. Arthur and Lancelot close; they touch hands, touch arms, embrace. Holding, loving, accepting. No answers, no explanations, no pardons. Silently loving. Rebellion is over. I, the Grail, have seen it. I whisper it."

THE LAST JUDGMENT

"Anger is over. Rebellion is over," said the Grail. "Pain and inadequacy, sorrow and impotence reign in their stead. It is as if a death has stolen over the land. But this is no land where they stay. This is no earthy reality where the Three remain in their death. This is truly a Purgatorial Realm, a place of No-Heaven, No-Hell, No-Earth. An inbetween place, a true place of death. But the Three have been purged in the Purgatorial Place. The Three have been loved and judged, punished and praised by the Four.

"Anger and Rebellion are gone, but where is the Metamorphosis? Where is the change? Where is the rebirth into life, or a least into the vibrancies of Hell or Heaven? It is not there. For more, much more, must happen before this can take place. Come now, you Three, and come now, you Four; look and live with the last pair of cards of the magical, fortune-telling, meditative set. Look now at the final cards of the gift of Merlin the Magician. But you must look alone–that is the purgatorial pain. Even though the glass has worn away, even though you are together in silent, submissive, soft feeling, you must continue alone. To be all together now, would be to deny the other side of your Anger and your Rebellion, its virtue. For you have sought your Being and your Becoming. You have asserted your individuality through Anger and Rebellion. To be only with pain and inadequacy, sorrow and impotence, would be mere resignation. And that would be to deny that God worked within you. That would be to deny all your struggle, all your integrity, all your valiant and creative life! I, the Grail, will not permit such a resignation! I must urge you onward, and alone.

"So then Guinevere, you first. Look at the next card–Judgment. Look at it, with the man, woman, and child rising out of coffins. They are grey, like you in Purgatory. They denote another dimension than ordinary life–they are the opposites after struggle and death, ready for rebirth. They look up to the great figure of the angel, the cosmic fire and breath of Gabriel, the angel of the Lord. His wings are outstretched and he blows his horn in seven great notes. The seven, the seven notes of the scale, the harmony of these seven, radiating like the sound which issues from breath, which issues from air, which issues from heat upon the water, which issues from the creation of God. For in six days did He create and labor, and on the seventh did He rest. And look at the banner, with its red cross on a white field. The red cross of valiant feeling, belonging to Knights, to the servants of God. But look too at the blue robe of the Angel, the spiritual figure which transcends all particular faiths, and is both water and heaven, both higher consciousness and unconsciousness in one. Look at the mountains beyond the waters below. Look at their stark, snowy whiteness; think of the heights of thought, the abstractions of the end, the final mathematics of the relationships of life and death. Look at all these, Guinevere, and reflect."

"I look, Grail, I look," said Guinevere. "I see the Angel, his trumpet, the three naked figures of man, woman, child. I see the snowy mountains, I see the red-crossed banner. I see all that. But I see nothing. I see that I am alone. I see that I have not loved enough. I see that I am inadequate. I see that I have not seen. I see that I have not had my own vision, that I have merely loved two men, loved deeply, but have had no stance of my own. Where can I stand? What can I serve? How can I love? What can I be? If I am to be born again, I must, as you say, face all these questions anew. Grail, I am alone. I accept it."

"You accept, but you humiliate yourself. You do not value yourself enough. You were too far off, now too far down. Think and speak. Remember what you have learned. Remember your meditations, and the help of Dog and Son of the Knight, Mother and Daughter. Remember and take in."

"I remember, though weakly. It is as if my blood flows thinly. That which coursed through me in passion and ecstasy now flows watery and thin. I remember. I have loved. But, I am weak. Let me die anew. Let me enter the coffins of the picture of Judgment. I judge myself and find myself wanting."

"So be it, Guinevere, so be it," said Grail.

"And You Arthur, King. You. You of the Sword, of the mighty vision, do yo have the strength to embrace your aloneness? Can you stand and be counted for your individuality?

"I cannot. I am weak. Where there was vision is now blindness. Where there was anger and firm resignation, now there is only watery blood, feeble eyes. I feel like a very old man. Let me die then. Let me too die anew. Let me enter the coffins of the picture of Judgment. I judge myself and find myself wanting."

"And you, Lancelot, Knight. You, handsome, loving, courageous, Knight, ladies' man and hero, can you stand alone for your value, for your love and your life? Do you remember all that you have learned and have assimilated?

"I remember all and nothing. I am weak. I am without strength, without courage, without love. I feel like a weak boy. I too can look at the picture and wish oblivion, which is more even than death. For death brought me only here to a purgatory of pain and struggle. I am weak. Let me die then. Let me die anew. Let me enter the coffins of the picture of Judgment. I judge myself and find myself wanting."

THE GRAIL SPEAKS

"The Three enter the coffins and, as is their wish, they die anew. Let them go into the depths of the dark space of death once again. Let them vanish from the last vestiges of life, of vitality and energy and viewpoint. They were large and vital and great. Now they are small and sapped, aged and weak.

"For what are they, really? Are they anything? Are they real or only a figment of the imagination or a fairy tale? Or if not a fairy tale, and they have lived and suffered and loved, then what? Perhaps only a fantasy in the mind of God. And who, then, is God? Is it he who writes this? He who speaks this? He who reads this? Yes.Thou art God. Arthur is God, Lancelot is God, Guinevere is God, were they but to know it. But they know it not, and I cannot tell them. Yea, I, even I, Grail and Vessel, Container and Speaker, I cannot tell them.

"But I, as Angel, will send them on a voyage in their death. They will go deep, deep into the earth of dreams. They will be utterly alone as one is in sleep, in death, yet they will have the same dream. Each will dream that he is with the others, yet alone. For how else can they be utterly alone, and utterly dead, and utterly together? Only in the depths of sleep and dreaming and in the mind of God, who is themselves. So come, you Four, and come you who reads this and participates thereby. Come to them, separate and independent, and together dream of Arthur, King, Lancelot, Knight, Guinevere, Queen."

"In this dream," says Grail, "Arthur is old and enfeebled, has lost his vision. In this dream, Guinevere is wrinkled, haggard, with unlovely, blood-filled eyes. She is loveless and no longer beautiful. In this dream, Lancelot is thin, flabby-skinned, gaunt, hawk-nosed. He is loveless and no longer handsome nor courageous. They are enfeebled. The walk along as the blind leading the blind, weak holding up the weak, the fearful protecting the fearful. They walk along a cold sea, beneath snowy mountains.

"The scene is much like that of the Judgment, though no coffins nor triangle of male, female and child is present. Nor is an Angel present, at least to their eyes. We are the Angel, the Four, you reader, and I, the Grail. We are the spiritual viewers, we are the summoners, we are the participators in the plight of the pale, weak, defeated triangle. No one can judge them more. No one can say that Lancelot is a deceiver, that Arthur is a fool, that Guinevere is incapable of loving two men. No more world to judge them. For only you, you Four, and you One who reads and I, are there. And we do not judge, for we know. We know, for we have seem and, having seen, do not judge, for we know. We know, for we have seen and, having seen, do not judge.

"These poor Three walk along the beach of this cold sea. They feel the cold wind coming from the heights of snowy mountains. No green is there, only white of snow, blue of sea and sky. They are alone, though together. Feeling pain and weakness and cold, though dead.

"But now a trumpet sounds. It is the Last Judgment? Is it the Angel? If so it does not appear, does not show itself. Only seven short notes. A scale, ascending, descending. These Three look up to see from whence come these sounds, but no trumpet shows, nor Angel either. They hear, but they do not see. But now they sense something else. It is a ship, anchored some yards off. It is a sailing ship, not large, but big enough to contain a crew of seven or eight, perhaps. The ship startles the Three.

"The Three go aboard the ship and find it fair and seaworthy. It is of handsome construction and beautifully designed, but the furnishings are tattered and foul. They wander through the ship, the cabins thereof, and come to a large room in which lies the one piece of furniture which is different from the rest–a large canopied bed, richly designed and polished, laden with heavy mattresses and down quilts. It startles the eye. The canopy is made up of flowers of every hue tucked in a latticework structure. The flowers seem perennially fresh and beautiful. Also upon his bed lies a richly jeweled scabbard with flashing sword half emerging from it.

"The Three are told, from the same imageless place from whence came the musical notes, that this is a Ship of Solomon, constructed thousands of years ago by that great King and master who was so wise and loved so well. Upon the bed lies the Sword of David, waiting for the true Knight, the favored one and blessed one, to remove it from its scabbard. Ship and blade wait for redemption–to redeem and be redeemed, but only those who can pass the test will be so honored.

"And the test? Aye, the test. It connects with the ugly and tattered furnishings. Solomon, despite his wisdom and his love, was embittered and pained by life, particularly by a bitter experience of women. And David? Well, the world knows of Bathsheba, and his pain. Here, with wisdom beauty, love, lies the tattered curtains of pain and agony. Only she who can resolve the riddle of love and soothe its pain will furnish this ship as it should be–such was the task given by a wife of Solomon. And only he who can brandish the sword with understanding, with the repair of destruction, with the wisdom of unravelling the meaning of love, only such a Knight can see the Grail and be blessed. And the bed? Well, the bed. The three will have to try to see if they can pass this test of the bed.

"First comes Guinevere, tired and weak. She sees the bed and her eyes open up wide. For she has had such an image all of her life. Such has been a vision of hers, never fulfilled. How many times did she dream of trudging up a mountain through thorny brambles, with a wanted lover behind; how many times did she dream that at the top of the mountain, in an Ark like Noah's, lay a bed just as this; how many times did she see the magnificent canopy, the flowers, the downy quilts; how many times did she dreams that she had at last arrived, only to find the unknown lover gone; how many times? Yes, Guinevere, the great and good and many-lovered Guinevere had dreamed this dream, felt this pain many, many times. For the final moment, the consummation, the union with the Gods, was always denied. Always, from within, the unknown lover vanished. Always. Whether Arthur, Lancelot, or other unnamed, always the God was present, present, present, and gone at the end. Who will understand this, who will know what is meant to live in Paradise, to struggle to Paradise, to taste Paradise, and to have it snatched away at the last moment?

"Thus does Guinevere view the scene. The bed is here, the vision is here, the lovers are here. But she is old and weak, no longer attractive, having failed. She has failed as wife, as mother, as lover. Sit then, Guinevere, sit down upon this fair bed. Sit down and then lie down. Lie and wait and dream. For, though it is no longer a lovers' bed, it is a bed, and beautiful, and a place to rest. Sit, and lie and sleep. And dream anew, a dream within a dream. Dream on the dream that you are.

"Guinevere drops exhaustedly and contentedly onto the bed. She sleeps a sleep beneath a sleep. A woman comes to her, old and haggard. She speaks in the sepulchral tones of ghosts":

"Guinevere, Queen, greetings. Welcome to the Ship of Solomon, my husband. Welcome to the Ark constructed of that wood of the Tree of Paradise, which made both Vessel and Cross. Welcome. I know you. For such as you, did I weave these miserable curtains. For such as you did I prepare these terrible furnishings. For such as you, did I allow such tatters. But not out of meanness and anger and despair. No. Out of knowledge. For such as you know the pain of love, the deceit of love, the horror of love. For such as you know the terrors and tatters, just as I did. I, it was true, was bitter and cruel and resentful. I, it was true, was vinegar and acid. I, it was, who made Solomon grieve and be sorry and terrified of his pain.

"Do you know why? Of course you do! Because I was only one of the many, one of his harem and his frock! How I loved him and how I pained! How I was furious! For I would have been the one, I longed only to have been the one, and to have him be the one for me! But it was not so, it was not so, as all the world knows. He had two, and more, and many more! How hard this is for a woman; how hard this is for God! For God is a woman; God understand the need for the One! For He-She was the One, and demanded the One.

"Now you understand, Guinevere, you understand. For you have had two. You, a woman, have loved two. You have done what the men have done, you have done what Solomon has done, you have done it. Thus do you come. For you know what it is to be a lover of two. You know the pain. As woman you know my pain, but you also know the other. Thus, Guinevere, can you now go beyond the tatters of love, the tears of love, the agonies of love, to the joys of love? You come now to your bed, your dreamed of, longed for, canopied bed! This bed is the Bed of heaven with the canopy of stars, the flowers transformed into globes of light. The softness of the clouds transformed into the tender feel of earth. It is the bed of Heaven become Earth and earth, heaven. Know now that your dream is a dream of Paradise. Know that your ghostly lover is God Himself. Know now that it is the God of the above-below, the God who is demon and lover, one and many whom you carry, lead, follow and await. Know, now, that it is He!

"Sleep, now, Guinevere, sleep the dream of the dream within the dream. Sleep the dream and wait for God!"

UNTO WHOM ONE SERVETH OF THE GRAIL?

"Look now to Lancelot, all forlorn," says the Grail. "Guinevere sleeps and dreams and waits, enveloped in the Bed of Heaven and Paradise. He too sees the bed, sees the Sword, sees the beauty. he does not take the Sword, having done with tests of prowess, adventure, pride. He glances not at the scabbard, or the jewels. He falls flat on the bed upon his face, in exhaustion; he turns over on his back and sleeps a sleep beyond sleeps. He too is in the bed, but alone, as Guinevere is alone. But Lancelot goes back in memory, he returns to the last pains of love, the last talks before the battle, before the war, before the death. He returns to his memory of the pain of love, the tatters and tears. He tells Guinevere once more of his pain, he tells her of his drive and he tells as he told so often:

"Our love has been a vat of acid
 Our heat and passion have corroded all tenderness
 Our intensity has burnt and scorched every human value
 Many lie dead

Lies are broken
Hopes fall crushed
Such is the fruit of our love. Still do I love thee.

"Our love has been a trough of tears
Our words have stung and stabbed belly and heart
Our venom has poisoned all good will and fair intention
Many are appalled
Judgments stand negative
Pain holds sway
Such is the fruit of our love. Still do I love thee.

"Our love has made a good man a cuckold
Our love brings humiliation and distrust
Our love has crossed all laws
Many are disgusted
Stupid-cruel say the
Fools are we
Such is the fruit of our love. Still do I love thee.

"Our visions clash
Our values quarrel
What's right for me, hurts you
What's right for you, pains me

"Should we end it then?
Should we part, as friends?
Should we admit defeat?
Should we stop the pain?

"Yes

"But how stop the pain?
Without you, I weep more tears for the trough
Without you, my heart corrodes with belly-acid
Without you, the pain has no surcease

"No

"Why has God wanted this love?
   Why has He given us such horror?
   Why does He let us neither part nor unite?
   Why does He torture us?

"Why?

"Does God tell you?
   Does He whisper to you as He does to me?
   Does He shout at you as He does to me?
   I know He does, even if you do not tell me

"He tells me that He loves you, adores you
   He tells me that your trial is His trial, your pain His
   He tells me these things

"And I believe Him
   Yea, I believe Him
   Though I know not his intention, I believe Him
   Though He kills me, I believe Him

"Is this, then, a God of pain?
   Is this, then, a cruel God of torture?
   Is this, then, a beast-God, a tyrant?
   Is this, then, a devil-God I serve?

"Perhaps, Perhaps
   He is all of these, and more
   For love is these

"The fire, the acid, the words, the tears
   The people, the judgments, the horror, the dismay
   All are tests of love

"Love tests
   And love survives

"Such is our love

"Even if you leave me
Even if you reject me
Even if you kill me
Love survives

"Such is our love"

"Lancelot weeps and clutches his belly in his sleep, but now he speaks afresh. Now he sings anew, in different vein, remembering again:"

I remember the days of our love
Whenever there is music

"As soon as music plays,
 I weep
 With remembrance

"I remember the tastes

"Do you know how you taste?
 Sweet? No
 Tart? No

"Like an olive, maybe
 Good and fleshy and ripe
 Tart in vinegar
 Sweet in brine
 Luscious plain
 That is how you taste

"I remember the smells

"Do you know how you smell?
 Flowery? No
 Earthy? No

"Like an olive, maybe
 Earthy, flowery
 Fecund, rich as earth

Heavy, heady as flowers
Luscious plain
That is how you smell

"The tastes and smells, oh!
I adore you, devour you
You are my olive!
Unadorned, beautiful

"But the music, the music!
Olives do not sing

"Who will play the music
When you go?
Who will sound the notes?

"No one. Not even God
So, stay
No, go, if you must
But, return
No, stay!
I love you
My musical olive"

"Lancelot weeps anew," explains the Grail, "and is now visited by the same woman, wife of Solomon, who instructed Guinevere. She speaks, sadly and lovingly, to the Knight:"

"Lancelot, Knight, Lancelot lover, you are so much like David, the King, lover, singer, warrior, seeker. So much like the Father to my Son, my husband; yet the Father was more Son than Father, and the Son more Father than Son. You are like he and wise in your way. For you have been offered the Sword of David, the King. You have been offered it and have refused. You have refused and thus done well. You need not ask, but you have answered the riddle because you have not asked it. You have served the Grail without enquiring! Listen, now Lancelot, for the Sword is the Sword of David, the King, and, through him, of all the leaders of men and followers of God. He who attempts the sword, who would draw it out and lead, he it is who must answer the question:

" 'De quoi li Graus sert?' Unto whom one serveth of the Grail?"

"Unless one answer rightly, one has failed in the quest. But you, Lancelot, Knight, and leader, father of a Grail-finder, you have relinquished your pride. You have not sought to be the leader, you have not grabbed all for yourself. In this, you have redeemed yourself of your sin. You have chosen love and the service of love, and by this choice you serve the Grail. In this you are a true Hero and Knight. In this you have overcome the battle of the Three. In this, in your submission, you have gone beyond and through. In this, your battle with Arthur is finished. Welcome Knight, welcome Hero. For you serve love naturally, lovingly, without question, and with arrogance. Come now, and enjoy the fruit of your Grail, the vision of your soul., Guinevere. But know that Guinevere, the vision of your soul, is Gold!"

"So spoke the wife of Solomon to Sir Lancelot, Knight. So spoke she and informed him. Thus now does Lancelot await his bride, the image of Guinevere, his soul and vision of God. Sleep, now, Lancelot, sleep the sleep within the sleep. Sleep and unite with the Goddess!"

THE SWORD ONCE MORE

"As Guinevere and Lancelot sleep and dream, together and separately, in the Bed of Paradise, look now to Arthur, King of the Round Table" says the Grail. "He too has seen the vessel, has seen the tatters, has seen the bed. Before bed and more than bed, he has seen the sword.

"Oh, how ruefully he holds the sword in its scabbard. He can see its greatness, its specialness. He can see the jewels, the shining pommel and top of the blade. He can see. But above all men, he knows and remembers. He recalls how it was that he, Arthur, became King and leader of men! He thinks now on what sort of leader he was, how inadequate and blind. He thinks, with rue, of all the dead and injured in the cause of his jealously alone. He thinks and he weeps. He is old, haggard; he surrenders. He abandons his claim for leadership. He falls on the bed, wishing only to rest and find solace in totally unconscious sleep.

"As Arthur rests, a strange thing happens. Miracle that it is, the scabbard with its blade moves toward him! Arthur awakens with a start and finds that the sword moves of itself! It comes out of the scabbard, stands in the air, shining magnificently as if it were a vibrant and living cross, and slowly moves itself toward Arthur. At first it approaches with the point toward him, as if to kill him. Arthur flinches not, for he know that nothing can cause him more pain than he has already endured. The blade changes direction and the handle nestles itself in the outstretched and expectant hand of Arthur. Arthur, King, receives the blade. He does not seek it, but goes forward to meet it, to receive it. As he grasps the sword, he hears the voice of the Angel asking:

" 'Who serves the Grail? Whom does the Grail serve? The Grail:'" "God of the past, of the Fathers; God of the present, of the Mothers and Daughters; God of the future, of the Sons. Unto God, been, being, becoming. God of love, God of vision, God of ecstasy, God of knowing. The Grail, cornucopia, server. I, Arthur, King, serve. God the ever-present, ever beyond. I serve. In blindness, in pain, in pleasure, in knowing, I serve, as would answer all who have tasted life, defeat and love.' "

"Know, Arthur King, and Arthur Man, know that you are a God-Man," says the Grail. "You have served Christ, the God-Man, and followed the vision. You have served and suffered, having succeeded and failed. Know now, that this is the Sword of Paradise, hanging there since that first sin, that first failure, keeping men away. Keeping them away from the knowledge that they are God-Men, meant to be and to become. Know now. Know and enter the things, with the heaven of starry-flowers and mattress of downy clouds. Enter Heaven. Enter and see Guinevere.

"Arthur sinks into the Bed of Heaven, weeping and saying:

" I remember the beautiful girl of my heart,
  The smiling one, the laughing one
  I remember

"Those joyous lips, full and fair
  Those tender hands, soft and warm
  Those flaring nostrils, sensual and beckoning

"I remember and I weep
  The girl that I wed
  The treasure who adored me

"What have I done to her?
  What callous disregard?
  What brutal hurt?

"Her youth, her beauty
  Her joy, her gaiety
  Her trust, her simplicity
  Gone

"And I have done it
  Yes, I
  Not Another

"Through lack of love, of caring
  Through lack of love, of fathering
  Through lack of love, of husbanding"

> In Arthur's dream Guinevere speaks in answer:

"But no, Arthur, my husband,
  I love thee
"You are not to blame,
  It was I

"I, who longed for more
  I, struck by passion
  I, struck by love

"I thought that love was One,
  Meant for one, in two
  Two in one, one in two, thought I

"I was wrong
  Rueful woman am I
  I was wrong

"For love is two, and three
  God knows how

"Love is four, and more
  and love has no end

"Love scalds, and corrodes,
  Love boils, and bakes
  Love tortures
"Oh, how I would have stopped the pain!

"But, I love thee, husband
  I love thee"

"Now Arthur replies,"

"Oh, wife, come and be my wife again!
  Come and join me in holy wedlock
  Come and be my bride

"And be with me
  And me alone,
  When with me

"For I claim no more
  Beaten am I, broken am I
  No longer royal am I
"But loving I remain
  Come Guinevere, wife, beloved, come
  I love thee"

"Says Guinevere:"

"I come, Arthur, I come
  Thee I love, thee I love
  As the jackal loves it mate
  As the hyena loves its mate

"For such am I
  Jackal and hyena
  Thief and devourer
  Deceiver and traitor

"Such is their nature,
 But they love, too."
"Says Arthur:"

"Come then, jackal
 Come then, hyena
 Come then
 For I, Arthur, am animal, too

"No longer proud lion,
 No longer eagle
 But cub, perhaps, or bird

"No, a man. A king-man,
 But a man
 A God-man
 But a man
 A man who loves

"Says Guinevere:"

"Arthur, I adore you.
 I, animal-woman, Queen
 God-woman, Queen
 God-woman, flesh
 I adore you"

"Thus," says the Grail, "does Arthur dream within his dream of Paradise restored, with the return of Guinevere. But it is not enough that he so longs, so feels, so experiences in his soul. He forgets his vision, he forgets Camelot, the seekers after the Grail. The Knights of the Round Table, those who served their Ladies and served the seeking of God–all broken. What of that, Arthur? What of that broken leadership? What of that broken sword? The sword is not repaired on loving visions of wives alone! Arthur, Arthur! Speak!"

"I cannot speak, for it is true. I need a new vision, and await the God, or Goddess, who will restore me!"

METAMORPHOSIS

"Look," says the Grail, "The three lie dead upon the canopied bed in the cabin of the Ship of Solomon. Dead once, dead twice, dead thrice–a death within a death. The tattered curtains blowing in the wind, the creaky doors rocking back and forth make the only sound as the ship floats leaderless upon the gently waving sea.

"Look again," says the Grail. "Out of the sadness, out of the despairing hopelessness of death, out of the wicked waiting in the wind of tatters and sickening rolling, out of the relentless struggles in pain, there emerges a dark figure. A dark figure emerges–out of the ocean. Out of the cracking timbers of the Ship of Solomon. Out of the cold and frozen earth of land near the sea. Out, too, from the land under the sea, the land beneath sand and water, the land where caves of shells cover the blue light, the purple light, the yellow light of the Underworld, the Charioteer is emerging.

"He emerges not in sound and fury, not in rage, not in great trumpetings of the horn of the Angel Gabriel. Rather he emerges with the soft notes of the minor scale. He emerges out of the pain of man, and of woman. He emerges out of the impotence of rage, the despair of inadequacy, the pain of loving, the hunger of non-fulfillment. He emerges and slips gently into the room, into the cabin, onto the gorgeous bed of the Ship of Solomon. He approaches the three and takes the Sword of David in his hand. For He it is who will wield the Sword of David, He it is who will guide and lead, He it is who will touch the mind and heart and soul, He it is who will lead the leaderless ship. He slips gently into the room and gently into the figures on the bed. For He is they, and they, He. The Charioteer speaks:"

"Oh, Arthur King, I salute you! You are the Spirit. You are the man of vision, the seeker after the highest. And, Arthur, you are me and I am you. Your spirit is my spirit, my spirit yours. Your vision is my vision, and mine yours. Where you have achieved, so have I. Where you have failed, so have I. But we will make a new vision, you and I, and we will make a new Spirit. You and I are one. For you, Arthur, are the Sword, this Sword which I hold. You are the one who was chosen, in the beginning, in the middle, and in the energy and power, the leadership and passion from earth itself. You it was to whom it was given to use the sword to lead, to guide and to see far. And you it will be again, to lead, to see and to guide. You in me, and I in you–we are one.

"And you, Guinevere, Queen, I embrace you! You are Soul. You are the unity, the loving platform upon which the drama is enacted. You are the dish, the plate, the pattern upon which the flesh of body and spirit are united. You, Guinevere, Queen, you are love, and woman. You are soul, and, Guinevere, I am you and you, me. We are one. Where you have loved, I have loved. Where you have failed, I have failed. But we will love anew, you and I, we will make a new and more total experience of love. You and I are one. For you, Guinevere, you are the dish, you are the plate, you are the roundness upon which all is made manifest.

"But you, Lancelot, Knight. You, loving Knight, serving man, passionate friend, you are 'I'. Without you, there is no 'I', without you there is no particularity, there is no humanity, no life. You are the father of knights, the lover of loves, the one who errs and achieves. You, Lancelot, are the wand. You are the lance which I carry in my hand. You and I are one. We are twin brothers, you and I, indistinguishable and different. You will understand this, Knight, for you know.

"Now look you three, Spirit, Soul and Ego, look King, Queen and Knight, look to the bearer of the Grail! See you there the Fool as Page? See you there the great He-She of the Fool, the nullity which is the totality? See you there the body of me and you? For King, Queen, Knight, Page make a quarternity of wholeness. Just as Charioteer and Fool make a wholeness in duality-trinity.

"But your trials are not at an end. Your Page-Fool carries the Cup, he holds the Grail which is the last of the Hallows, holy name for the four–the Lance, Sword, Dish and Cub. Before you can drink, before you can recover from your dark sleep, before you can live that which you have earned, you three must know what the others of you have felt. Spirit from Soul, Soul from Ego, Ego from Spirit. And for this exchange among the three, and for the healing of the three, we need the four. In this wise were the four brought here. For this were Son of the Knight and Dog, Mother and Daughter brought here.

"So, now, you four, unite with the three, unite with the three upon the canopied bed. In the union with the three and the four, in the exchange of one and another, will emerge the healing unity of seven. And seven is mine, the union of four plus three, of six plus one. In seven days was the world created, and on the seventh did the Lord rest. Unite now, and know whereof I speak."

"Thus does the Charioteer speak. Thus does the Charioteer speak. Thus does he quietly announce his being and his mission. It is simple, it is true. But I, the Grail, must speak and tell of this Charioteer. I will describe this being of the cards, this figure who, combined with Judgment, can bring about Metamorphosis. This is how he is.

"Mighty is he, the Charioteer, mighty is he, but gentle. He comes as the flow of powers, above and below. Can you see the Chariot upon which he stands? Above is the starry canopy, the blue silk covering upon which stand the six white stars of David and Solomon–and the five white stars of the quintessence of Venus. For the Charioteer is beyond five and beyond six, he and has the music of seven, of the day in which the Lord finished his creation and rested. The canopy is heaven, which covers that bed of the Ship of Solomon, and covers thus the Chariot upon which the Charioteer rides, for bed and Chariot are one.

"Look now at the Chariot below, upon which he stands. Of stone is it made, a cube. A union of Father and Son, a stone of Abban, a carrier of the forces below, of the terrestrial powers of the earth, as the canopied silk carries the power of heaven. Four pillars support the canopied heaven–earth, air, fire and water. But these four come from below, they rest upon the car. The car is the vehicle, the vessel and the body upon which the Charioteer stands. Red lingam-yoni adorns the car, as do blue wings and yellow globe–the powers of passionate union, the flights of consciousness, of aspiration.

"Above and below–canopy and car. Both belong to the Charioteer. Mighty is he, but gentle. He comes as the flow of powers above and below. He comes as the powers of the universe. He is conquest in mind, in soul, in flesh. And he comes as man. He comes as Self, as God expressing himself in man. Without man there is no one to know that God exists, that the powers exist. Without 'I' there is no being. Such is the Charioteer, the total expression of the powers of the universe in man. A mighty knight, a servant of the highest, a Lancelot, triumphant in the living. Full does he live, much does he serve.

"Thus, is the Charioteer. There is more, much more–his animals which draw this car, sometimes sphinxes in black and white, riddle-asking, sensing; sometimes a horse, black and powerful; his wand of magic oneness; his crown of highest ruling. These and more. But let us ask no more of his symbols. Feel rather of his presence. Sense rather the union of the four with the three. Son of the Knight, Dog, Mother, Daughter, Arthur, Guinevere, Lancelot–all seven united, joined, come together. Such is the Charioteer.

"But what is the Vessel? What is the Grail? What is that fourth Hallow which comes after Sword, Lance, and Dish? It is the Cup, the vessel upon the four and the three, which holds the hallows of all. For even the human personality is more than an "I" of Lancelot, more than a soulful love of Guinevere, more than a kingly vision of Arthur. It is more that a being of Dog, a becoming of the Son of the Knight, a loving and serving of Mother and Daughter. The human personality contains God. It is the container for that which transcends the human personality. What is it that transcends? It is the unspeakable voice of God. It is from the silent time before the world was created; it is from God, before He knew He was God; it is from the everlasting, evercreating primal place from which come the All and the Nothing, the infinity above the wand, the eight beyond the seven. No more.

"Feel now, union of the seven in the eight. Feel now the seven become whole in the eight. Feel Charioteer unite with the Fool. Feel the birth of God in man, of self in the human personality.

"The music sounds in the trumpet of Gabriel. Judgment and Chariot–Metamorphosis occurs. Arise from the dead, you three! Arise, Arthur, Guinevere, Lancelot! Arise and live in the one."

LYSIS

"Now, said the Son of the Knight, "I speak for the human personality of all of us, weak and fragile as it is, demanding and powerful as it is, far-reaching and limited as it is. Speak, Charioteer, speak and fill those crevices of desire within the soul! Speak, Charioteer, speak those words of vision which enlarge the sight of man! Speak, Charioteer, speak the words of love, the happy words of man loving which make him expand beyond his littleness, his despair, his impotence and rage! Speak, Charioteer, we implore it and command it!

"I speak, when summoned. I need only to be summoned to speak. And I speak when summoned not. For God is always present, summoned or not, and I am that image of God which lies in man, in man in particular and ever-unfolding, I am God in man–becoming, God in man–being, God in man–loving, God in man–serving, God in man soul-filling, God in man–ego.

"What would you have me say? What would you have me be? Wish it and it is yours. Desire it and it is yours. For man can wish, desire, and have it fulfilled. His wish is his creation, his desire is his drive. God wishes and creates, He desires and fulfills in His creation, in man. Man is the vehicle. No other. So wish, man. Desire and create."

"I am man," responded the Son of the Knight. "I wish for the moon, I wish for more. I wish for peace. I wish for love. I wish for the surcease of pain. I wish an ever-expanding vision of man for man. I wish for little fishes to swim peacefully. I wish for stars to grow warm. I wish for clean air and blue skies. I wish for everything and nothing. I know not what to wish for. I wish only to serve God, to love God, to become God, and be God, alone and with my fellows. I wish to do that which I am told. I wish to find pleasure in my service. Such is my irrational wish."

"You speak well, man. For you speak the irrational speech of tongues. You speak the words which come. You submit, and you serve. Serve now a silence. Rest a little, as God rested upon the seventh day. Rest and let the world-vision come to an end. Rest and let the quiet soak up the past. Rest, before the new creation begins."

"I have rested, Oh Charioteer. I have rested and I have done your bidding. I have rested and heard the music. I have rested and felt the sun. I have rested and seen the sun. Speak, now Charioteer. Speak and answer my questions."

"I will speak."

"What, then, is the end of man? asked the Son of the Knight. "Why are we here? What do we serve?"

"God is the end of man," said the Charioteer, "Love does he serve. He is here to serve God."

"And what is the end of God? Why is He here? What does He serve?"

"Man is the end of God. Love does He serve. He is here to serve man."

"Are man and God one?

"Man is God becoming, God is man being. Yet man is God being, and God is man becoming. Identical and different. Two in one; one in two. But many in One and one in Many. For God is man in both one Man, and in all Men. One in Many, Many in the One."

"How do we serve? How can we live? Why is love so hard?"

"These words are old. These words are pale. These words speak not. Tell me, Charioteer! Tell me! Tell me!

Thou art God!

"I am god, Charioteer! I am God?"

"Thou art God!"

"I laugh, Charioteer, I laugh. Does God laugh?"

"God laughs."

"I weep, Charioteer, I weep. Does God Weep?"

"God weeps."

"I am impotent and futile. I am silly and childish. Is God?"

"God is."

"What am I that is not God?"

"Nothing. All of you is God."

"What is God that I am not?"

"The rest of mankind. The rest of animal-kind. The rest of plant-kind. The rest of matter-kind. Of the past, of the present, of the future."

"Then I am nothing. A grain of sand. An atom of energy."

"Yes, nothing. And everything. For without you, there would be no God. Thou art God!"

"What good to be God? What joy? What for?"

"Just so. Just so. For joy. For itself. For ecstasy. For peace."

"I am God then, I will make a world, a better world.

I am God then, I will make myself a better self.

I am God the, I will."

"Thou art God, then. Thou art God.

We will make a world, a better world.

We will make a self, a better Self.

We will."

"I see now the union of the seven," said the So of the Knight. "I see them, Knight and Lady. I see them, husband and wife, Father and Son, Mother and Daughter. I see them, Friend and Friend. I see them, two and by two. I, a man, like Noah, sailing on his ark, the forerunner of that Great Ship of Solomon, having survived the flood of God, the wrath of god, the unconsciousness of God, having survived the errors of God, having rescued what he could, having loved and helped and saved, having survived the ignominy of his fellows, I, a man, like Noah, do proclaim the rainbow. I proclaim the colors of God's peace. I proclaim the music of the circular rainbow of love and concord. I stand apart and look at the great rainbow of peace with God.

NEW FALCON PUBLICATIONS

**Publisher of Controversial Books and CDs
Invites you to visit our website
www.newfalcon.com**

- Browse the online catalog of all our great titles, including books by Israel Regardie, Christopher S. Hyatt, Robert Anton Wilson, Aleister Crowley, Timothy Leary, Osho, Lon Milo DuQuette and many more.
- Get special discounts
- Order our titles through our secure online server
- Find products not available anywhere else
    - One of a kind and limited availability products
    - Special packages
    - Special pricing
- And much, more more